FEASTS OF HONOR

# FEASTS OF HONOR

Ritual and Change
in the Toraja Highlands

TOBY ALICE VOLKMAN

Illinois Studies in Anthropology
No. 16

UNIVERSITY OF ILLINOIS PRESS

*Urbana and Chicago*

© 1985 by the Board of Trustees of the University of Illinois
Manufactured in the United States of America
P   5   4

*This book is printed on acid-free paper.*

Library of Congress Cataloging in Publication Data

Volkman, Toby Alice, 1948–
    Feasts of honor.

    (Illinois studies in anthropology; no. 16)
    Originally presented as the author's thesis (Ph. D.—
Cornell University, 1980) under title: The pig has eaten the vegetables.
    Bibliography: p.
    Includes index.
    1. Toradjas—Rites and ceremonies.   2. Toradjas—Social
conditions.   I. Title.   II. Series.
DS632.T7V65   1985      306'.0899922      84–16123
ISBN 0-252-01183-X (alk. paper)

To my parents, Florence Pincus and Jacob Volkman,
And to Mama' Agus Lies Kombonglangi'

# Contents

Acknowledgments                                            ix

Chapter 1. Introduction                                    1

Chapter 2. The Historical Context                          20

Chapter 3. The Pregnant House                              44

Chapter 4. Status, Shame, and the Politics of Meat         59

Chapter 5. Capturing the Wind                              83

Chapter 6. Change at To' Dama'                             116

Chapter 7. The Undertaker Becomes a Big Man                142

Chapter 8. "Our Umbrella-dom Has Disappeared"              153

Chapter 9. The Ritual Dilemma                              161

Epilogue                                                   173

Notes                                                      175

Appendix A                                                 189

Appendix B                                                 191

Glossary                                                   197

Bibliography                                               201

Index                                                      209

# Acknowledgments

My thanks go to many people who have shaped my thinking about anthropology and Indonesia. At Cornell University, where this book had an earlier incarnation as a doctoral dissertation, I am indebted to Robert Ascher, Benedict Anderson, Bernd Lambert, and James Siegel for their stimulating teaching as well as their support and criticism. Bob Ascher deserves special thanks for encouraging me to turn the dissertation into a book. Terance Bigalke, Jason Clay, and Gail Ringel offered valuable comments on the manuscript in its early stages, and more recently the text has benefited from the thoughtful criticisms of Elizabeth Coville, Erika Duncan, Robert Hefner, Nancy Smith-Hefner, and Charles Zerner.

The fieldwork on which this study is based was undertaken in Indonesia from 1976 to 1978, supported by a Fulbright Hays Doctoral Dissertation Research Abroad Fellowship, with additional support from the National Science Foundation and the Center for International Studies at Cornell University. The Cornell Southeast Asia Program supported the write-up of this research, and the National Science Foundation also supported several years of graduate study. In 1983 Documentary Educational Resources gave me the flexibility of time that enabled me to complete the manuscript. I am grateful to all these institutions.

In Indonesia my work proceeded smoothly thanks to Lembaga Ilmu Pengetahuan Indonesia in Jakarta, and to the sponsorship of Dr. Mattulada of Hasanuddin University, Ujung Pandang. I am also grateful to the government of the Regency of Tana Toraja, and to Bupati Andi Lolo.

Special thanks are due several friends in the field. Shelly
Errington introduced me to Bugis culture and to the family of
the late Opu Tosinilele in Palopo, with whom she had worked.
Both introductions proved invaluable. I am grateful to many
members of this family, and especially to Andi Anton Pange-
rang for his insights and friendship. Shelly Errington's own
work among the Bugis has enriched and sharpened my understandings of the Toraja and of the contrasts (and similarities)
between the highlands and the coasts. In the highlands, special
thanks to Terry Bigalke, whose penetrating historical research
forms an integral part of this book. I also wish to thank him for
enjoyable hours of palm wine and good conversation in the
field. Thanks as well to Shinji and Yoshimi Yamashita, whose
insights about the southern Toraja region provided a measure
of the tremendous richness and variability in highlands' culture, and whose good spirits and hospitality were well appreciated. Another perspective on the north was offered by Liz
Coville, whose fieldwork was undertaken after I had left
Indonesia and who generously provided a communicative link
with friends on Mount Sesean.

For hospitality in Ujung Pandang, thanks go to Gene and
Betsy White, Harry and Marian Cummings, Tim Babcock and
Helen Cruz, Dr. Werner Meyer, and the family of Dr. Pange-
rang. In Rantepao, Pastor Patrik Decavele often shared his
knowledgeable views of Toraja as well as his high-spirited
humor. For friendship and help in countless ways, up and
down Mount Sesean, Motohiko Okumura of P. T. Toarco Jaya
deserves special thanks.

To Charles Zerner, my husband, myriad thanks are due: for
reading most of what I have written and offering incisive criticism; for sharing his own perceptions and interpretations of
Toraja; for fine drawings of plants and architecture; and, most
of all, for sharing two years of living and working in the field.

My debt to the people of Tana Toraja cannot possibly be
repaid by mere acknowledgment. Still, words and names are
terribly important to the Toraja, and it is my hope that they
will recognize this story as their own. Many people helped me
immensely through their kindness and knowledge: in particular, Guru J. T. P. Pirri', Hakim John Mangayung, Pak Kila', Pak

Banti Pempe, Ibu and Pak William Tambing, Pak Sarira and his family in Pantilang, *to minaa* Ne' Tandi Datu, and the family of *to minaa* Ne' Lumbaa. Young Kombong, who died in 1984 in Kalimantan, gave generously of his imaginative tellings of Toraja tales, his songs, and his guidance during my initial months on Mount Sesean. To the people of To' Dama'—to Mama' Agus, Ne' Leme, Agus, Ruben, Limbong, Maria, Elis, and the whole "family bamboo clump" on the mountain, a Toraja thank you: *ma'kurre sumangat, ma'pole paraa; denno upa ta si tammu pole.*

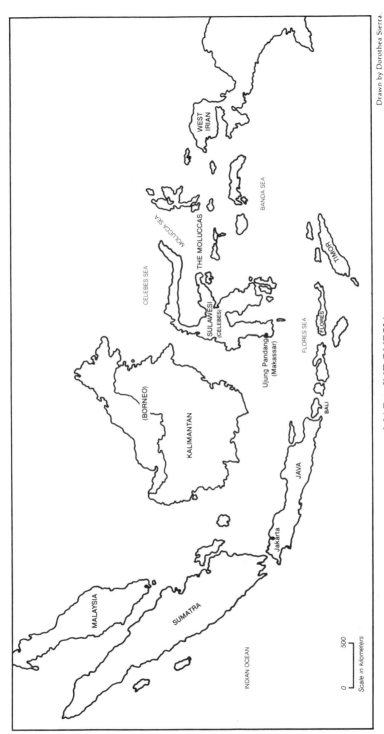

MAP 1. INDONESIA.

SEKO

LUWU

*Mt. Sesean*

MAMASA

Rantepao ●

● Pantilang

●| Palopo

GULF OF BONE

● Makale

TANA TORAJA

ENREKANG

SIDENRENG

● Pare Pare

MAKASSAR STRAIT

BONE

Ujung Pandang ●
(Makassar)

GOA

*0      50*
*Scale in kilometers*

MAP 2. SOUTH SULAWESI.

# CHAPTER 1

# Introduction

On a map the island of Sulawesi at once catches the eye: like the petals of a windblown orchid, its peninsulas stream into the Celebes, Molucca, Banda, and Flores seas. Few writers have resisted the temptation to give this oddly shaped piece of land a floral or faunal identity: a giant crab, a mutant starfish, an octopus, a spider. Alfred Russell Wallace, the great nineteenth-century naturalist, was fascinated by the zoogeographic anom-alies of Celebes (as the island then was called), anomalies now thought to have been produced by the collision of frag-ments of several ancient continents.[1] Today Sulawesi lies between two massive continental shelves, making it a most active island, geologically, with erupting volcanoes, earth-quakes, and dramatic coastal uplifting.

Cultural life on Sulawesi is no less active. The southwestern province known in contemporary Indonesia as South Sulawesi is the homeland of four major ethnic groups and several minor ones. The Bugis (3.2 million) inhabit the extensive coasts and much of the fertile, central lowlands. The Makassarese (1.5 million) are concentrated in the south and around the port of Makassar, a steamy metropolis of 700,000 once famous for exporting hair oil to Europe. Along the peninsula's northwest-ern coastal strip are the Mandarese (400,000), said to be the finest sailors of Celebes (Pelras 1975:6). In fact, all three peo-ples are renowned throughout the archipelago for their excel-lent small boats, their role in interisland trade, and, especially in the Bugis case, their skill and fearlessness as seafarers and former colonizers of distant coasts. The land as well as the sea sustain these peoples, who practice various combinations of rice cultivation, gardening (coconuts, bananas, maize, cassava, sesame, pepper, cloves, nutmeg), silk weaving, lake and ocean fishing, as well as trade (Pelras 1975:6). Since the early seventeenth century the lowlanders have also practiced Islam, which was first embraced by a Makassarese prince of Goa, a kingdom on the peninsula's southwestern coast. In former kingdoms and petty states, as in everyday contemporary life, rank and status were, and still are, paramount concerns, elaborated in finely graded hierarchies of "blood" and spiritual potency.[2]

In the northern reaches of the peninsula, fertile plains and rolling hills give way to rugged mountains with 3,000-meter peaks. These mountains are the homeland of 550,000 people collectively designated as "Toraja" and known locally by such names as Mamasa, Rongkong, Seko, Maki, and Mambi (Pelras 1975:6). The best known of these highland peoples are sometimes called Sa'dan (or Sadang) Toraja, after the great river that courses through the mountains. The area now defined by the Indonesian government as the "regency" of Tana Toraja, or "Toraja Land," includes just over 3,000 square kilometers and a population of approximately 330,000. Here rice is cultivated in steeply terraced, irrigated fields that cover mountain slopes, interrupted by clearings for small villages and towering stands of bamboo. Cassava, maize, and coffee are also grown, and water buffalo, pigs, and chickens are raised for ritual consumption. In the past highlanders were scorned by their lowland neighbors as kingdomless headhunters who wore little more than loincloths, ate pork, and worshiped pagan (non-Islamic) deities. Today other stereotypes prevail. In Indonesia the Toraja are often viewed as highly educated, energetic, ambitious Christians. In the West the Toraja have become well known in recent years for their elaborate mortuary rituals, which have attracted the attention of both European tourists and, not surpisingly, anthropologists.

## Who Are the Toraja?

Until this century "Toraja" as an ethnic group or category scarcely existed except in the minds of others. The term was applied in the seventeenth century by the Makassarese (*to* = person; *raja* = north) to the highland peoples whom they raided; and the Bugis used the term (*to* = person; *ri aja* = of the interior, above) to include all highlanders of both southern and central Celebes (Bigalke 1981:14–15). Dutch missionaries in central Celebes borrowed this broad usage in the 1890s, although the American anthropologist Raymond Kennedy attempted to restrict "Toraja" to the peoples of the central highlands, calling the southerners simply "Sa'dang" (Bigalke 1981:16). By the 1930s the name "Toraja" had taken hold among the southern highlanders, who by the 1970s were enthusiastically reformulating the cultural terms of that identity (Volkman 1984). The fluidity of these ethnic categories is paralleled linguistically. Mills (1975:205), who distinguishes seven languages or dialects that originated from a "Proto South Sulawesi," warns that in "an area like South Sulawesi, where all the languages have been in prolonged and intimate contact with each other, the decision as to what is a 'dialect' and what is a 'language' is often difficult."

The earliest European mention of the Toraja appears in the account of the French Jesuit priest Gervaise (1685), based on descriptions obtained from two Makassarese princes studying in Paris (Nooy-Palm 1978:165). The princes spoke of "le royaume de Toraja," a land rich in gold, bamboo, and forests. Gervaise (1685:80–81) also wrote of the arrival of two Makassarese vessels in Siam, laden with "the most wild and untameable" Toraja natives for sale as slaves. In the mid-nineteenth century the Englishman James Brooke (the White Rajah of Sarawak) traveled extensively in the lowlands of Celebes and recorded these impresssions of "the Turajah, who inhabit the hills":

> ...in dress, or rather no dress, they bear a resemblance to the Dyaks of Borneo. They are not converted to Islam, and are said to seek heads on the occasion of a great chief's death.... I saw about twenty of them in the market-place at Palopo, but they spoke no Bugis, and were very shy and frightened.... [They] bore marks of great poverty, and had brought down small quantities of paddy for sale, from the produce of which they buy salt

and other necessaries. An intelligent native told me their language somewhat resembled that of Goa; and, from the few
words I heard them speak, I thought it soft and pleasing. They
have no written characters. (1848:156)

Not until the end of the nineteenth century did Europeans
actually penetrate the Sa'dan highlands: a Dutchman, Van Rijn
(1902), and two Swiss scientists, the Sarasins, left descriptions
as well as photographs of their expeditions. One photograph
stands out in my mind: two emaciated Toraja men, enchained
and for sale as slaves in the Palopo market (Sarasin 1905:201),
a reminder of the turn-of-the-century turmoil that plagued
even the remote highlands.

These days it is not difficult to travel to Tana Toraja. A
rickety Mercedes bus leaves the provincial capital of Makassar
(now Ujung Pandang) in the early morning hours. The road
winds north, through countryside dotted with strangely bul-
bous limestone formations, reminiscent of Chinese landscape
paintings. It hugs the coast, passing salty Bugis fishing villages
that look out onto the Makassar Strait, with their faded pastel,
wooden slat houses standing tall on stilts, and marshy stretches
of *nipa* palms. At Pare Pare, a Bugis city of 75,000, the road
leaves the coast and turns east to traverse a broad, fertile pla-
teau where cattle graze. Foothills gradually give way to steep
mountain gorges and cool, clear air. The scenery becomes more
breathtaking, until the bus pauses at a spectacular mountain
pass in Duri, the Islamic highlands just south of Tana Toraja:
dry, rough terrain peppered with mosques and goats. Passengers clamber out of the bus and are besieged by pretty girls
selling mounds of red palm sugar wrapped in leaves. Older
women sit by the roadside with piles of papayas, and long
curved bananas hang from stalls like clusters of yellow horns.

Some 180 kilometers and ten hours after the journey began,
depending on one's luck, the Liman Express lurches into the
first Toraja town on its itinerary, Makale, in a valley 800
meters above the sea. There it drops off passengers and, after a
seemingly interminable wait, makes its way to Rantepao, 18
kilometers to the north, crossing a landscape of lush, irrigated
rice fields broken only by the distinctive swooping roof of an

To' Dama' landscape: towering bamboo, fields to be planted, and mist.

Toraja men for sale at a Palopo market. Photographed
by Paul and Fritz Sarasin in 1895.

occasional Toraja house outlined against the sky. In the distance, approaching Rantepao and beyond, loom the great craggy peaks of Mount Sesean.

At 2,000 meters Mount Sesean is the highest peak in Tana Toraja. It is also the home of the mythical Suloara, the first great priest or *to minaa*, "the one who knows." Far below Suloara's invisible cave, jagged basalt rocks give way to barely cultivable slopes. Solitary, delapidated houses of wood and bamboo appear on clearings that nearly vanish in the mountain's shifting fog, and occasional pigpens, cassava gardens, or plots of coffee trees are in evidence.

Descending further the landscape continues to change; and at about 1,500 meters, well-worked *sawah* (irrigated rice fields) come into view, with large, black volcanic boulders in their midst and bright yellow sunflowers growing at their edges. Rows of substantial houses stand opposite rows of substantial rice barns, enclosing well-swept dirt yards and framed by luxurious stands of bamboo, cassava gardens, red-leaved cordyline and sandalwood trees, and pens filled with pigs. Dozens of such house clusters make up the "village of the earth," Tondoklitak. Within this village is a smaller settlement, at 1,400 meters above sea level, known as "the place of dammar," To' Dama'. Although dammar, the fragrant tree resin used in making lamps and varnishes, has not been traded at this site for many years, To' Dama' retains its name along with its character as a lively, changing place.

## Ritual and Change

"The folk here are meat-mad," wrote Kennedy (1953:191) on a visit to the highlands in 1949–50, and he also observed that they were obsessed with death. More than thirty years later, meat and mortuary ceremonies remain vital and ever-changing symbols in Toraja culture. Funerals, in particular, have flourished in recent years and in the process have become vehicles for social transformations and the critique of fundamental cultural premises. Many Toraja are engaged in dialogues about the meaning of their beliefs and rituals, the construction of their personal and cultural identities. The present study is an examination of some of those dialogues, using the funeral as a lens. The Toraja themselves most often focus on funerals, and in funerals they are most sharply focused—not only to outsiders but to their fellow Toraja.

Ritual, and much of what Indonesians refer to as "custom and culture" (adat dan kebudayaan), has become problematic for the Toraja. Changes initiated in the Dutch colonial period (1906–42), and intensified with Indonesian independence after 1950 (including abolition of slavery, the spread of education, Christianization, increasing monetization, and most recently out-migration and tourism), have transformed the dynamic interrelationships between ritual performance and social status. In the past ritual was thought to affirm a person's "place" as noble, commoner, or slave, distinctions based upon descent ("blood") and, at least ideally, coincident with wealth. Today many commoners and former slaves who have acquired education at home and wealth abroad return to their natal villages and stage expensive funerals for their traditionally low-status relatives. For these Toraja family name and status are enhanced through previously restricted ritual channels, as money from the outside is converted into symbolic capital at home. For Toraja who are now declining nobility such rituals are visible reminders of their own loss of power and prestige, of the waning of their once expansive, sheltering "umbrella-dom" (kapayungan).

Rethinking ritual has thus become a significant cultural activity in Tana Toraja. To some, ritual is a source of renewed dynamism; to others it is the object of a nostalgic romanticism; and to still others it is a burdensome legacy that leads to squandered wealth and energy. Through ritual the Toraja enact, elaborate, and reflect upon images of themselves and their society. In recent years new actors have moved to center stage and new observers have begun to view the scene. The responses of government officials, tourists, and anthropologists, in turn, influence the Toraja's own experience. Through tourism in particular the Toraja have come to see themselves as popular performers in exotic spectacles which increasingly define their value and identity in the wider world.

However thin the line may be between the creative construction of cultural identity and its reification into neat anthropological or touristic packages, it is clear that the village funeral ceremony remains the symbolic arena in which the Toraja self is validated. Here, competition between inherited status and newly acquired wealth emerges in what the Toraja call *inflasi* (inflation) of the ritual stakes, a battle on the ceremonial field between blood and money.[3] Inflation, of course, is more than escalation; it also implies devaluation. "Inflated" rituals evoke responses sometimes expressed as loss of power— "Our umbrella-dom has disappeared" *(ta'de mo tu kapayungangki)*— or sometimes as loss of authenticity, originality, or truth. "It's no longer authentic/original," people say in Indonesian *(tidak asli lagi)*; or, in Toraja, "It isn't true" *(tae' na tongan)*.

The Toraja themselves thus touch upon the anthropological preoccupation with the problem of meaning. "Man," as Clifford Geertz (1973:5) reminds us, "is an animal suspended in webs of significance he himself has spun." Through these symbolic webs men and women attempt to make sense of their lives; and at times they get caught in the sticky threads. A symbolic form such as ritual is of interest not only because the anthropologist may unravel hidden strands of meaning, but also, as Geertz (1973:448) argues in his now-classic analysis of the Balinese cockfight, because (in this case) "it provides a metasocial commentary upon the whole matter of assorting human beings into fixed hierarchical ranks. . . . Its function, if you want to call it that, is interpretive: it is a Balinese reading of Balinese experience, a story they tell themselves about themselves." The cockfight is such a story because of the myriad ways in which the Balinese manage to connect "the collision of roosters with the divisiveness of status."

In the present study the Toraja funeral is also seen as a "story" about status, one in which the key symbolic action is not rooster collision but meat division. Here I have not separated the social from the interpretive function. The Toraja funeral most certainly affects the worldly wealth and status of its participants, as well as their understandings of that wealth and status and of their relationships with each other and with their gods. That both these relationships and these understandings are changing is a central theme of this book. We may even carry the textual analogy a step further: ritual in contemporary Toraja is something to be analyzed and criticized, accepted or rejected, reviewed and revised.

A ritual worth its salt in Tana Toraja is one in which people care deeply about the splendor of buffalo and pigs, the ways in which their meat is divided, and the honor or shame that is thereby bestowed or aroused. Yet this very engagement may be a problem: "the problem of meat," or "the problem of honor/ shame," as the Toraja put it. Like the Balinese cockfight, the Toraja funeral may be read as a depiction of struggle within the culture. The Toraja funeral is also interpreted, by at least some Toraja, as a struggle *with* some of the culture's most steadfast symbolic webs.

In this book a history of To' Dama', a single village, and the stories of a woman, Mama' Agus, and her family, are told against the broad outlines of the history of the Toraja highlands and an analysis of Toraja society and ritual. It is a local history that emerges through the eyes of the people of To' Dama' and the surrounding area, a history in which symbols, ritual performances, and social processes are reinterpreted and charged with new meanings in a profoundly changing world. It is also an account of how one family experienced the colonial and postcolonial era in Sulawesi, and the symbolic forms through which they attempted, and still attempt, to make sense of their lives.

## Fieldwork

When Charles Zerner and I arrived in Indonesia in December 1976, preparations were underway for the four-month national election campaign. As a result, foreign researchers were restricted to living in major cities. We were fortunate to be able to settle in Rantepao, Tana Toraja's largest town (pop. 11,000). By contrast with the surrounding countryside, Rantepao is a lively urban center with shops, hotels, and restaurants; an enormous, thriving market; a new sewage system; electricity, schools, hospitals, churches, and a post office; and a rapidly growing fleet of Colt minibuses. In its fine stone houses live many of the once politically active elite, now retired, and a younger, well-educated elite who hold government jobs in the district capital, Makale, eighteen kilometers to the south. We had studied Indonesian (*bahasa Indonesia*) in the United States, and once in Rantepao we began to study the Toraja language, sometimes referred to as *bahasa Tae'*. This was not, however, an ideal situation, since most people in Rantepao also speak excellent Indonesian and were not inclined to speak their "old-fashioned" language with Americans, especially with a *doctorandus* (Ph.D. candidate). Our Toraja tutor, a judge in Makale, was teaching his three young daughters only Indonesian, believing that in the future it would prove more useful to them than their native tongue. The attitudes and contradictions revealed here were perhaps more significant than the actual Toraja language training.

Rantepao proved a base for daytime forays into the countryside, and through trips and conversations I came to choose Mount Sesean as the area for my research. I had been interested in studying the resiliency of a traditional ritual system within a largely Islamic nation, and more immediately within the context of Christian missionizing in Tana Toraja. Initially I had been drawn to photographs of magnificently austere wooden effigies, carved for the noble dead, and I sought an area where effigies were still being made and ritual life was still active. Sesean seemed a promising choice: it had a reputation as an area where rituals were "still authentic" or "original"—*masih asli* in the local (Indonesian) idiom—and still vital in everyday life. It had fewer converts to Christianity than many other areas, about 40 percent in the village I eventually chose. European tourists, who had begun to flock to Tana Toraja in the early 1970s, had not yet discovered the area—a somewhat miraculous occurrence since it is only three hours by a bumpy, winding, dusty mountain road from Rantepao, traversing some of the most stunning scenery in Indonesia: cascading, terraced *sawah* laced with huge volcanic boulders; bamboo stands a hundred feet tall; and chilly morning mists that rise from the valleys.

Ritual not only flourished on Mount Sesean, it was also in flux, and it was this flux that quickly came to intrigue me.

Conflict was evident on the first day we visited To' Dama', in May 1977. We were invited to a ceremony marking the ground breaking for a new Japanese coffee factory, a kilometer down the road from the whitewashed wooden house that was to become our home. There was particular irony in this ceremony: coffee had lured outsiders to Toraja in the last quarter of the nineteenth century, when Bugis traders sought not only beans but also Toraja slaves, causing considerable upheavals in the highlands. In the early twentieth century Dutch commercial interests encouraged coffee growing, but during the Japanese occupation (1942–45) the price of beans plummeted and local people allowed their trees to die. Now the Japanese were back, promoting coffee and modernity with the first factory in the Toraja regency. One sensed both excitement and trepidation at the unknown implications of the factory. Ambivalence toward this installation emerged more clearly that afternoon at an animist funeral held in a nearby village. Traditionally, rites of life and death cannot be held in a single community on the same day. At this funeral most of the afternoon was spent debating the proprieties of continuing the death ceremony in light of the morning coffee initiation. At last the problem was resolved by declaring the coffee rite to be purely Christian (in this context, akin to secular), and hence not affecting or conflicting with the animist death rite. Later I came to understand that land and local politics played as much a role here as did the rules of religious separation.

Two months later we moved to To' Dama', a cluster of houses by the roadside, at an altitude of 1,400 meters. To the south, layers of rice terraces descended into the Rantepao valley, a three-hour walk for a fast, strong-legged Toraja. North of To' Dama' the mountain rose to a steep, irregular ridge that was frequently shrouded in fog. Directly above To' Dama', ten or fifteen minutes on narrow trails in several directions, were rather prosperous settlements surrounded by lush rice fields, with traditional houses, granaries, and planting patterns. Farther up the slope the land became drier, cassava gardens replaced the rice fields, and instead of neat clusters of houses in rows there were isolated, small houses on criss-crossed log foundations. The higher up the trails one walked, the less chance there was of meeting anyone who spoke even a few words of Indonesian.

The prosperous lower settlements, the poor upland houses, and the roadside To' Dama' are part of an administrative village unit (*kampung;* pop. 1,200), which is in turn part of a larger unit known as the *desa* or *lembang* (pop. 5,500 in 1978). In everyday talk, however, these boundaries are disregarded and people use the old name Tondoklitak to describe a community that sees itself as linked (if not exactly unified), both socially and ritually. Of still greater relevance for daily interaction are the house clusters, such as To' Dama'.

In 1977-78 To' Dama' consisted of five main houses with several others located peripherally off the road. Two of these houses included coffee shops, or *warung,* and a third large *warung* was built along the road during our stay. The settlement also included a clinic, which housed the paramedic and his family, and a whitewashed, wooden Protestant church. The concrete foundation for a new church building was laid just before our departure. The constant population of To' Dama' was about fifteen adults and ten children, but at any time there were at least ten or twenty visitors of all ages, some for extended stays of weeks or months. Children and grandchildren, at school in Rantepao, would appear in the village on weekends. On Rantepao market days (every sixth day) the population swelled enormously with crowds of market-goers awaiting minibus transportation along the road (a phenomenon that increased visibly during our stay). Other market-goers, tired and footsore from the long walk, would pause to rest and gossip in the *warung.* At these times the *warung* buzzed with activity. Traders of both coffee and onions would also spend the night in the *warung,* sleeping or playing cards.

In spite of its small size To' Dama' was often lively because of its special location—a meeting or resting place for traders, gamblers, old women from high up the mountain who came to buy a little betel or tobacco, and rowdy children who attended school just above the road. In addition to all this, life in To' Dama' offered me a chance to study the influence of the Dutch.

Not only was the village indirectly created by the Dutch, who built the road it straddles, but Dutchmen figured prominently in the lives of its inhabitants, especially Mama' Agus.

We were fortunate to be introduced to Mama' Agus, thanks to her cousin Wym, whom we had met in Rantepao. Wym, the son of a German geologist and Mama' Agus's mother's sister, worked at the technical high school in Rantepao. He suggested that on our trip north to Mount Sesean we might look up Tanta ("Aunt") Lies, as he called her. We did, arriving by minibus on a Sunday morning just as services were ending at the Protestant church. She emerged, dressed in a pale blue cotton blouse and sarong, and welcomed us. We talked politely over coffee and spent the night, captivated by this tiny, slender woman with waist-length black hair, strong features, and serious eyes. She did not look or seem her nearly seventy years, but clearly she had already lived a long and complicated life. We left the following day, promising to return. In July 1977 we moved into her house at To' Dama', where we lived until September 1978.

Mama' Agus was born a kilometer or two east of To' Dama'. Much of her childhood, however, was spent in the company of three of her mother's sisters and their Dutch or German husbands. With them she lived in the Islamic cities of Palopo (on the Gulf of Bone) and Makassar, where the men worked for the colonial administration, engineering waterworks or building bridges. With one uncle, the German geologist, she traveled as a girl into the jungles of central Celebes and by sea to the tiny islands of Celebes's southeastern arm. By the end of World War II, Mama' Agus was in her early thirties and still unmarried, having lived much of her youth between two cultures. With the collapse of Dutch power and the departure of some of her closest relatives for Holland, she was persuaded to marry an older Toraja man, a district head in the Dutch-administered regency. He died in the 1960s, and during the 1970s all of their three children left the village for jobs or school in Jakarta or Ujung Pandang. In the late 1970s she found herself in a large, quiet house, together with a twenty-year-old niece. Mama' Agus, who seemed to feel that she lived very much alone, welcomed our company and the chance to talk about her life.

A large part of my fieldwork consisted of conversations with

Mama' Agus. Initially we spoke in Indonesian, in which she was fluent, and eventually in a mixture of Indonesian and Toraja. Her stories spanned the late nineteenth century, through memories of her grandparents' tales, and stretched across the twentieth century: her colonial childhood, the Japanese occupation, and the struggles of postindependence Indonesia. As the months went by she began to realize that her own life was as important to me as the more general precepts about kinship or ritual that she was also skilled at explaining. Gradually a personal and family history unfolded during many afternoons sitting by the kitchen fire while the rice cooked, or during long chilly evenings around our pressure lamp. I never taped these sessions, having learned from experience that to do so would have drastically altered their intimacy; and depending on the tone I did not always take notes. But Mama' Agus knew that I remembered and later wrote down much of what she said.

Intimacy was more variable with other people. At times the most satisfying form of fieldwork was to sit in Papa'na Anis's coffee shop down the road, where a few villagers or passersby would gather, and talk or simply watch and listen. At other times Ne' Nipi would sit around the kitchen fire with us. Eighty-four years old, stooped, wizened, and sarcastic, Ne' Nipi was also funny and endearing. She would joke about her erstwhile husband, Wym's father, the *Balanda* (Dutchman), jokes that I knew concealed a bitterness she felt toward the man who had long since abandoned her. But beyond the wry jokes Ne' Nipi did not want to talk about this or any other period in her life.

Ne' Leme, Mama' Agus's white-haired older brother, was considerably more loquacious. He often came to visit from his house across the road, after a long day's work, a large plaid cotton sarong or a wool overcoat across his bare shoulders. He would relax with some Scotch or cigarettes and begin to talk slowly about politics, or slavery, or agriculture. He introduced us to his son-in-law, a tireless, erratic fifty-year-old schoolteacher with an analytical bent, who walked up the mountain from Rantepao on numerous weekends to give me what he felt was a more coherent understanding of Toraja. My friendships with a younger generation, in their twenties and thirties, were

invaluable but all too rare, as this age group is rapidly migrat-
ing from the villages. In particular, though, the two sons of
Mama' Agus were devoted "younger brothers," and the contrast between them was enlightening: Agus was fascinated by
the complexities of traditional Toraja thought and ritual, while
Ruben rejected the village and its old-fashioned ways in favor
of his image of modernity. Agus was an exceptionally gifted
assistant for the few months before he returned to complete
his accounting degree at the university in Ujung Pandang.
Kombong, a zany, uneducated youth from a nearby settlement,
was also a valuable assistant. Lacking both formal education and
high status, he was rich in imagination, spontaneity, and a flair
for the expressive arts of song and narrative. He too left To'
Dama' after several months, to seek his livelihood raising and
selling vegetables with relatives in Kalimantan.

I also worked with ritual specialists, both *to minaa* (*to* = person;
*minaa* = to know), or "priests of the right" (*to minaa kanan*), and *to
mebalun* (*to* = person; *mebalun* = to wrap), or "priests of the left"
(*to minaa kiri*). *To minaa* are associated with rituals affirming life
and fertility; *to mebalun* are associated with rituals of death. Ten
minutes up the trail from To' Dama' lived Ne' Tandi Datu,
acknowledged as the foremost "man of knowledge" in the area.
A good-natured, energetic man of about sixty, with white hair
and twinkly eyes, he knew no Indonesian (deliberately, I
thought) despite a lively interest in local politics. Even when I
barely understood Toraja he would answer my awkward questions at great length, as if convinced that by the sheer force of
his speaking I would understand. Eventually our communication became more substantial: we spent long nights recording
myths, and other long hours explicating rituals in which he, as
*to minaa*, so often played a leading role. His counterpart, the *to
mebalun*, also came to figure prominently in the story that
unfolds here.

One of the striking patterns that emerged in many fieldwork
contexts, and an occasional cause for frustration, is the Toraja
penchant for order and completeness. To discuss a ritual sequence, for example, one must proceed from the beginning to
the end and leave out nothing in between. This has the ethnographic advantage of providing fairly thorough and orderly
information, but it leaves little room for interpretation. In an

early conversation, for example, Agus grew increasingly irritated with my interest in the everyday meanings of a word used in an obscure (and untranslatable) ritual metaphor, and almost insisted that I not write them down. He was equally upset that in my notes I was using abbreviations (including one for his own name) and made me promise that later I would write everything out in full. There is a strong sense among Toraja that anything in progress (unfinished) is "not good" (*tae' pa na melo*). I was fascinated, for example, with the emergence of an effigy from bamboo poles and heaps of necklaces and cloths, and often photographed the process. Inevitably someone would interrupt me, insisting that it was not good until it was finished. It was fine, even desirable, to photograph it once complete, especially a direct frontal view. This canon of propriety had little to do with thoughts of hovering ghosts or the like, for exactly the same thing happened with the building of a house. Eventually people became accustomed to my quirky interests in imperfect things-in-progress.

Related to this concern with completion is a concern with something like "truth" (*tonganna*). When anthropologist Shinji Yamashita visited our house and told a version of a myth from southern Toraja, Mama' Agus remained politely silent, as she told me later, although she knew that he was "wrong." But when a Toraja Protestant minister gave me a poetic, rather formal version of a myth that Mama' Agus herself could tell with far more eloquence and wit, she refused to repeat her own account, insisting that I now had the "true" story from the minister, a younger man of great prestige.

In spite of this attention to order, accuracy, and completeness, some kinds of inquiry met with the most elusive responses. Even a village survey had to wait until my stay was almost ended. People are generally suspicious of one another and reluctant to answer direct questions even among themselves, much less with an outsider. When I did begin, with the help of a young local woman, she only surveyed about fifty households before a powerful man (employed by government, church, school, and the new coffee factory) insisted that she stop. I learned that he was engaged in a long-standing rivalry with her father, a more traditionally based big man. The limited survey did prove useful, however, especially for infor-

mation about migration and education, as well as for what was
revealed though omissions and data-collection problems.

Certain kinds of data were unobtainable from almost any
source—for example, land ownership. One cannot ask a person
how much land he owns or how much *padi* he harvests in a
year. Resistance to reply is deeper than the simple fear of
government taxation. Although land is fervently desired and
valued, it is embarrassing to say you own too much, to boast of
your riches. On the other hand, you do not want to admit how
rich your neighbors are, so asking other people yields vague
answers. Government records are often inaccurate and list
landholdings areally, whereas most people who own land do so
in several areas. The other important form of wealth, buffalo,
was also difficult to estimate for similar reasons: people often
have buffalo that are being raised in distant villages. In sum, it
was impossible to ascertain definitively the distribution of
wealth or its relation to status.

Status is a sensitive subject, too, and slavery is supposedly
unmentionable. Once a certain level of trust was established,
however, I found people surprisingly willing to discuss these
issues. For an understanding of the historical dynamics of
ritual slaughter, it would have been useful to have figures
from past rituals for comparison with current figures, but such
information is at best scattered and sporadic in official records.
People seem to distort accounts of rituals in the distant past by
exaggerating their grandness; and in the more immediate past
embarrassment may inhibit any statement on how much of
what was actually sacrificed by whom.

Aside from "family," assistants, neighbors, ritual specialists, a
survey, and occasional government records, the main sources
for this study were rituals and travel.[4] Fortunately my presence
was welcomed at rituals, since Toraja think of "culture" as ritual
anyway, and they assumed that this was what I had come to
study. I attended several house celebrations (*maro* and *ma'bua'*), a
full cycle of planting and harvesting rites, and parts of approximately twenty funerals; seven of the latter were Christian, the
rest were "animist" (*aluk*). I never participated in a complex
funeral from start to finish, because in a sense there are no clear
demarcations. There is always a prefuneral planning session or

postfuneral inheritance division that stretches into weeks, months, or sometimes years. Funerals are definitely processes, not events. In attending I would select several days, as systematically as possible (but also depending on how many sleepless nights I thought I could endure), and come and go. This is the way any Toraja attends funerals, although for different reasons. Only the closest relatives are constantly present, and they, at the end of such an experience, are said jokingly to be "half-dead" (Indonesian *setengah mati*).

Performances provide a chance for native exegesis, observation, and a key to symbols that recur in other ritual and non-ritual contexts (Turner 1967). Since rituals also involve much sitting around and waiting between the highlights, there are many chances for conversation with participants about what they think is going on, who is participating, what are the kin relationships and the debt relationships, and who is bringing, dividing, and receiving meat. Seemingly endless ritual hours were spent in trying to unravel the complexities of these interactions. Beyond the specifics, these situations also offered opportunities for talking about the ritual system in general, as people's feelings were usually stirred up—feelings about slaughter, meat division, nobles and slaves, Christianity and indigenous religion.

If rituals were a means of delving into local culture, travel provided an often needed outward movement, a more distant perspective from which to view To' Dama', Sesean, and Toraja as a whole. A week spent with a charismatic, gifted young *to minaa* (priest) and his family in their small bamboo house offered an experience of life in the relative hinterlands. In this area, about six hours' walk west of To' Dama', status hierarchy was rudimentary and poverty a pressing fact of life. Traveling in the other direction, we lived for several weeks in a settlement an hour's drive from the city of Palopo on the coast of the Gulf of Bone. There lived a branch of Mama' Agus's family, refugees from the mountain village of Pantilang that had been destroyed in guerrilla warfare during the 1950s. Old Pantilang was located midway between Toraja and Palopo, for centuries the center of the Luwu kingdom. In many ways Pantilang was culturally between these two realms as well, and so provided a kind of foil against which to view Sesean Toraja. Finally, in Palopo itself we stayed often with a family of Bugis nobles, former rulers in the kingdom of Luwu. The contrast with Toraja was extraordinary and enlightening, and each time we would return to our mountain home as if with new eyes.

The shape of the fieldwork reflected in this book was thus an oscillation toward a center and out again: a movement between the intimacy of Mama' Agus's recollections and the sort of questions one would ask a priest; between "high speech" recitations, translations, and interpretations and the gossipy banter of the *warung* palm-wine drinkers at dusk; between the passion of a meat fight at a funeral and the cool coastal noble's comments on such fights. Ultimately all the sources produced new questions and elicited new responses from Mama' Agus, whose anecdotes, interpretations, and styles of being in the world shaped my perceptions of Toraja. Because of Mama' Agus's past, and because in a remote way she shared a bit of our Western traditions, we had from the start a means of bridging our otherness. Yet our apparent ease of communication concealed differences in our perceptions and evaluations of those traditions. For example, it was ironic that we were welcomed in part out of nostalgia for her colonial past. And her easy surfaces sometimes disguised her more truly "other" Toraja persona. Discovering that person was made more difficult by her ability to objectify her own lived world as well as ours.

Far more difficult was discovering ways of communicating with others, particularly low-status people, poor people, or former slaves. This study deals with change in Toraja status, but most of the conversations on which it is based were held with people of relatively high status. In a general way this reflects the structure of status groups in Toraja, in Southeast Asia, indeed in most parts of the world. Usually the elite are accessible, articulate, and wealthy enough to welcome strangers into their homes. They conceive of themselves as having a voice and the right to express it. When I began fieldwork I had been advised by a social scientist with experience in Sulawesi that to talk directly to "small people" might alienate not only those important, "bigger" people above them, but even the poor and former slaves themselves. To begin at the top, presumably, would earn me the respect and confidence of people at all levels. However, the bonds between Toraja leaders and followers, high and low, are relatively weak. In spite of my position as a "daughter" in a high-status family, few lower-status people seemed drawn or compelled to speak to me for this reason. More commonly such people answered questions with a repeated "I don't know": in the hierarchical organization of knowledge, they were not expected to "know." Once an old woman, a former slave, cried out in exasperation: "Why are you asking me? You're questioning a cat!"

Mama' Agus and her family represent a small, elite level of Toraja society. In a way this study is about the perceptions and lives of this unusual elite, even more unusual because of their relationships, through marriage, to Europeans or Toraja of the Dutch colonial administration. These ties to the *Balanda* (Dutch) affected our relationships in To' Dama', and whatever traces of nostalgia for the colonial past emerge in these pages have their basis in this family history. It is particular and positioned people, shaped by their own histories and temperaments, who respond to their situations and may reshape them. Mama' Agus and her brother Ne' Leme are surely atypical, connected both to the taproots of Toraja cultural tradition and to a Dutch colonial topsoil. In these atypicalities we begin to know them as living people in a particular time and space, still, to be sure, "other" people, Toraja men and women in a distinctively Toraja place.

# CHAPTER 2

# The Historical Context

According to the royal genealogists of Luwu, Batara Guru was the first heavenly being to descend to earth (Errington 1978). He came to Luwu, the navel of the world, and with him were forty lesser first cousins who were sent to surrounding mountains and islands to rule. One of these destinations was Toraja. Thus the Bugis of Luwu explain their relationship with their mountain neighbors. The cousins eventually intermarried, and to this day high-status Toraja still marry with Luwunese.

The Toraja too acknowledge their long-standing relationship with Luwu, but they explain it differently.[1] Theirs is the tale of Karaeng Dua', the elder of twin sons born to an earthly Toraja father, who lived in a forest clearing, and a spirit-mother in the form of a large white pig. Karaeng Dua' grew up in his father's house, where his father would hand him down through the floor when he needed to be suckled by his pig-mother. He became a radiantly handsome man. With his brother he collected rattan in the forest and took it to distant marketplaces. One day, when he went to sell his rattan in Palopo, he was seen by the ruler (*datu*) of Luwu, a woman. The *datu* was awestruck and was determined to marry this glowing young man. Karaeng Dua' at first refused, ashamed about his mother; but at last the *datu*'s slave persuaded him that it did not matter if his mother was a piece of wood! So Karaeng Dua' married the *datu* and lived with her in Luwu, along with his mother. One day a mischievous, wandering highlander named Dana' appeared and noticed a pig in the rafters of the *datu*'s house. "Eeeee," Dana' proclaimed to all the Luwunese, "the *datu*'s mother-in-law is a pig!" Shamed and angered, the *datu* scooped all the sun into her own house and refused to release it to darkened Luwu until, after three days of unlimited pig feasting, every remaining pig in town was returned to the forest. There would be no eating of pigs forever after, she declared. And indeed, say the Toraja, this is the history of why the people of Luwu do not eat pork.

Toraja are proud of this myth, for it demonstrates their connection to the kingdom of Luwu through marriage, and not an earthly marriage at that. At the same time, however, they voice trepidation lest the Bugis are outraged at unthinkable implications of pig ancestry. I was warned by a Toraja schoolteacher not to repeat the story to Bugis friends, who might "slit our throats." Characteristically what emerges is ambivalence: the kingdom with its ideology of heavenly descent and high nobility is both attractive and disturbing. Luwu, in centuries past, had a strong, well-organized polity, centered at the court and in the person of a single potent *datu*. The Toraja highlands, in contrast, had hundreds of scattered settlements, little competing cones of power,[2] and endless variations on pagan *aluk*.

The relationship between Luwu and the highlands is perhaps best summed up by the rite of *medatu* (*me* = to gather up; *datu* = a ruler, or something of the highest, most respected level). Each year in the past, before new rice seed was sown, Toraja descended the mountains to pay tribute to Luwu's ruler, as did other peoples of Celebes in similar tributary relationships. Men from northern Rongkong, for example, might have brought a buffalo horn filled with gold; other regions contributed cloths or slaves. Symbolically and practically the presentation expressed submission to the center, Luwu, in exchange for which the rice was blessed (van Lijf 1947–48:531). Fertility originated at the navel, and mountain people depended on the *datu*'s magical potency to ensure their own agricultural success. Yet in one Toraja tale the *datu* of Luwu is pregnant and long overdue. Unable to give birth, she is advised by Dana', the Toraja trickster, to squat in a field of mud that he digs up. She does so and indeed gives birth to rice. The source of rice is thus Luwu's ruler, but without the clever assistance of Toraja it would not have come forth (typically, Toraja in these stories are clever but dependent). Dana' is then wily enough to steal the royal seed and bring it to the mountains, where the Toraja,

in their own estimation, have far surpassed the Bugis in the
order and beauty of their rice fields.

Toraja responses to submission to Luwu emerge indirectly in
many stories, in the form of tricks. One story, for example,
tells of a Toraja leader who goes on a visit of submission to the
*datu* (Decavele 1978). A contest is proposed whereby the Toraja
and the *datu* could prove their respective strengths: who could
produce the superior excrement? The *datu* fixes a sumptuous
banquet but produces a shapeless, stinking heap. The Toraja,
on the other hand, eats simple pumpkins and green vegetables,
and excretes a stylish, solid mound the color of fine gold. Everyone has to agree that the Toraja has won: the *datu* is not only
outwitted, but out-shitted.

## Toraja in South Celebes

The history of the Toraja cannot be understood in isolation
from the wider history of South Celebes, nor from the still
wider European struggles in which the island's kingdoms and
petty states became embroiled. Unlike the Bugis and Makassarese, the highland peoples never had a written script, and so
much of what we know of their early history is based on the
chronicles of their literate coislanders (Noorduyn 1965). Also
unlike their lowland neighbors the highlanders never had a
centralized polity or kingdom, no concentration of potency in
the person of a godlike ruler, no expression of his potency in
the organization of a court. Instead, Toraja consisted of numerous small, often competing *tondok*—a word roughly trans-
latable as "settlement," an elastic concept referring to a unit as
small as a cluster of two or three houses hidden under a stand
of bamboo, or as large as the highland world. Between these
two extremes lay a shifting *tondok* defined largely by marriage
and ritual interaction, which could link distant house clusters,
and warfare, which could separate ones nearby. The dimensions and power of a given *tondok* rose and fell with the strength
of its "big men" (*to kapua*): individuals of high status, wealth,
and charisma who could attract substantial followings. Big
men owned large amounts of land, particularly wet rice land,
and numerous retainers or slaves (*kaunan*), who worked this

land in exchange for food. The big men's status and power were repeatedly expressed (and often challenged) in ritual performances, which defined both individual position and relationships between dispersed *tondok* in the hills. The ritual medium was most frequently meat: through sacrifice of water buffalo and pigs, and distribution of their meat, big men affirmed their "names" and followings. No courtly titles, no permanent office, no potent regalia ensured their continuity.

Quite different was the situation in the lowlands, where Indic-style polities had waxed and waned for centuries. The kingdom of Luwu had seen its heyday in the fifteenth century (Andaya 1979:362). In 1511 the port of Malacca on the Malay Pennisula fell to the Portuguese, resulting in a diversion of the spice trade to Makassar. Consequently the Makassarese kingdom of Goa flourished, as sandalwood, pepper, and other spices that had previously flowed from the Moluccas, Timor, and Solor to Malacca and then to Egypt now passed through Makassar. The port, on the southwestern coast of Celebes, was located strategically at the intersection of shipping routes in four directions (Lineton 1975a:12; Vlekke 1960:52–53). By the mid-seventeenth century Goa exercised considerable influence over surrounding Bugis states and other parts of Indonesia. Among other actions the Makassarese invaded the Toraja highlands in the seventeenth century, for the purpose, according to Gervaise (1685:6–7), of establishing the "True Religion," Islam, which had been accepted by Goa early in that century.

The expansion of local kingdoms and of Bugis, Makassarese, and Malay trade was so successful that the Dutch finally intervened in an attempt to regain control over their spice monopoly in the Moluccas. To do so they played on "the delicate balance of power between Goa and the Bugis states" (Lineton 1975a:13) and enlisted the aid and troops of Arung Palakka, a prince of the Bugis kingdom of Bone. Arung Palakka had fled Celebes in 1660 after leading an abortive revolt against powerful Goa, and he appealed for help to the Dutch East India Company. Six years later he and his Bugis troops set sail with the Dutch to attack Makassar, which fell to the invaders in 1669.

The resulting treaty gave the Dutch East India Company the monopoly of trade in the port of Makassar, which led to a vast

expansion of Bugis smuggling, piracy, and conquests throughout the archipelago. Closer to home these events had ramifications on the political scene in South Celebes, as Arung Palakka
eventually became the ruler of Bone and "the principal archi-
tect of the reorganization of the power structure" (Andaya
1979:364) in South Celebes. The new leader conducted military campaigns against the major Bugis states (Luwu, Mandar,
Wajo, Sidenreng), and even against the scattered highland *tondok* in the north. Arung Palakka's invasion of the highlands late
in the seventeenth century has become a Toraja legend: with
one exception all the major Toraja *tondok* are said to have united
to repel the invaders. The exception became an outcaste village, its inhabitants until Dutch times considered a legitimate
source for human heads (required at important funerals), and
today still stigmatized as "cowards." For all its mythic import,
however, the unity of the Arung Palakka episode was fleeting.

   The highlands again became deeply involved with lowland
kingdom rivalries in the last few decades of the nineteenth
century. In 1861 powerful Bone was attacked by the Dutch,
after which its "younger brother" kingdom Sidenreng, on the
western coast, emerged vigorously upon the local scene. In the
late nineteenth century the three kingdoms of Bone, Sidenreng, and Luwu all sent traders and raiders to the Toraja highlands, seeking both coffee and slaves.[3]

   The dynamics of the coffee and slave wars of this period
have been admirably documented and analyzed by Bigalke
(1981: chaps. 2–3), who shows how trade in the two commodi-
ties must be viewed in conjunction. Although coffee may have
been planted in the highlands as early as the seventeenth century, when Goa was busy raiding in the area, its real expansion
did not occur until the mid-nineteenth century, when the price
of beans was increasing dramatically on the European market.
The excellent arabica coffee of the highlands became highly
desired by the lowland kingdoms that began to compete for
control of its trade. Luwu, with its eastern port of Palopo (Gulf
of Bone), and Sidenreng, with its western port of Pare Pare
(Makassar Strait), took the lead. In the 1870s and 1880s agents
from Sidenreng began to operate in the highlands, offering
firearms (recently obtained from English gunrunners) in ex-

change for coffee beans. Later Sidenreng sent bands of armed men into highland villages, terrorizing the population and succeeding, by 1897, in controlling the coffee flow. At this point Luwu called on its more powerful ally, Bone, which sent a contingent of red-hatted troops into the highlands, the Songkok Borrong ("Crimson Hats"). This Bone army swept through the coffee routes, but soon after their departure the highland traders turned again toward Sidenreng.

On the opposite side of this coin was the trade in slaves, which became substantial in this period. In part, Bigalke argues, the slave trade was tied to growing labor shortages on the coasts, where land was plentiful and manpower scarce (the opposite of the highland situation where land was already in short supply).[4] Significantly the slave trade also seemed to stabilize a fluctuating coffee market. Bigalke shows that when coffee prices plunged, slaving increased, and it declined when prices rose again. Apparently the trade in persons simply utilized already established long-distance coffee networks between Toraja elite, who controlled the routes, and the coastal courts.

In most Toraja *tondok*, now and in the past, the social world consists of at least three categories of persons: nobles, commoners, and slaves, or *kaunan*. The "slave trade," however, did not necessarily trade only *kaunan*. It often happened that ordinary folk were captured, bound, and sold, should they be ambushed along a trail or taken as captives in war. An old woman on Sesean remembers seeing men and women grabbed and tied and marched away, while their small children lay abandoned by the path. "It was a time of fear," she shuddered. Women did not stay alone in houses, nor could market-goers travel without a protective entourage. At times people were attacked while harvesting their fields. In these years many *tondok* were surrounded by stone or earthen walls and were connected to neighboring settlements by long underground tunnels. These tunnels, wide enough to allow the passage of a long-horned buffalo, were sometimes laced with sharpened bamboo poles, sticking out at lethal angles to spear an unwary or fleeing enemy.

Although thousands of slaves must have been captured,

others were simply sold. Sesean villagers speak of certain people who sold their own brothers "like buffalo or vegetables," and of others who gambled themselves into debt-slavery. Children appear to have been exchanged in gambling as well: van Rijn describes a "half-starved child" in a highland market in 1897, being sold for ten rijksdollars. He was told that "most people who are traded in public are weak and rundown because their not well-to-do owners, who have obtained them in gambling, cannot afford to feed their living property for long and try to sell them as quickly as possible" (quoted in Bigalke 1981:73–74).

The vicissitudes of slaving and raiding in the late nineteenth century created an increasingly tense situation in the highlands. Sesean villagers remember vividly their grandparents' stories of warfare: men fought with spears and blowguns equipped with poisoned darts, and women incited them from the rear, dancing with sarongs lifted, feet stamping rhythmically, and bodies spinning as they waved shields and horsehair banners and whooped a piercing cry. By the late nineteenth century even the style of warfare had begun to change, as firearms came into use. And what were perceived as local dramas between rival big men were now usually episodes in a larger play. The directors were the lowland kingdoms, the key actors their slave and coffee traders. The Toraja elite were not merely pawns the lowlanders chose to cultivate or manipulate, but, as Bigalke has shown, they too were actors in this play. The pawns, unfortunately, were some twelve thousand highlanders who found themselves sold as slaves.

## Transitions: The *Balanda* in the Highlands

On another level the play within the play was moving rapidly in the highlands, as growing power struggles developed between several Toraja big men, struggles that were abruptly halted with the entry of the Dutch. Most notably, Pong Tiku of Pangala' (in the northwest) and Pong Maramba of Kalambe (near Rantepao) each controlled a major coffee route, and each was allied with a different lowland kingdom and port of trade (Sidenreng and Luwu, respectively). Each could exploit the kingdoms' rivalries to ensure their own support. Thanks to the availability of firearms and Bugis military advisors, each was able to capture land and people to a degree unprecedented in highland history. Each created his own growing reign of territory and terror. Pong Tiku is remembered on Sesean for his violence. He took politically valuable women as wives, both to expand his influence and in a series of fruitless attempts to father children. When "necessary" he murdered the husbands and burned homes in recalcitrant *tondok*. Pong Maramba is remembered on Sesean for his voracious greed: he is said to have been very fat, capable of devouring an entire pig at a single sitting.

In 1905 and 1906 Dutch troops attacked and occupied all the major kingdoms of South Celebes: Bone, Sidenreng, Goa, and Luwu. The Dutch then proceeded to move into the Toraja highlands. With rumors of Dutch conquests on the coasts, Toraja leaders braced for an attack, and for a brief period internal fighting gave way to a consensus to resist (Bigalke 1981:100). Both Pong Tiku and Pong Maramba were assigned strategic roles. Meanwhile the Dutch in Luwu used Arab traders' reports to penetrate the less cohesive side of highland politics, and learned of internal conflicts between the major *tondok* and Balusu, a region with close historical ties to Luwu. In fact the son of a Luwu official was married to the daughter of a Toraja noble (*puang*) in Balusu. Bigalke (1981:102) tells this story: "Almost surgically, the 'culprit' was separated from his Torajan in-law and arrested in Palopo, after which time the Puang did an about-face and sent 190 retainers to Palopo to assist the Dutch entry into the north. With this group of porters, a column of 150 troops led by 3 officers entered tondok Balusu on March 13, 1906."

The outcome of these events has become almost legendary in Tana Toraja. While most other big men capitulated to the armed newcomers, Pong Tiku and his troops resisted Dutch attacks for many months. In part because of the rugged mountains of Pong Tiku's northern fortresses, in part because of his military experience, and probably in part because of his sheer brazen courage, Dutch troops found themselves fighting something like a guerrilla war on terrain the natives knew best. In fact the Ambonese, Javanese, Timorese, and Batak forces complained about the cold (Bigalke 1981:108). Not until heavier artillery arrived could they penetrate Pong Tiku's lesser forts, and the main fort remained unyielding. At last the governor general began to be embarrassed, fearing "that the authority of Netherlands East Indies troops in South Sulawesi might be undermined by a prominent symbol of resistance. He thus dispatched the civil and military Governor of Celebes to personally conduct the final assault against Pong Tiku" (1981:110). In October 1906 the long siege ended. Pong Tiku and his troops, who fought fiercely with everything from hot pepper-juice sprayers and spears to cannonballs, surrendered. In the 1960s Pong Tiku received the official title of "National Hero." But in 1906 the Dutch were finally ensconced in the highlands of South Celebes.

The Dutch arrived in the highlands at a time when the local scene had been shaken by unprecedented territorial expansion and consolidation of power; by incipient economic changes such as the penetration of cash from coffee trading, Bugis-introduced gambling, and new patterns of land ownership; and the general climate of fear. The latter, in particular, is remembered by old people on Sesean who were children in precolonial times, and who often told me how the Dutch came with peace, initiating the "present world" (lino totemo). The residue of several decades of insecurity was still real for children born after the Dutch arrival: Mama' Agus, for example, who was born in about 1910, recalls that when she was three she saw the ghost of a to sallang, which means both "enemy" and "Muslim" in Toraja. She recognized him by his crimson hat (i.e., he was a Songkok Borrong from Bone), as he stood by the entrance to an underground tunnel. He was there, her grandmother explained, because as a Muslim he knew no "ritual" (aluk) and therefore had had no proper burial. To appease the ghost her grandmother brought eggs and betel to the gateway and told him to go away and not to bother them.

The Dutch did, indeed, bring peace to the troubled highlands, although not always an easy peace, and they inspired fear as well. Ne' Bulaan, a very old woman on Sesean, was guarding her grandfather's water buffalo when she first saw the *Balanda*, as the Toraja call the Dutch: "I was just a girl, and then they came, thorns on their feet and smoke pouring from their mouths! Waduuh, I was scared," she laughed, adding that she and her friends grabbed rice, cooking pots, and whatever else came to hand and ran to caves in the hills. Boots, cigarettes, white skin, "white" eyes (or "cats' eyes"), and outlandish size all suggested an alien, almost spiritlike aspect of the newcomers. Their food was strange (especially the canned fish they ate with bread when they camped on people's granaries), and so too was their speech: an incomprehensible birdlike babble.

The *Balanda*, like the Bugis before them and like the spirits (*deata*), were viewed with an ambivalent mixture of respect and fear. In one ritual verse the Dutch are described as "above the sun." They cook with its heat and use brass pots and golden spoons, and are as pleased with their power as if delectable durian fruits had fallen at their feet. Another verse expresses a more direct opinion: "Dutchmen go home!" (*Sullemo ko Balanda*); while another proclaims ambiguously, "Trick the Dutch!" or "The Dutch trick!" (*Kena kena to Balanda*).[5] The Dutch were seen as tricky and spiritlike even in military contexts: Toraja who had seen Dutch exercises at Pare Pare, before the invasion of the highlands, observed that rows of men fell down when shot and rose again (Bigalke 1981:100), like so many figures in Toraja myth who died and were returned to life.

The Dutch, for their part, came as a result of the Netherlands' new Ethical Policy, which professed at the turn of the century that the colony was to be governed not (only) for the sake of the mother country, but also for the sake of its indigenous inhabitants. Until then Dutch interests in South Celebes had not reached substantially beyond control of the entrepôt of Makassar, with its lucrative trade. In the nineteenth century it was still the case that "with regard to the Celebes, although it yielded a small supply of coffee, the opinion generally prevailing was ... 'the less one heard of it the better' " (Furnivall 1939:177–78). By the end of the long and costly war against the Islamic Achenese of North Sumatra, the Dutch were persuaded that a more penetrating presence was required in the Indies. "It was only by effective occupation that

Government could ensure the welfare of the people," Furnivall (1939:237) observed; ". . . moreover, by this time oil had been discovered in Sumatra and Borneo. In the name of righteousness therefore, and in the interest of capital, Government took up the task of bringing the whole archipelago under Dutch rule." Capital was not the only interest. One of the effects of the war in Aceh was increasing concern about the spread of Islam. Among its other attractions the highlands of Celebes offered the promise of a large, as yet non-Islamic population that could someday convert to Christianity. Pagan Toraja might become a steadfast Christian island in a vast sea of Islam.

## Colonial Days

Within a few years after their arrival in the highlands the Dutch had created two company towns; a clearly bounded territory carved into thirty-two districts, in turn subdivided into hundreds of villages; a system of taxation and corvée labor; schools; and an indigenous, local-level administration. They also abolished headhunting, which seems to have been carried out infrequently on the occasion of major funerals, and the sale of persons. Of the estimated twelve thousand highlanders who had been seized for slavery and transported to the lowlands, about a third returned before the 1911 deadline set by the Dutch (Bigalke 1981:141). In spite of all these changes, however, most Toraja today are emphatic about one thing: the Dutch wished to keep the status hierarchy exactly as it was, so that nobles remained nobles, commoners remained commoners, and slaves remained slaves.

The delineation of fixed boundaries was far from the indigenous (and typically Southeast Asian) manner of defining power, which was centered in persons (and in Toraja, in houses) rather than bounded by geography. Nonetheless, this seemed to be an inescapable feature of the colonial administration. The whole region of Toraja became two subdivisions (onderafdeeling) of the larger division of Luwu (afdeeling), a revival, in a sense, of the highlanders' declining tributary relations with that Bugis state. The two Toraja subdivisions, Makale in

the south and Rantepao in the north, were governed by a
Dutch *controleur* stationed in Makale. In an attempt to fit this
system with local norms the Dutch borrowed Toraja names.
Districts, for example, were labeled *bua'*, a southern Toraja
term for "ritual community," and district heads were called *to
parengnge*, "those who carry (something) on their backs," a
southern term for "leader."[6] Districts, in turn, were divided
into villages, or *kampung*. A tax collector on Sesean who had had
to memorize the twenty-nine villages of Tikala District while
in Dutch school was still able to recite the list to me, in geo-
graphical order. Below each village head were lesser officials or
*bandoro*, responsible for such tasks as collecting taxes or calling
the men out to work.

In theory the district head (*to parengnge*; or *Kepala Distrik*, as he
was known in Indonesian) was elected by the adult males,
although the Dutch *controleur* retained the right to judge him
"fit" or not (Bigalke 1981:126). In their efforts to understand
exactly how (and for whom) the social hierarchy worked, the
Dutch sent Ambonese genealogists into the hills to discover
which were the respected, feared, wealthy, and powerful
families in each area. Not surprisingly the Dutch supported
established power, and some big men became legitimized
"heads." Depending on the local context, the new officials may
sometimes have been slightly lesser but more cooperative
nobility. This seems to have been the case in Tondoklitak,
where in spite of the village head's official position via the
Dutch, he lacked the all-important Toraja power to divide
meat. That power continued to be exercised by the traditional
leader, or *ambe'*, "father" of the *tondok*. At all levels the new
colonial headmen were able to maintain a form of patron-client
relationship with their followers, since their position entitled
them to a certain number of days of labor from each adult male
under their jurisdiction. The legitimation of such relationships,
of course, now came from above rather than below. This
system also allowed some officials to extend their landholdings
relatively unchallenged, relying on the vast labor supply at
their disposal.

Headmen received salaries in addition to free labor, but

initially the circulation of money was quite limited. Precolonially coffee had brought some cash into the economy, but
most trade at local markets took the form of barter, while
larger markets were dominated by Bugis traders. On Sesean
old people remember receiving coins from Dutch soldiers in
exchange for carrying their belongings, or for the occasional
purchase of a pig or chicken. In fact coins had been popular in
the highlands precolonially, when Portuguese and East India
Company coins were used as ornaments or melted down into
thick, highly valued silver bracelets worn by high-status
women. Coins were treated like other treasured, exotic items,
such as bird-of-paradise plumes that hinted of distant trade
routes to New Guinea, or woven *ikat* cloths from the northern
forests of Makki. They might decorate a noble person's effigy
or be placed in boiling water to give the water healing powers.
At first the coins brought by the Dutch may have been treated
in a similar way.

Taxation required the transition from coin as potent object
to coin as medium of exchange. What had previously been a
restricted luxury became a periodic necessity, as first a head
tax and later a slaughter tax were imposed. Many people were
forced to sell precious *padi*, pigs, or even land to avoid arrest or
forced labor for lack of payment. To Napa, the great priest of
Sesean, is said to have blinded himself in rage and fear that he
would be required to pay taxes, although as it happened ritual
specialists were exempted from this burden. Taxes continued
to be resented (as they still are), but gradually, in the course of
over three decades of Dutch administration from 1906 to 1942,
a modest cash economy began to penetrate the area. Larger
markets became more cash-oriented, and officials, policemen,
teachers, and office clerks became a new class of salaried labor.
Money slowly came to be a standard and a means, though still
restricted, of obtaining status.

Status was still largely expressed through participation in
the traditional ritual system, however: through the sacrifice
and distribution of animal wealth to fellow-men, gods, and
ancestors. This Toraja reality, Dutch missionaries soon realized, would have to be confronted.

## The Mission: Two New Religions

Precolonially the Toraja language had no word for "religion," nor did it have a special word for "ritual" or "custom." Ideas and actions, with regard to both human and spirit actors, were fused in the single conception of *aluk*, which touched all that was believed in, said, or done. *Aluk* was the wisdom of the ancestors, brought by the great *to minaa* Suloara; it was the multitude of spirits who inhabited mountain peaks, or streams, or house rafters; it was the speech of the priests, or *to minaa*; the speechless gestures of the mortuary priest, or *to mebalun*; the number of buffalo slaughtered; the countless (or 7,777) prohibitions that informed daily life; the proper performance of every prayer and ceremony. All this and more was part of *aluk*, until the mission succeeded in dividing it so that *aluk* came to mean "religion" (Indonesian *agama*), while the neutral Indonesian word *adat* was adopted to mean "custom."[7]

A large part of the knowledge spread by the *to minaa* Suloara concerned the proper performance of an array of rituals, informed by an opposition that permeated all aspects of life and death: smoke-rising (*rambu tuka'*) and smoke-descending (*rambu solo'*). Smoke-rising referred to that which was on the side of life, growth, prosperity, and the rising sun in the east. Smoke-descending was death, decrease, and the setting sun in the west. To please the gods mankind was required to separate these realms carefully, and numerous taboos (*pemali*) maintained the separation. The time of year, crops planted, food consumed, animals sacrificed, and even the vocabulary employed were all distinguished according to which way the smoke was moving.

The major smoke-descending ritual, or *aluk rampe matampu'* ("*aluk* on the western side"), is the funeral, which serves to transport the soul (*bombo*) from this world to the next. The grave is sometimes called the "house without smoke"; it has no kitchen fire burning. Puya, the world of *bombo*, is located to the southwest, possibly between Enrekang and Kalosi (Nooy-Palm 1979:112). Existence in Puya replicates existence in this world: there are ranked statuses, wealth, and buffalo. *Bombo* in Puya became "ancestors," *nene'* or *to matua* ("the old ones"), but at times they may still bother the living. In dreams, Pak Kila' said, "we sometimes see them, or hear them going '*krak krak krak.*' Maybe because we made some error in their *pesta* (ritual)." Because ancestors do not lose contact with the human world, men must continually respect and honor them; they may be pleased or angry, may bless or harm the living. A few rare individuals may make direct contact, those with the power to "visit" Puya.

Depending on the actions of men on earth, some *bombo* may eventually become *deata*, or spirits, if their descendants perform the proper ceremonies. *Deata* are associated with the northeast (*aluk rampe matallo*, "*aluk* on the eastern side"), in contrast to the southwesterly direction of the dead. They are also everywhere. Some have been around from the beginning; others are former ancestors transformed. Some are named and have definite characteristics; others are associated with particular rocks, trees, springs, snakes, or houses. Still others are ancestors who are thought to be, in Pak Kila''s words, "up there somewhere with the stars and clouds; they return to earth in falling rain and mist, and we meet them at the spring." One cannot pinpoint them; they permeate the universe and its contents, including, at certain rituals, men and women who may become possessed.

*Deata*, ancestors, and a third figure, Puang Matua, are called and fed at rituals. Puang Matua (*puang* = owner, lord; *matua* = old, great) is one of many mythical ancestors but not the first; he forged mankind from his golden, heavenly bellows and is always mentioned and given special offerings. The rising smoke of burning incense or offerings, the *to minaa* Tandi Datu explained, is like the aroma of freshly roasting coffee beans: it lures the gods and ancestors and Puang Matua, and they fulfill our wishes.

In Toraja cosmology hundreds, perhaps thousands, of spirits and ancestors are named, their genealogies traced, their stories told. Few people, however, know the contents of this elaborate (and regionally variable) mythic history, except for a small number of *to minaa* whose job it is to retain this specialized knowledge and periodically reveal it in poems, chants, and supplications. Nonetheless, all *aluk* adherents know that ancestors and gods are everywhere, and that a hierarchy of rituals must be performed so as to please, appease, and beseech these spirits, and keep the universe in good order.

If *aluk* was a total phenomenon, its ritual expressions were most conspicuous and bothersome to the Calvinist mission that arrived soon after the Dutch administration. In particular the paganism of a world populated by spirits that required feeding and frequent sacrifice at every ritual was distasteful to the mission's "civilizing" impulses. Still, sensitive to the importance of ritual in Toraja life and thought (and its role in maintaining a hierarchy of nobles, commoners, and slaves), the mission initially avoided meddling in this domain. When A. A. van de Loosdrecht, the first missionary from the Dutch Reformed Alliance (*Gereformeerde Zendingsbond, GZB*), arrived in Rantepao in 1913, he avoided all questions of ritual or theology, seeking instead to cultivate good relations with the nobility. He urged them to accept schools, believing that religious education would then come easily. He met resistance to his school campaign, however, and his tactics of rounding up truant children and jailing their parents did not endear him to his target converts. Nor did villagers appreciate his insistence on their contributions of labor and materials toward school construction, or the contemptuous attitudes of Minahasan and Ambonese teachers toward their less worldly mountain pupils (Bigalke 1981:62). Eventually van de Loosdrecht grew impatient and altered his approach, appealing (or so he hoped) to lower-status groups and criticizing the inequities whereby the wealthy owned much land and many others had none at all. He blamed the situation on the death feast, observing (correctly) that people often pawned and lost their land as a result of ritual obligations. But the missionary's attacks on death rituals touched a vital nerve, and rumors spread that he conspired with the governor to abolish the death feast altogether, while converting the whole population to Christianity. This, combined with his well-known opposition to cockfighting and the exile of several prominent (unconverted) headmen on extortion charges, proved to be the last straw. In 1917 several years of grievances culminated in plans for serious rebellion, to be orchestrated by village headmen with the goal of driving the

Dutch away. Of many subplots only one was realized: a spear was plunged through van de Loosdrecht's chest.[8]

Van de Loosdrecht's murder and the subsequent uncovering of plans for wider rebellion marked the end of active Toraja resistance to the Dutch, as well as the end of the mission's frontal assault on ritual practices. By 1923 the mission had established a council composed of missionaries, teachers, and elders to determine the proper accommodation between ritual and the new religion (Bigalke 1981:221). The outcome was the development of a simple but decisive strategy: the formal separation of custom from religion, as two complementary but distinct domains. Now one no longer had to renounce everything traditional in order to convert, since "custom" (adat), being secular and social, was deemed acceptable. Only aluk, by definition both religious and heathen, was threatening to the Church and would be forbidden.

The problem, of course, became one of distinguishing which was what, and this the council did by a series of pronouncements. Almost all smoke-rising or fertility rituals were declared heathen and hence banned to Christians. Rites of death, on the other hand, were acceptable with revisions. The slaughter of water buffalo, for example, could be seen as a perfectly secular custom (at least if you were Dutch). It was permissible, according to this logic, for Christian converts to sacrifice buffalo and to share the meat among the living, but spirits could not be presented with a portion of the sacrifice. The mission thus attacked the fundamental premise underlying sacrifice and made this emphatic in a decree: "You must not think that the dead takes the slaughtered animals from him ... (since) these animals do not have an eternal soul. What is slaughtered is not the provisions ... of the dead, but is offered merely as a repast to the guests and the family" (quoted in Bigalke 1981:224).

In attempting to regulate what the Toraja "must not think," and to reduce ritual to sociology, the Dutch laid the foundation whereby ritual practices might flourish while the beliefs in which they were once embedded waned. Thanks to the mission dichotomy which split aluk, Toraja could join the Christian church, attend Sunday services, and still share in their traditionalist relatives' sacrificial meat. This was providing, of

Following the murder of missionary van de Loosdrecht in 1917, Toraja involved in rebellion plans were arrested by Dutch authorities. The men in this photograph are identified by an inscription as (*from left to right*): Bujang (?), Ne' Matandung (district head of Balusu), Tandi Bua (district head of Pangala), and Pong Massangka. Photograph courtesty of S. J. Sarunggu in Rantepao. Archival reproduction by C. Zerner.

"Hats, hats, and more hats," wrote dance researcher Claire Holt (1939:42). "The whole market looked like a bobbing sea of wide conical straw hats." Holt, who photographed the Rantepao market in 1938, was also reminded of "a continuous big restaurant." Photograph from the Claire Holt Collection, courtesy of the Dance Collection, The New York Public Library at Lincoln Center. Archival reproduction by J. Petticrew.

"In places where real trading was done, we came to a section where the whole ground was covered with sheaves of golden rice," Holt (1939:43) wrote. The clay cooking pots and woven bamboo baskets in this 1938 photograph are identical to those produced today; the loin-cloths and rattan headbands mark this as a preindependence scene. Photograph from the Claire Holt Collection, courtesy of the Dance Collection, The New York Public Library at Lincoln Center. Archival reproduction by J. Petticrew.

Near the Rantepao market, 1938. Photograph from the Claire Holt
Collection, courtesy of the Dance Collection, The New York Public
Library at Lincoln Center. Archival reproduction by J. Petticrew.

course, that they did not believe in the spirit world toward which much of any ritual was directed. In spite of this possibility, less than 10 percent of the highland population had converted to Christianity by the close of the colonial era in 1942. Only a fraction of the conversions that did occur were effected through the budding school system that van de Loosdrecht had been so eager to establish.

In spite of widespread resistance to schools in the first decade of mission activity, a number of three-year mission schools eventually were built in villages throughout the highlands, as were government continuing schools in Makale and Rantepao (and later mission continuing schools as well). In theory the primary schools were open to any child, while the secondary schools were restricted to children of the elite. Ironically, in the early years the elite sometimes substituted slave children for their own, fearing the unknown implications of this foreign, compulsory institution. Gradually, as it became evident that schools could provide access to a certain kind of power, the nobility began to send their children to school rather than hiding them in the hills. Some of the young graduates came to form a new, small class of bureaucrats and teachers: capable of communicating in Malay (a new language even more exclusive than Toraja ritual speech); literate (thereby surpassing the oral wisdom of the *aluk* priest, or *to minaa*, who without the ability to read could still be tricked); conversant with and often, although not always, converted to Christianity. This affiliation led to jobs as teachers, evangelists, policemen, or low-ranking civil servants, and the new power and prestige that such positions (and their salaries) might entail.

By 1930, however, only 1,700 Toraja, or less than 1 percent of the population, had been baptized; in 1938 the total number reached 8,200, or 5.5 percent, and the conversion process was dormant for the remainder of Dutch rule (Bigalke 1981:227). Surprisingly, Bigalke (1981:240) shows that the vast majority of early Christians were not former students but were in fact from peripheral areas where Islam encroached more forcefully at the edges. Not until the late 1950s did fears of the *to sallang* (Muslims) converge with increasingly strong Christian education to produce massive conversions in the highlands.

## An Era Ends

In March 1942, just thirty-six years after their arrival, the Dutch suddenly left the highlands. The Toraja found their land occupied by new strangers—Japanese soldiers. As in many parts of Indonesia the departure of the *Balanda* was a shock, especially to the majority of villagers not in touch with nationalist thinking on Java. To many Toraja the *Balanda* had appeared to be installed indefinitely in power. When the Japanese first arrived, said a Rantepao man who was twenty-one at the time, "they touched our arms and said, 'the skin is the same; the eyes are the same; the hair is the same.' " But he added, "Although we knew that they were Asians too, we soon learned that our lives could not fit with theirs. Finally people almost returned to liking the Dutch. It was our most bitter time."

The Japanese occupation is remembered "bitterly" by many Toraja as a time of deprivation, primitivity, violence, and the first unravelings of social order. The deprivation was most simply a consequence of the fact that Japan was busy supporting its war effort. Especially rice, but also pigs, salt, sugar, coffee, and whatever else the Toraja deemed precious, seemed to be demanded by the occupying forces. Japanese quotas for such goods were enforced by village and district headmen, who would be beaten if the quotas were not met. Whenever possible people hid food or other possessions; salt, for example, was stored in clay cooking pots and buried in the ground, with just a little bit taken out when needed.

Not only were rice, salt, and other essentials scarce, but so too was cloth. The lack of cloth during the three years of Japanese occupation epitomizes to many Toraja the bleakness of this period, even a reversion to what was felt to be a more primitive state. One of the great delights of Dutch colonialism was the introduction of soft, ready-made cotton cloth. Among other reasons women liked it because they no longer had to sit for days weaving pineapple fiber at their back-strap looms; men liked it (or so a man told me) because it felt much nicer than coarse woven pineapple for loincloths. Both sexes liked it because cloth, an important item throughout Southeast Asia,

was associated with well-being, prosperity, and ancestral blessings. When cloth suddenly became scarce during the Japanese
occupation, people were forced to turn again to the laborious
tasks involved in processing the pineapple plant and weaving its
stiff fibers. The less fortunate lacked even pineapple cloth; and
some, it is said on Sesean, went naked. Another sign of the
primitivity of the time was the lack of kerosene; in its absence,
dammar (resin) torches and candles were used as in the past—a
product of the forest rather than the civilized, *Balanda* world.

In other fundamental ways the occupation was experienced
as dehumanizing. The Japanese link between respect and fear
was resonant with Toraja values, but although the Toraja were
terrified of the Japanese, their respect for the apparent irrationality and severity of Japanese violence was less than abso-
lute. From the Toraja perspective much was taken and little
given in return: something had gone awry in the basic conduct
of reciprocity. The Dutch, although deeply resented for their
taxes, forced labor, and other forms of control, seemed at least
to offer something in exchange: peace, institutions such as
schools and clinics, medicines, imported cottons. Combined
with the perceived lack of reciprocity on the part of the Japanese was a frightening violence. If you did not bow properly
three times to any Japanese you might be beaten, and stories
are often told of men being hung from trees along the road to
Palopo, burned until their heads exploded. Sesean women were
sent to remote eastern islands to serve as prostitutes for Japanese soldiers, and, closer to home, a large prostitution business
operated in Makassar. Mama' Agus, who lived in the city for
much of this period, was the object of several attempts to per-
suade her to work in huge buildings that "stored women," as
she put it. Once a Japanese woman "friend" took her to such a
house, asking her if she wanted a "seamstress" job. When they
arrived she saw a long room with women dressed up and made
up; before each woman was a number. Japanese soldiers would
enter, look over the women, and pick up a number; that
woman followed him into a room. "They were treated like
animals, *aduh.*" The people who brought new women, of
course, were paid, like Mama' Agus's "friend."

For many Toraja the Japanese occupation is remembered as
a time when "things began to be chaotic" (*sudah mulai kacau*);
when, for example, slaves could freely join the paramilitary
youth corps. For people such as Mama' Agus, whose closest
relatives were Dutch (or Germans who apparently became
Dutch nationals), these years of occupation were particularly
harsh. The Dutch (and their Toraja wives and children) were
dispersed in Japanese camps throughout South Sulawesi, and
Mama' Agus spent much time trying to locate, and secretly
visit, her aunt and uncle and their children. When the war
ended in 1945 there was jubilation both in Makassar and in the
countryside. In the highlands chickens were cut in celebration,
and women brought out their best yellow sarongs from their
hiding places. Mama' Agus remembers walking with a friend in
Makassar when suddenly they saw hundreds of tall, uniformed,
American soldiers coming toward them. She raised her hand
and saluted, "hip hooray!" and all the soldiers did the same.
And then they shook hands with all the hundreds of soldiers; it
took hours. The war, to everyone's great relief, was over.

In Java, shortly after the Japanese surrender, Sukarno and
Hatta proclaimed the independence of Indonesia on August 17,
1945. Within months the Dutch had reestablished their control
in the highlands: Australian troops reached Makale-Rantepao
in November, stayed briefly, and were replaced by Gurkhas
(Bigalke 1981:352). The reinstatement of the pre-Japanese
order was accomplished by Dutch officers attached to the
Allied Powers, or to NICA (Netherlands Indies Civil Affairs)
(1981:353). A small nationalist movement that had grown up in
the Toraja towns was quickly crushed, although in 1946 a local
victory was achieved: the "regency" of Tana Toraja was at last
granted autonomy from Luwu. Elsewhere, especially in Java
and Sumatra, Indonesians waged a revolution against the
Dutch. Four tumultuous years later, in December 1949, independence was achieved. The Toraja found themselves again
without the *Balanda*, by virtue not of their own but of other
people's actions.

The implications of nationhood in Tana Toraja were not
immediately apparent. True, it was no longer good to have
been "one stomach" with the Dutch, as were some members of

Mama' Agus's family who sailed several years later to Holland. This was doubly hard for Mama' Agus, who had married a lifelong collaborator who served the administration as district head from 1920 to 1946. But in actuality condemnation was not so harsh: her husband, for example, was gently deposed, only to be replaced by his eldest son (by his first wife). Power remained in the family. The slaves and followers who had enlivened the house, worked its fields, and (wo)manned its cooking pots hardly disappeared all at once.

One consequence of independence was felt quickly, however: the return of local warfare. With the end of the revolution young South Sulawesians who had fought the Dutch in Java and in Sulawesi wanted recognition and a role in the new national army (Harvey 1974). Discontent with the dominance of Javanese and Minahasans in the military and the government was channeled into a full-scale rebellion that brought unrest to South Sulawesi from 1950 to 1965, led by Kahar Mudzakkar. Kahar, a Luwunese Muslim who had been active in the war in Java, was recalled to Sulawesi where he led guerrilla fighting against the Dutch. At the end of the revolution the military command of East Indonesia was established, but Kahar was not given a position that was equal to his expectations. Angered by this slight he joined forces with the young guerrillas who were demanding recognition. By 1953 his rebellion was linked with the Darul Islam movement of West Java, and by 1956 much of the South Sulawesi countryside was controlled by his forces (Harvey 1977:30). Although Kahar's forces did not directly enter Tana Toraja they did control much of the surrounding area, including Pantilang.

To the Toraja it seemed that the lowlanders were once again attempting to Islamize the highlands. Thousands of refugees from areas attacked by Kahar's guerrillas streamed into the regency with tales of pillage, pig slaughter, and forced conversion. The presence of Andi Sose, a Duri (Islamic) warlord who commanded a battalion of the Indonesian army in Makale, only heightened the atmosphere of suspicion, culminating in his expulsion by armed Toraja Christians in 1953. In 1958 Andi Sose's troops were again sent to Toraja, and again local Christians led an armed uprising against them, forcing their retreat.

All this contributed to the growing climate of fear and anti-Islamic sentiment, while the rate of Christian conversion rapidly increased.[9]

The early years of independence were also marked by turbulence closer to home, particularly in relation to scarce land. Even in the beginning of the twentieth century, when the population was about 123,000, land shortages were so acute as to cause thousands of freed highland slaves to remain in the lowlands rather than return to their homeland (Bigalke 1981:83). By 1947, when the population had grown to about 210,000, the Dutch *controleur* van Lijf observed: "The shortage of cultivable space is acute, and people are prepared to make great sacrifices to get (*sawah*). . . . Nowhere in Indonesia is the price of *sawah* so high. Before the war people would pay f400 to 500 for an average hectare of *sawah*, and now f3,000 to f4,000" (quoted in Bigalke 1981:398–99). In the early 1950s a series of small uprisings occurred against large landowners, often based on grievances dating back to land seizures made in the heydays of Pong Tiku, Pong Maramba, and other expansionist big men. A virtual insurrection occurred among the peasants in the Makale area in 1953 in their attempt to challenge a noble's disputed *sawah*. Several people were killed, while others fled the region (Crystal 1970:132). In the north, on Sesean, "people fought and beat each other in the fields." In the government the man who held the position of regency head (*Kepala Daerah*) happened, remarkably, to be of low status and a supporter of land reform. During this period branches of the Indonesian Communist Party (PKI) attracted a good deal of support from hundreds of small, struggling landowners, from the landless, and from some large landowners with long-standing grievances. By 1953 some five thousand plots of wet-rice land were in dispute (Bigalke 1981:418). It is not surprising that land should have been a focus for intense conflicts in this period, given the legacy of colonial expansionism and growing population pressure.

Another sensitive issue, and a stimulus to the actions of peasant groups, was meat. Crystal (1970:200) reports an incident in the 1950s in which villagers demanded that not only the head but also the esteemed hind quarters of the pig be given to the former slaves who bore the animal to the ritual. In the north some big men adapted communist rhetoric to their own Toraja style, including one village leader who exhorted everyone, rich and poor, high and low, to perform *ma'bua'*, the most prestigious (and expensive) smoke-rising ritual. "Are you not ashamed (*ma'siri'*) to eat everyone else's meat?" he challenged. "Do your own *ma'bua'* and pay it back!" The headman's encouragement of equal participation in the ritual system, according to the man who told this story, thinly disguised his intention to increase the flow, and hence his share, of meat.

In 1965, in the terrible aftermath of the abortive coup in Jakarta, hundreds of thousands of Javanese, Balinese, and other Indonesians suspected of being sympathetic to communism were brutally killed. The repercussions of these events were not as immediately or painfully apparent in the outer islands, although several Toraja did lose their lives and many others were arrested, later to be released. More than a decade later, however, highland villagers were still clearly frightened of being labeled "communist" or "atheist." Closer to home, the year 1965 was also marked by the death of Kahar Mudzakkar and his long rebellion. South Sulawesi was at peace for the first time in two decades, and with roads and bridges passable again, the highlands were no longer cut off from the lowlands or the world beyond. The "New Order" regime of President Suharto welcomed foreign investments, which poured into the oil- and forest-rich islands of Kalimantan (Borneo), Irian Jaya (West New Guinea), and elsewhere. For young, overeducated, underemployed highland villagers, the accessibility and promise of the growing multinational world beyond the highlands meant the possibility of migration. In the late 1960s a new era in Toraja history began—an era of unprecedented movement, bringing with it infusions of wealth, social mobility, and a simultaneous blossoming of both ritual activity and doubt.

# CHAPTER 3

# The Pregnant House

As one approaches the Sa'dan highlands on the road from Ujung Pandang, a massive gateway suddenly spans the road, announcing in Indonesian, "Welcome to Tana Toraja." Atop this structure stands a full-scale replica of a Toraja house, replete with carved and painted walls, a roof of many bamboo layers, and a stately sculpted water buffalo head. Inquisitive tourists may pause in their journey to climb the gateway and circumambulate the model house before proceeding to drive across the threshold into "Toraja Land."

The house provides an entrée into Toraja, especially into those ideas of personhood, social ties, and links with ancestors and the divine that are expressed in and sustained by ritual performances. The present story of ritual and change, of the "blossoming of both ritual activity and doubt," must be told against the background of the many meanings of the traditional house. These meanings, of course, are also changing, as the welcome gate suggests. In recent years the *tongkonan*, a physical and conceptual entity inadequately translated as "house," has become a self-conscious symbol of Toraja cultural identity. Miniature carved wooden houses are for sale in souvenir shops in Rantepao, and tour guides are sure to include visits to traditional houses on their itineraries. Toraja are discouraged from modernizing old architectural forms, for example by using corrugated tin roofs instead of bamboo, in the interests of maintaining authenticity (for tourists). Internationally the house is an accepted and convenient symbol as well: by chance I was present when the head of Tana Toraja presented an elegant "miniature" house (at least a meter tall) to the visiting ambassador from New Zealand.

Toraja traditional houses are, in fact, physically remarkable. Constructed entirely of wood and bamboo, without a single nail, a house consists essentially of a rectilinear box of wooden panels set between a frame of sturdy horizontal and vertical beams. This structure is raised on wooden posts (from about two to five meters high), numbering eighteen or thirty-two, with from three to five posts in the front, depending on the size. The panels on the outside of an elaborate house are incised with intricate geometric designs that represent buffalo, rice, insects, and symbols of prosperity, and are painted red, black, and yellow. A realistically carved wooden buffalo head and a more abstract, long-necked cock may be prominently displayed in front, where rows of buffalo horns are hung from past funeral ceremonies. Perhaps the most striking feature of such a house is its roof, assembled from layers of split bamboo in a great swooping arc, a shape that from the side recalls the curve of a buffalo's horns.

## The Family Bamboo Clump

Although its distinctive physical qualities lend themselves to ready appropriation as a symbol by the outside world, for the Toraja the symbolic meanings of the house are embedded in social action. The Toraja social world consists, most broadly stated, of family and other people. In this respect the Toraja resemble the Bugis, for whom, as Errington (1979) has shown, these two categories define the trusted and comfortable as opposed to the unknown and potentially threatening. Not surprisingly family relax in the interior of the house, which is sealed off from outside penetration, for example by carefully closing all the apertures. In Toraja, as in Bugis culture, neither family nor other people define bounded or enduring groups. Rather, in accord with principles that underlie the conception of how people are related, groups with different names take shape in different contexts. Hence we find a multitude of Toraja terms for what is occasionally glossed in Indonesian, via Dutch, as pamili ("family"), and other assortments of persons.

The substance of common ancestry and social bonds in

Toraja is expressed in terms of blood and bones. The Indonesian word for family is often translated as *rarabuku* (*rara* = blood; *buku* = bones), a shortened version of *sang rara sang buku*, "one blood one bones." The aspect of shared substance that Toraja stress is oneness or unity. To fight within the *rarabuku*, for example (a common enough occurrence), is said to be like separating the whites of the eyes from the black irises. It is *pemali*, "taboo." Other terms for family also emphasize this shared biological substance and the ideal unity that it implies. *Sangdadien*, for example, means "one birth." *Sikande rara* is "to share blood," with the sense of being so closely joined that there is no gap, like broken bones that grow together (*sikande*) as they heal. From this physiological oneness it is thought that oneness on other levels follows: the family members should be "one word, one breath" (*misa'kada, misa'penaa*).

The ideal of unity is also expressed in terms of the plant world. Several nuclear families that share a common ancestor are called *sang sape*, a single branch of the rice plant. A cluster of *sape* is called *sang to'*, the clustered strands of a rice plant. When many people (many "clustered strands" or *to'*) acknowledge a common ancestor, the term *sang rapu* or *pa'rapuan* is applied. *Rapu* is a clump, as in a dense bamboo stand or a group of coconut trees, growing together as if from a common root, but with each tree branching separately.

Although in theory ancestors never vanish, and their descendants always remain together, in practice this is not the case. The persistence of the family group is reaffirmed at each ritual occasion when members must contribute animals or rice or money. If members fail to contribute to rituals, or even to attend them, their ties to the group are attenuated. After many generations ancestors and ancestral houses may eventually be forgotten. Conversely, persons without the biological link of blood and bones may be incorporated into the *rarabuku*, most frequently by adoption. A small ceremony is held at which a pig is sacrificed and a few drops of its blood dabbed on the forehead of the child. A symbolic bond is thus created, and the adopted child acquires inheritance rights and the obligations to participate in family rituals.[1]

If blood establishes one kind of symbolic bond, cooking, eating, and sharing food establish others. It is no accident that the kitchen or hearth, *dapo'*, is literally and figuratively at the center of the house, and that the household is referred to as a *dapo'*. *Sang dapo'*, "one hearth," includes a married couple and others who eat together in one house. To marry is to "become" or "plant a hearth" (*mendapo'*, *untanan dapo'*). "Half a hearth" is the situation in which one spouse has died; "to divide the hearth" is to divorce; and "to return to the hearth" is to remarry a divorced spouse. It is to the *dapo'* that meat is publicly divided at a ritual, and it is from women's constant centers at the hearth that rice (a symbol of unity) is apportioned to the family.

The hearth is physically the center of the house. All houses have at least two rooms; some have a third, an optional front porch (*paluang*) where guests are received and sometimes sleep. The central or main room (*sali*) contains the *dapo'*, a firebox framed in wood in the middle of the east wall. In small houses the *sali* may be no more than three meters square, and the *dapo'* dominates the space. Even in larger houses, however, its presence is strongly felt. There the family congregates, women cook rice or boil water, children play, and neighbors and relatives chew betel and gossip. Meals are eaten sitting on woven mats around the hearth, from which women spoon out rice or boiled cassava roots. After eating the mats are swept clean, later to become sleeping mats and blankets. People sleep virtually anywhere in this space as long as their feet are not pointing west, in the direction of the land of the dead. The space around the fire is preferred because it is warm and cozy, especially on cold mountain nights.

If the *sali* is the liveliest room in the house, the most sacred space is entered through a small door in the south wall. This room, the *sumbung*, is reserved for honored guests, at times the household heads, and for the marriage ceremony. It is said to be the "root" of the house, for all horizontal timbers in the house are laid with their roots toward this southern end. The roots must be "fertilized," a *to minaa* explained, so that the "branches and the leaves" (the front of the house) will be beautiful. For this reason sacred heirloom cloths and swords are sometimes stored in the *sumbung*.

In the past a house would have been occupied by many

people who ate and slept there, while carrying on most of their social life outdoors, in the well-swept yard, at the river, in fields or gardens, or whiling away their time under the granary. The granary, which is like a smaller version of the house, stands opposite it, facing south (houses always face north). Beneath the granary proper is a bamboo platform on which people sit, casually chewing betel or mending baskets, on ordinary days. When important guests arrive they are given a mat and a place of honor on this platform; at rituals a seat on the granary is a sign of status and respect. From this vantage point one cannot help but gaze at the display of horns and carvings, the "branches and leaves" that grace the house facade. The house interior, in contrast, source of fertilizer (heirlooms) and nutrients (the kitchen), is small and dark, lit only by shafts of light that filter between the boards, a tiny window, or perhaps an opened door, no more than a meter high. This is a private, family space. Public attention is always directed toward the impressive exterior, the "face" or "front" (*lindo banua*).

The close connections between houses and personal identity were revealed to me in the first few months of my stay in To' Dama', when I often found myself confused about people's names. Introductions typically took the form of "this is my older brother," or "here is my grandchild." At the beginning, when I asked people their names, they would reply with something like, "I have a house up there," or "my grandfather's house is in that village." Mama' Agus, advising me on preparing questions for a household survey, taught me the polite way to inquire about a person's identity. Begin by asking what the house is called, she said, then for the name and sex of the founding ancestor and from what previous house he or she came, and then you may continue with questions such as "Who did this person give birth to?" "Which ancestor gave birth to you?" and so on. In this way one never need ask the respondent's name, only his relationships to others linked through his house (or houses). The important aspects of an individual's identity are not names but houses, with their associated ancestors and descendants. Names simply serve to emphasize the links in both directions, past and future.

The Toraja reckon kinship bilaterally, giving equal weight

A big man and his family pose proudly before their finely carved and painted house.

An elegant granary is adorned with drum and buffalo hide, roofed
with many layers of split bamboo, and supported by smooth cylindrical
trunks of palm. The leg of the *to minaa* who owns this granary is visible
in the doorway, as he collects seed for the year's planting.

At the year's first agricultural rite (*medatu*) women use their feet to separate rice seeds from stalks. At other times rice is pounded in a large rectangular wooden mortar. Photograph by C. Zerner.

Seed is then sifted in winnowing trays and transferred to woven bamboo carrying baskets. Photograph by C. Zerner.

The rice-filled baskets are brought to flooded fields where they will be immersed for several days. A sacred red-leaved cordyline (*tabang*), associated with fertility, has been planted on the rock. Photograph by C. Zerner.

It is unusual to see a buffalo drawing an agricultural implement, here a rakelike iron tool that turns the muddy earth.

Pigs arrayed in bamboo stands at *ma'bua'*, awaiting sacrifice.

Detail of an heirloom cloth (*sarita*) made by an ancient stick-batik method and used to adorn the "tree of desire" at the *maro* ritual. Photograph by C. Zerner.

to male and female ancestors and ideally creating as large a family as possible. In the family (*rarabuku* or *rapu*), kin terminology serves to minimize distinctions within generations. Aunts and uncles, for example (*indo' ure, ambe' ure*), are addressed and often referred to simply as "mother," "father" (*indo', ambe'*), although some Toraja use the Dutch-derived terms *tanta* and *om*. Their children are addressed and referred to as Ego's elder or younger siblings (*kaka', adi'*), their parents as grandparents (*nene'*), and so on. Distinctions between generations are marked, continuing through great-great-grandparent and -grandchild, for which there are reciprocal terms. Beyond five generations, however, all ancestors merge into a collective category known, like ordinary grandparents, as *nene'*. Biological age is no longer important; even a child becomes a *nene'* after death. Like spirits (*deata*), which they may also become, ancestors exist in the upper world where they watch, listen, and influence events on earth. This is why at any ritual the *nene'* must be given offerings and their blessings requested. It is the core of *aluk* belief and practice, succinctly called *pa'kandean nene'*, "feeding the ancestors," on Mount Sesean, and exactly what the Christian mission prohibited.

Ancestors are remembered on earth, not just through offerings but also by the practice of naming grandchildren after them: a respected ancestor's name is continually recycled. The pervasiveness of the name is heightened by the practice of teknonymy, so that a parent is called by the first child's name. Mama' Agus, or more formally, Mama'na Agus or Indo'na Agus, is Agus's mother. Should her first grandchild be named Kalua', for example, her teknonym would become Nene'na Kalua', "grandmother of Kalua'." If her own mother's given name had been Kalua', she might well spend her last years bearing her mother's name. Also, by having contributed to generational continuity (in the form of a grandchild), she earns the respectful title *nene'*. Her own personal name, which may have been derived from yet another ancestor, may emerge again in future generations. Teknonymy here is less a matter of genealogical amnesia, working as in Bali to reforge statuses (Geertz and Geertz 1964), than a means of keeping ancestral names in circulation within the family. The particular people to

whom they are attached at various points in time matter less
than the continual presence and movement of the names
throughout the *rarabuku*.

If ancestors link past and present, the *lolo*, "umbilical cord,"
links the present and the future. Ancestors connect people on
earth to the upper world; the umbilical cord roots people in the
earth and to their houses. Before the advent of hospitals and
clinics, births were accompanied by a little ceremony in which
the newborn was placed in a rice-sifting basket and rocked up
and down to cries of *yu hu huu* (if a boy) or *hee heee he yo* (if a girl).
This was to protect the baby from being startled later. The
midwife then cut the umbilical cord with a bamboo knife and
tied it quickly so that at this dangerous moment the breath
(*penaa*) would not escape to the afterbirth.[2] The following day
the *lolo* was placed inside a woven pouch (*kapipe*) and buried by a
man along the east side of the house. It was carefully marked
by bamboo stakes and covered with rocks for protection.

Alongside any house, then, are scores of *lolo* planted for its
progeny. In a sense the house exists to guard these *lolo* and as a
sign that there are *lolo* in that earth. The house is sometimes
called "the place where the *lolo* are buried" (*inan lamunan lolo*),
and its inhabitants are called "the guardians" of that burial
place. Even if the house itself no longer stands, the family
eventually may hold a ceremony on the land, planting a piece of
wood (a symbolic house) and sacrificing a pig.

The *lolo* is connected to fertility in its widest sense. The word
also means "straight, unblemished." *Malolo pa* means "still
young, virginal." The *lolo* is "planted" on the east side of the
house, since east is the direction of the rising sun and all
fertility-associated rites. That it is placed in a *kapipe* is note-
worthy, for this reed pouch normally holds cooked rice, associated with fertility. Also, the expression "large *kapipe*"
colloquially means "vagina, womb." It is sometimes said that
the *lolo* is always inside the woman, emerging in sections with
each new child. Hence one expression for siblings: *to ma'polo lolo,
to si turu' tai bai*, roughly translated as "those who are cut from
the umbilical cord, who follow each other as pig shit."

Lest this expression be misinterpreted, let me stress that
children are highly valued. Aside from their economic value (as

laborers in fields and houses), their social value (they join houses in alliance), their ritual value (they sacrifice animals for their parents), and their emotional value (they are generally adored), they are valued as affirmations of self (childlessness is considered a severe and pitiable lack) and as a sign and promise of good fortune (*dalle'*). All the riches in the world mean nothing, people say, without children. "If our fortune is good, we will bear one child on each hip and another on each shoulder; they are our treasure." The *lolo* thus symbolizes not only the continuity of descendants but all other forms of riches which are felt to follow from a child's birth.

## Celebrations of the House

There are two words for house in Toraja: *banua* is an ordinary house; *tongkonan* is an ancestral house. In everyday speech the two are not always distinguished, but in practice certain rituals must have been performed for a house to become a *tongkonan*. The viable definition of a *tongkonan* on Sesean is that the children, or more usually the grandchildren, of the person who built the house must hold a ceremony at which the roof is repaired, pigs are sacrificed, and the meat distributed among the founder's descendants. It is also usually the case that the *tongkonan* is built according to traditional and elaborate architectural norms. The simpler style houses—which are smaller, closer to the ground, and sometimes built of woven bamboo or of unpainted, undecorated wood—are not usually candidates for *tongkonan*-hood, although their basic layout is the same.

In theory a person has claims to membership in parents' houses, grandparents' houses, and so on, as far back as can be remembered. As in any system of cognatic descent, in practice people cannot affiliate with all their houses. Most Toraja, however, prefer not to admit this possibility, so strong is the belief that one should so affiliate. The more houses that Toraja can claim as their own, the more extensive the family and the greater the pride. In time, however, certain houses are simply forgotten or are too far away. Few people can name more than four or five houses in which they actively participate. In addition to inherited houses, Toraja might claim a spouse's house.

But affiliation with the latter is contingent on the birth of children and the duration of the union. If the marriage "has results," the offspring will hold or join all of their parents' houses in new alliances.

Marriage rules reflect a tension between the need to expand the house and to consolidate its wealth and power. Marriage on Sesean is prohibited between siblings, first, second, and usually third cousins (although in recent years the latter marriage is said to be more common). Beyond third cousins marriages within the house are encouraged, and are called *sulle langan banua*, "returning to the house." Such marriages reinforce the system whereby everyone is interrelated and intertwined, as Toraja love to explain; expansion occurs but the house and family still keep close enough to its center to avoid the problem of "other people." In fact these in-house marriages were surprisingly rare in Tondoklitak. They appear more common among higher-status people for whom there is some wealth and power to consolidate; ordinary people tend to marry "anybody" (*sembarang*).[3]

The word *tongkonan* derives from the root "sit" (*tongkon*). In Toraja, as in much of Indonesia, where and how one sits are signs of status. It is not surprising, then, that the *tongkonan* quite literally defines a person's place in the society. In cosmic orientation every house is equal: the simplest bamboo shack and the most statuesque *tongkonan* face directly north, toward the rivers' source, ensuring that the right side of the house faces east (toward life) and the left side faces west (toward death). Rituals are always performed in accordance with these directions: smoke-rising rites are held in the northeastern corner, smoke-descending rites in the southwestern corner. In fact this cardinal orientation is so strong that the members of a family who have lived for twenty years in a resettled village, in a house that faces southwest, still speak of going to the rear of the house as going "south."

In social space, however, not all houses are equal. Houses generally form a neat, straight row, opposite their granaries. In any row the most important house or houses, and their corresponding rice barns, may be especially large, handsome, and elaborately adorned. Truly special *tongkonan* are marked by the plants that grace their yards: sacred red-leaved cordyline terminalis (*tabang*) and sandalwood trees are signs of rituals performed in years past. Precolonially such signs were closely restricted to the nobility, when all details of construction and decoration corresponded in theory to the status of the *tongkonan*, or rather of its descendants who could be considered members of a single cognatic descent group. Precolonially it also was the case that great *tongkonan* were surrounded by rough bamboo shelters around the back and sides of the master building: these were the quarters of the slaves.

The house, then, represents a person's ties with his history (ancestors) and with his contemporaries. It is a kind of focal point, a concentrating center for the often dispersed energies and interests of one cognatic descent group of which he is a part. Only a few people live in the *tongkonan* or even nearby, but hundreds of others feel deeply attached to it. The major way these connections are made manifest or activated, if temporarily, is through the ritual cycle. Of all the house-related ceremonies the inauguration of a new roof for an old house is perhaps the most highly charged. Unfortunately I was not able to witness more than parts of such an event. I did, however, see several other house-related rituals, two of which, the *maro* and the *ma'bua'*, are among the most dramatic and symbolically rich performances in Toraja. Here a brief account of the *maro* and *ma'bua'* will highlight some dimensions of house, personhood, and potency in Toraja thought and action.

Until recent times both *maro* and *ma'bua'* were performed only by families of the very highest noble rank, in part because of strict prohibitions and in part because they both require a great deal of wealth. They are the two most elevated rituals in a hierarchy that culminates with *ma'bua'*; no stage in this hierarchy may be performed without completing those that precede it. *Maro*, on Mount Sesean, takes place when the rice has just begun to poke its bright green shoots out of the seedbeds. It is said that *maro* will "finish off the business of death" by transforming the ghost (*bombo*) of a recently dead ancestor into a spirit, or *deata*. The apparatus for "reversal" (*pa'balikan*) is a tall tower of three lengths of bamboo, some seven meters high, to which scores of sacred cloths are tied. This apparatus, called a *bate,* is an inversion of a similar structure erected when the deceased in question had been given a funeral. This time, however, the *bate* is inserted into the earth in the direction in which the bamboo naturally grew, signifying growth and renewal, and topped with lush red cordyline associated with the *deata.*

All members of the *tongkonan* who possess heirloom cloths contribute them to the *bate,* whether ancient blue-and-white *sarita* batik or garish modern synthetics. The cloths are said to be gifts from the spirits, or from ancestors, or from Java, and are considered potent and normally subject to strict taboos. Their assembly on the *bate* is thus a concentration of sacred stuff that is otherwise dispersed among the *rarabuku.* This sacred concentration is heightened by the addition of ancient iron blades *(la'bo to dolo),* again from various family members.[4]

For several nights prior to the final day a crowd of *to minaa* gather in the main room of the house in which the *maro* is being performed. Into the dawn they chant in ritual speech, retelling myths and genealogies and exhorting the spirits to give blessings. "Here is the family bamboo clump" *(indeto ma'rapu tallang),* they proclaim, inviting the spirits to draw near:

> We will make a water channel for you to come
> We will build a stone bridge
> We will make a golden waterworks
> It will arrive here
> The sea will encircle the earth
> There will be no brokenness.

The spirits are advised to take notice of the great gathering of the descendants of the house, and to grant their wishes, as the *bate*

> ... bends like a tree-top toward Mamasa
> It sways for a while
> It becomes branches of gold
> Becomes leaves of all kinds
> Everything that is used
> All that is eaten.[5]

On the climactic day, a large crowd gathers on a ritual field ringed with *bate* from the several houses that may be holding *maro* concurrently. People enter trance as the *to minaa,* chanting and singing under the hot sun, call upon the *deata* to approach. Men, and more particularly women, are possessed or entered by the spirits; they whirl about and dance, loosen their hair, jump on drums, stamp on sharp, upturned blades, and cut themselves with swords while (ideally) drawing no blood. Should blood appear the leaves of the magical cordyline plant are applied to stop its flow. Long ago, I was often told, when there was more power in such things, people even cut off their own heads and danced in trance until they were ready to replace them, sealing the cut with a leaf of cordyline. Even without this added drama the trance day of *maro* is quite spectacular, and it is easy to understand why the Toraja say that the *bate* and the whole ritual field are "hot," "aflame." This excerpt from my field notes is illustrative:

> The field seems to vibrate with the sun, palm wine, the seven richly colored swaying cloth towers (all facing east), and the countless circles of men, women, and children who dance and whirl together or in pairs, voices chanting, drums beating.... One old woman spins dizzyingly into view, waving a casuarina branch and encircled by a singing crowd, while two men place a sword upon the ground, holding up its gleaming edge. The woman's hair comes down, her mouth is open and her eyes downcast. Then her bare heels are rocking on the blade, and now slowly to her toes, and heels again, arms swinging, and again still harder, moving back and forth and hands on the two men's heads, till at last she jumps firmly off, stamping on the earth as if to erase the soreness of her soles. Now she takes the sword and presses it beneath her blouse, bends over forward, hops, screams; men hold the sword as she leans onto it, her muscles tensed.... She stamps and pulls back her hair, sways, sits dazedly on the ground....(November 13, 1977)

Throughout the afternoon, people are possessed by the *deata*; they are, for a few extraordinary, incandescent moments that they cannot "remember," *to ma'langi'*, "people of the sky." Late in the day the *maro* draws to a close: the spirits have gradually departed, and the *to minaa* "bless" and "cool" (*umpasakke*) the fiery *bate*. It is stripped of its cloths and swords, which are dispersed to their guardians, while the green bamboo frame is carried home, to be stored in the rafters of the newly blessed house.

The presence of this bamboo gives the house a special quality, subjects it to new prohibitions, and allows certain plants to
be grown on the east side of the house. Most importantly
everyone who participated, by giving and eating chickens and
rice, by dancing or trancing, can now say, "Our house has done
the *maro.*" By contributing people affirm their membership in
that *tongkonan* and expect to share in its future blessings and
prosperity. So strong is the obligation to give to one's ancestral
house that Mama' Agus once gave us one thousand *rupiah* (a
large sum by her standards) to take to a *maro* up the mountain,
because, she told us, she had a *nene'* there, though she could not
remember them. It is also desirable to be associated with an
ancestral ghost transformed into a spirit; some say that the
ancestor takes with him into the spirit realm the entire
(deceased) membership of his house. In death, as in life, the
little people follow the big, and the still-living hope that they
too will benefit from the move.

Once a *tongkonan* has completed the *maro* it is possible to
undertake the culminating ritual, *ma'bua'.* Now, as in the past,
*ma'bua'* is a rare and expensive celebration. It is also probably
one of the most intricate of Toraja rites, in part because of its
sheer length (a full year), in part because of its great prestige.
Like the *maro* a particular *tongkonan* sponsors the *ma'bua'.* It
involves the selection of a very high-status (and wealthy)
woman to assume the ritual role of *Tumbang* (literally "jump"),
and several other high-status women to be her "assistants."

The *Tumbang* in particular holds a multitude of prohibitions
during the year of *ma'bua'.* She may never attend a funeral, she
may eat nothing that originates at a funeral, she may eat no
corn (associated with funerals). In fact she may eat nothing but
rice and occasional chickens, so clearly she must have sufficient
wealth in her own fields to sustain her for a long period. This is
even more the case because she cannot purchase anything. She
is obliged to offer rice to any visitors, who are frequent since
the *Tumbang* is thought to possess life-enhancing powers.
Should there be an argument in the area the parties involved
come to her house to make peace. Whenever the *Tumbang* eats
she must also offer food and drink or betel to her counterpart:
an effigy called the *ana' dara,* "sister" or "virgin." For the duration of the ritual year the *Tumbang* and the *ana' dara* virtually

live together, the *Tumbang* always sleeping at her side. The *ana'
dara* physically occupies the center of the house; she is fastened
to the building's central "navel post" (*a'riri posi'*) just alongside
the hearth in the main room, and she reaches nearly to the
attic. She consists of bamboo lengths wrapped in straw and a
massive palm-leaf skirt or sarong (*dodo*), although when I asked
*to minaa* Lumbaa what she was "made of," he answered "many
poems (*gelong*) are put inside."

The *ma'bua'* is clearly a pig ritual, as the Toraja put it. On one
of the first days of the ritual year dozens of pigs, perhaps a
hundred, are brought to the house yard where they are
installed in a row of fresh green bamboo platforms topped with
crimson cordyline leaves, each within its own container, or
*lempo*. On this day the life-oriented quality of the *Tumbang* is
represented in a dramatic moment, as she and her assistants
sit, legs outstretched and dressed in brilliant yellow, on the
house's narrow front porch. The mood is jubilant and noisy as
priests play tiny, snakeskin-covered drums and hundreds of
women in pink, lime green, and bright blue sarongs strain for a
better view. A *to minaa* takes a long iron blade with several rice
grains balanced on the tip and "implants" these grains in the
middle part that cleaves the *Tumbang*'s hair. Her forehead is
then dabbed with pig's blood, and nearby women clamor for a
sprinkling of blood themselves. Witness to all this human
commotion is an audience of pigs, lined up like enthroned
(imprisoned) spectators and squealing enthusiastically before
their imminent slaughter.

At the end of a year the *ma'bua'* is brought to a close with
another series of rituals. Again the descent group gathers,
some people coming from great distances, dressed in their
brightest smoke-rising colors (no black). On the crucial day
*Tumbang* is carried from inside the house, totally wrapped in
cloth: "exactly like a dead man," she is described. But she comes
quickly to life after being placed on a drum and turned around
three times. At the same time her "sister" the *ana' dara* is also
removed from the house and carried to a ritual field. There her
palm-leaf sarong, or *dodo*, is placed by a beringan tree and her
bamboo frame is taken to a rice field, where it remains. One
stalk of rice must always be left in this field at harvest.

The house, during the whole period of *ma'bua'*, is said to be

"pregnant" (keba'tang). After the Tumbang and the ana' dara have
come forth from it, it is no longer pregnant, although I am not
sure that Toraja would say it has given birth. Toraja do say
that now everyone and everything else will give birth: chickens, pigs, buffalo, people. It is as though the maro gathers up
ancestral energy and potency into the tongkonan, while the
ma'bua' impregnates it and, after a long gestation, releases its
fertility to crops, livestock, and human descendants.

After ma'bua' a circle of long palm leaves which had been
hung around the periphery of the house—its sarong, or dodo—is
now rolled up, to be kept always in place. The house, in the end,
remains an image of the body.[6] Bones and feather mobiles are
hung from rafters, and a sandalwood tree is planted at its eastern edge. From now on the tongkonan is said to be kabusungan—
powerful, dangerous, sacred. A stranger may not enter without
first taking three sips of uncooked water from the cistern. The
state of the house is qualitatively altered, and another chapter is
added to its ritual history.

# CHAPTER 4

# Status, Shame, and the Politics of Meat

"Pregnant" houses that bear fruit, like "hot" multicolored cloth and bamboo towers that attract the spirits, may diffusely benefit the collectivity. At the same time, however, nothing in Toraja society serves to define differences within the collectivity so powerfully and so visibly as ritual. Great performances such as *ma'bua'*, *maro*, and the major death feasts, which in the past could be sponsored only by the noble few, sharply distinguished those few from their crowds of loyal but lesser-ranked followers, who were in turn distinguished from the slaves who served them all. Rituals were the most dramatic expressions of status differences, but such concerns informed the shape of everyday life as well. Status is still a central issue in both ritual and everyday life, although its contemporary expression may be less clear than in the past. To approach the question of changing status in Toraja, this chapter sketches the social system that divides mankind into ranked levels in accord with blood; the symbolic dimensions of wealth; the conceptions of honor and shame that, depending on one's perspective, motivate social action or provide an idiom in which to discuss it; and, finally, an introduction to status in action, the meat-sharing group known as *saroan*. The themes of genealogy and wealth as alternative sources of status, power, and prestige reappear in later chapters, when blood and money do battle on the contemporary ritual field.

## Nobles, Commoners, and Slaves

There are at least two ways of thinking about rank in Toraja. One is the formal system referred to as *tana'*—literally a stake to which a horse or buffalo is tethered, or a stake that marks a boundary. In the present context *tana'* marks hereditary boundaries between levels of a social hierarchy, in a material idiom (in descending order): gold, bronze, iron, *karurung* (the hard black bark of the sugar palm), and *kua kua* (a common *sawah* plant). On Sesean only four levels of *tana'* are recognized (bronze is excluded), and even those levels do not figure prominently in everyday life or conversation. *Tana'* appears to be more significant in areas such as Pantilang, which is wealthier and is closer to Luwu and to Bugis status preoccupations. *Tana'* in such areas is also clearly tied to blood. In Pantilang, people ranked as *tana' bulaan*, "gold *tana'*," are said to have 100 percent pure blood, bronze have only 80 percent, and so on down to *kua kua*, who have none at all. The practical importance of this ranking is in matters of marriage and divorce. *Tana'*, like everything else, is inherited equally from both parents; a child's *tana'* is midway between that of his parents. Although a man, unlike a woman, may marry down, he must still be careful to protect his children's rank from dropping too precipitously. Persons of higher status have more to lose by being careless of their *tana'* in marriage, which probably explains the greater interest in this system in more stratified areas. *Tana'* also determines the amount of *kapa'*, a fine that must be paid in buffalo if the union is dissolved. Such fines may be considerable for high-*tana'* marriages and virtually inconsequential when the *tana'* at stake is low.

More to the point on Mount Sesean is a nameless system that operates according to the same genealogical principles and ranks persons as either nobles, *to makaka* (*to* = person; *kaka* = elder sibling); commoners, *to biasa* (*biasa* = common; alternatively *to kamban* = the dense ones; *to bulu di a'pa* = those tied like a bundle of slender grasses; *to buda* = the many); or slaves, *kaunan*. Since status in this case is also an average of parental status, many fine gradations are possible. It is said that a person with any slave ancestry will always know his mixed blood, but in fact fractions of low blood may be forgotten over generations, just as modicums of higher ancestry are well remembered. In this way mobility is (and was) built into the system.

Diversity is also a feature of the status system, which varies throughout the highlands and sometimes between nearby *tondok*. In southern Toraja, the region that includes Makale and Sangalla', four status levels are recognized, with *puang*, "lord" or "owner," as the highest nobility. *To makaka* are relegated in the south to the rank of commoners. Northern Toraja, such as those on Mount Sesean, equate their own top *to makaka* with the southern *puang*, but southerners reject this notion. At the same time Sesean people are quick to distinguish their more democratic style from the oppressive domination of the southern *puang*, who were notorious in earlier times for claiming the buffalo of ordinary folk merely by feeding the animals a lick of salt. Sesean villagers suggest a reason for the north/south difference: land is more abundant and fertile in the south, and the topography quite level. There a few families could concentrate their holdings in vast, productive fields. In the north the topography is steep and rugged, the land more marginal and difficult to control. Far smaller terraced fields are carved into the mountainside, and even a poor, low-ranking northerner might own a bit of land, and with it some rice and dignity. It is probable that these slopes were gradually cleared of forest by settlers who pushed upland and north from the wealthier, populous, and tightly hierarchical valleys of the south. If one continues to still poorer areas north and west of Sesean, or up the slopes beyond Tondoklitak, the three status categories merge into two (*to makaka, kaunan*), and even distinctions between respectful and informal terms of address are minimized.

As this overview suggests the ranking of persons, while expressed in terms of blood and genealogy, was closely tied to land. Myth implies that such was the case in the beginning: Puang Matua, the heavenly ancestor-forger, created Potto Kalembang (Clay Bracelet), the ancestor of hard-working slaves or *kaunan*, so that his descendants would labor on the land. Land is, of course, the source of sustenance, and a slave by one Toraja definition is simply "someone who is fed," *to dipakande*.

Land may have been a scarce resource in the highlands as early as the turn of this century, according to Bigalke (1981:79), who uses 1913 data to reconstruct population densities. He concludes that in some areas, such as Tikala, densities may have been as high as three hundred persons per square kilometer; in steeper terrain, such as Pangala', the density was about ninety per square kilometer. The fact that older people on Sesean speak of land as plentiful in the past may simply reflect their contrast with the present: by 1980 the population of Tana Toraja was 333,000 (Kantor Statistik 1982:147). It is probable that by the beginning of the twentieth century much of the cultivable land was already worked as *sawah*, for then, as now, rice was considered food, in contrast to all other edibles, which were mere side dishes or poor substitutes. In addition to rice land a well-to-do family would also cultivate gardens, with a few species of cassava for people and pigs. Land was required for bamboo as well, which in its serveral varities was indispensable for firewood, building materials, kitchen implements, sunhats, baskets, and countless other creations.

Much of the best land, however, belonged to certain powerful families. This was especially true in the southern Makale region but also in the fertile valley areas surrounding Rantepao. In Tikala, for example, Harahap (1952:64) reported that 20 percent of the *sawah* was owned by three rich men, and 20 percent of the population owned none at all. It often happened, then, that a person did not have enough land to support himself and his family. This situation could arise in various ways: his parents were poor and the little they had could not provide for all their children; or the parents had enough but other siblings inherited the larger share because they had cut more buffalo at the parents' funerals; or gambling, cockfighting, and other forms of betting had depleted their resources. Especially in the late nineteenth century land was often lost in war. The solution to moderate poverty was to work others' land in various sharecropping arrangements. Typically the landlord received two-thirds of the harvest, and the worker the remaining one-third. The solution to dire poverty, however, was to enslave oneself, and in so doing to make all of one's descendants hereditary slaves.

The term *kaunan* actually encompasses a number of different relationships ranging from those most easily glossed as "slave," in which *kaunan* are clearly property of their owner (*puang*), to others which more closely approximate a form of dependency or clientship with wealthier, more powerful patrons. For simplicity I follow the Toraja usage of a single word, *kaunan* (or the Indonesian *hamba,* servant or slave).[1] The generality of the term may reflect the fact that the precise conditions of slavery or subservience were less stressed than the existence of a relationship based on domination and subordination. Its generality may also reflect inherent ambiguities in the categorization of *kaunan* and other statuses, and tensions between blood and wealth as alternative, sometimes conflicting sources and measures of rank and power.

In precolonial times there were several different kinds of recognized *kaunan. Kaunan tai manuk,* "chicken shit slaves," were clearly owned by their *puang,* "lord" or "owner" (not to be confused with the highest-ranking southern nobility who are called *puang*). The *puang,* according to Bigalke (1981:87), could even have been a wealthy *kaunan,* although it is not clear whether this was true in the Sesean area. Like other forms of wealth "chicken shit slaves" were inherited. Yet while in theory the low status of such *kaunan* was determined by birth and blood, the Toraja clearly recognized a means by which a person might become a slave, seeking protection or escape from poverty and other dire circumstances. To this end a simple ceremony was performed: a person freely volunteered submission to a strong or wealthy patron, who prepared and slaughtered a pig. The pig was given in its entirety to the would-be slave and his immediate family, who consumed it all. By this gross metaphor a bond was established whereby all of the slave's descendants would be the *kaunan* of the *puang* and his descendants; not hungry but not free. Such slaves were known as *kaunan mengkaranduk,* from *randuk,* "to begin."

This type of relationship became especially common in the tumult of the late nineteenth century, when even landowners sought military protection against the possible ravages of the slave trade (Bigalke 1981:86). Unlucky persons captured and sold in the endemic warfare of that period were known as *kaunan diali,*

"purchased slaves," a condition thought to be beneath all dignity. Less lowly were *kaunan indan*, "debt slaves," who might
achieve this status through a passion for cockfighting or other
gambling, losing not only possessions but freedom. However,
such *kaunan* could usually work their own land as well as their
master's, and could, with diligence, repay their debts. Finally
there were *kaunan bulaan*, "golden slaves," poor members of a
family who might enslave themselves to their own brothers.
The ancient priest Suloara is said to have prohibited this type
of *kaunan*, and on Sesean people find the thought of it abhor-
rent. However regional variation is great, and elsewhere *kaunan*
*bulaan* were in a favorable position, attached to the important
*tongkonan*, working choice land, and helping with household and
ritual tasks (Bigalke 1981:85–86; Crystal 1974).

Whatever the regional patterns, there were hierarchies of
*kaunan* reflected in the kinds of work prescribed. Some were
assigned backbreaking labor, working in the fields or cutting
firewood. Others pounded *padi* in the wooden mortar behind
the house, fed the pigs, or cooked the rice. Some performed
intimate bodily tasks for their masters (*puang*). In Pantilang, for
example, one slave accompanied his *puang* to the river when he
relieved himself, in order to wipe the *puang*'s posterior. Nooy-
Palm (1979:166) mentions a slave who was charged with re-
moving maggots from a *puang*'s corpse. Other slaves, however,
were favored by their *puang*, sleeping in the main house, perhaps rising in the middle of the night to light a fire or heat
some water for their chilly master. A *kaunan* of this sort always
preceded his *puang* on a path and was known affectionately as
"the one who carries the betel pouch."

From a noble's point of view slaves and masters might have
good, mutually supportive relationships. One evening while
the rice was cooking Mama' Agus told me about her grandmother Ne' Lale and her slaves:

> In the past, slaves who were close felt free to ask for whatever
> they needed: betel nut, unhusked *padi*, rice, salt. They were not
> ashamed (*ma'siri'*), and they were given whatever they asked for.
> After all, they lived from us, they had nothing else. When people
> were short of food, or in debt, they came to my grandparents
> who always cut a big pig just for them and took good care of

their people. The pig was the ceremony for becoming a slave. In those days, they say, no one stole.

Ne' Lale used to sleep in the corn huts with her slaves when they were harvesting corn in the fields. And Ne' Tandi Allo (her husband) would go with the buffalo boys and wash the buffalo with soapy leaves. He had many, many water buffalo!

When the meat was divided the slaves were given some from the *puang*'s share. They really did have enough to eat, my grandparents' slaves! They even had meat. If there was just a little, Ne' Lale would have it cooked. If there was lots, it was divided raw and portions given to the slaves. The same with buffalo milk, which everyone prized. If there was enough, Ne' Lale would call the slaves who were mothers and give them each half a bottle of milk mixed with water and say, "take it home to feed your babies."

When Tandi Allo died, Ne' Lale could not take care of all the slaves because she had been so spoiled. She even handed her own children over to others to hold them and do all the child-care work. In fact, she didn't know how to do much at all when it came to responsibilities; she never even left the boundaries of the *tondok.* There were scores of slaves then, living in bamboo shacks on all sides of the house. After a while, she told them, "It's like this, little children (*susite, pia*), it's not as it used to be. Our head is gone and food is short. So you must choose. If you want to go somewhere else and make a living on your own (*tuo kalena*), you may. As long as you don't become a slave for another *puang* (*mengkaunan penduan*). If you want to stay, that's o.k. too, but be patient; it's not the way it was before." After a few years, one or two left, and built houses and gardens. After a long time, almost everyone left, until just a few slaves remained.

Mama' Agus contrasted this rather idealized account of Ne' Lale and her "soft" attitude with the crudeness of another ancestor who always measured out the rice he gave and beat people in anger. Because of his "high heart," she said, this man had few slaves. No rough bamboo shacks encircled *his* house.

Everyday interaction among the three status categories was governed by a host of prohibitions, or *pemali,* which ensured their separation. The rules for behavior between slaves and nobles were especially stringent. In the presence of

his *puang*, or any other noble (*to makaka*), a *kaunan* would fall to
his knees. If he needed to approach or ask for something his
outstretched arm would maintain distance as he virtually
crawled toward the noble. Only the politest forms of address
could be employed, punctuated by frequent "excuse me (*tabe'*),
mother" (or "father," "grandparent"). The slave, on the other
hand, was simply addressed as *iko* (informal "you"), regardless
of his age. If he sat inside a noble's house he would crouch in a
corner and make himself as small as possible. One of the several wives of Mama' Agus's father was a slave in Pantilang; she
could not even reach inside her husband's betel pouch, nor
could they eat from the same plates.

At rituals the functions of slaves were most publicly apparent: they carried pigs, led buffalo, hauled water, and poured
palm wine from long bamboo tubes, hovering around the edges
of the rice barn where honored guests were seated and served.
If not at work the slaves sat on the ground, behind the granary,
or at best on mats that they themselves had brought. At these
crowded affairs everyone was especially careful to separate the
drinking cups and dishes of slaves and nobles, as mixing them
could lead to illness. Such mixing was called *mabusung*, a viola-
tion of hierarchical relationships between men, and also between men and the spirit world, that was thought to lead to
swollen stomachs and sometimes death.

Although the bottom line of slavery was that one person
worked for another, and in return was fed, cared for, and protected, not only *kaunan* had such relationships with those who
possessed more land or power. Many commoners, in fact,
owned far too little land (and in earlier times were too weak
militarily) to work entirely for themselves. Commoners, therefore, were also typically involved in relations of dependency,
most frequently as sharecroppers on another's land. In exchange for labor they usually received one-third of the harvest
and, depending on the particulars, the protection and occasional kindnesses of the landowner. The line between *kaunan*
and commoner-dependent at times may have been difficult to
distinguish. One category clearly straddled this division: the
warrior, or *to barani* ("brave man"). In precolonial times such
men received rice, betel nut, and other necessities in exchange

for their military support. Sometimes they also received a child of the landowner's family; Mama' Agus, for example, was raised by a *to barani* of her mother's village, and to this day she is not sure if her adoptive parents were commoners or slaves. Whatever they were they gained prestige by their association with her family, and at their funerals she slaughtered buffalo, as would a daughter.[2]

If commoners sometimes resembled slaves in that they exchanged labor and loyalty for rice and protection, slaves sometimes resembled commoners in that they too had access to economic (and status) mobility. Slaves might be given small plots of land to work on their own; they might raise the *puang*'s pigs or tend his buffalo in return for which they received a certain number of the animals' offspring. In this way an industrious *kaunan* might substantially increase his wealth and even, in theory, purchase his freedom. If he wished to do so he could perform a ceremony in which he provided his *puang* with a hundred of "everything": buffalo, pigs, horses, needles, plates, and so on (one person's list included brassieres). Needless to say, only a much smaller symbolic version of such a ceremony ever occurred. Bigalke (1981:87) reports that redemption was possible by paying two-thirds of twenty buffalo to the *puang*, and Nooy-Palm (1979:47) notes that only three buffalo might be sufficient, whereupon a feast would be held.

In its ideal version the ceremony suggests the utter hopelessness of the attempt to overcome low status with wealth; in its reduced praxis it reveals that under some circumstances riches might redeem one's lowly birth. Such redemption, to be effective, would be accompanied by strategic marriages. In theory men were absolutely forbidden from marrying up, but women could do so with impunity. As women rose in status their fractions of mixed blood would be forgotten, until eventually a rising family might perform once-forbidden funerals or other rites. The carvings on their house might be made more beautiful, buffalo horns might be hung from formerly bare house posts, and red cordyline and sandalwood trees might be planted to mark the enhanced status of the "family bamboo clump." Although a person with even a trace of *kaunan* blood "still knows himself," it is also acknowledged that persons could sink to slavery through poverty, war, or awful luck, just as they rise above it through diligence, wise marriages, and careful manipulation of the ritual system.

Toraja myth abounds with stories about rising and falling fortunes. Pong Pa'pak, for example, was a poor man, perhaps a slave, who found a kind of tree bark, or *pa'pak*, in the forest that could be chewed with betel to keep the teeth strong. He brought it to market and sold huge quantities, until he gradually acquired a wife, a garden, rice fields, chickens, dogs, pigs, buffalo, precious cloths and beads, and swords. He had a carved rice barn and a carved house, and when the first rice barn was filled with *padi* he built a second one. He was truly rich, and many people came to share his wealth: "When *padi* was brought down from the granary, people came; when it was dried in the sun, people came; when it was pounded, people came; when his wife poured it into the cooking pot, people came; when she turned the pot over hot ashes, people came; when she spooned the rice out, people came; and when she ate, people came."[3]

The status hierarchy in Toraja was clearly no mere title system divorced from economic and political realities. On Sesean this is made apparent in the almost interchangeable use of three terms: *to makaka* (noble), *to kapua'* (big man), and *to sugi'* (rich man). The Toraja frankly appreciate wealth and consider it a concomitant of high blood and power. In his classic analysis of Javanese conceptions of power Anderson (1972:7) has written that power is "that intangible, mysterious, and divine energy which animates the universe ... a formless, constantly creative energy." In Toraja the tangible manifestation of such intangible energy is wealth, made visible in rituals and shared with others. A rich man is one who must be favored by the gods; his riches are signs of their blessings. It is only natural, therefore, that he should command the respect and loyalties of less favored, ordinary folk.[4]

### Wealth

A Toraja rich man (*to sugi'*) not only concentrates wealth, he also uses it, most notably by distributing it in lavish rituals. In doing so his wealth does not diminish; on the contrary, only when the legendary Pong Pa'pak's wife began to hoard her husband's wealth did it become depleted thanks to the anger of the gods. The most obvious level at which wealth is distributed is the sharing of food, especially meat, to the community of ritual participants. The idea that distribution enhances wealth is suggested by the gesture of tossing meat from a tall bamboo platform to the ground below, an action known as *massea'*, "to distribute meat" or "to broadcast seed." Koubi (1982:99) suggests that the meat of sacrificed animals is "sown" to promote the fecundity of livestock. On another level the rich man also shares by simply demonstrating his wealth, or *kasugiran*. *To sugi'* are said to have many followers or "friends" who wish not only for a share of meat but also that a bit of their leader's *kasugiran* will accrue to themselves. The presence of these many friends makes for the desired ritual atmosphere: crowded, colorful, noisy, and tense, in short *marua'* (Indonesian *ramai*). Danger and black magic may also threaten as so many distant people converge, but *marua'* is nonetheless the quality to strive for. The worst possible imaginable state is its opposite, *makarorrong*, quiet and lonely.

Wealth, with all its Toraja connotations, emanates from the *to sugi'*, as radiance from the traditional Javanese ruler (Anderson 1972), in waves of diminishing intensity as distance from the center increases. The material medium for this emanation is meat. To understand the ways in which meat becomes so powerful we must first turn to Toraja relations with their animals, which are both a source and a standard of wealth.

The Toraja raise water buffalo, pigs, and chickens. Buffalo are associated with men and, with few exceptions, death. Pigs are associated with women and both life and death. Chickens are usually associated with the *deata* and with life. Both buffalo and pigs are essential components of a person's wealth. One is not a Toraja without a pig in the yard, they say, and indeed I felt uncomfortable when for several months our household's pigpen was conspicuously empty, the last pig having repaid a funeral debt. I was relieved when Mama' Agus finally bought a small pig, for I no longer felt vulnerable to other people's queries about our empty pen. Also, I realized that Mama' Agus's days were fully occupied again. Even the smallest pig is quite de-

manding: a special cassava garden must be tended, and each
morning huge bundles of leaves are picked, cut up, and boiled
in a large pot for at least an hour while the fire is watched. The
animals are fed twice daily on their own specially carved wooden
plates, and they are served with care: the food must be warm,
but not too hot; the pigs must not knock over their plates, and
so on. The vegetables are called "pig rice" and they are cooked,
it is said, because pigs are "our friends, like us" (solata).[5]

Strong as the identification is between pigs (bai) and women
(baine), pigs are different from people in that they are exchanged and sacrificed at rituals. Since they are used in both
smoke-rising and smoke-descending ceremonies it is important
that they be available at short notice, to repay old debts, to
initiate new ones, or to confirm one's ties to the performers of
the ritual.

If pigs are a commonplace sign and source of wealth, buffalo
are its most spectacular manifestation. It is often said of a rich
or important person, "He has a lot of buffalo" (buda tedongna).
Although buffalo are the sign of their (precolonial) prerequi-
site, wealth in rice lands, only rarely does one hear, "He has a
lot of land (or padi)." The more frequent, more visible, and
more admired form of wealth is the water buffalo.

The buffalo, like a walking version of the house, lends itself
nicely to status distinctions. Pigs come in many sizes but only a
limited number of shapes and colors. Classification of the buffalo, on the other hand, is a fabulously complicated system.
Different shapes and curvatures of horns are named, and a set
of terms based on the human arm describes horn length. Other
sets of terms distinguish the color of the coat and tail, spots
and patterns, kinds of eyes, and types and locations of swirls of
hair. All of these factors and their permutations, combined
with size, strength, and general good looks, are considered in
the animals' evaluation. Today, when buffalo are sold for cash
in the market the price ranges from about U.S. $100 to nearly
$1000 for a castrated, exceedingly large and long-horned
animal. Even more prized is the rare and expensive piebald
buffalo with pink spots and glassy blue eyes, a breed the Toraja
know as bonga. The Toraja believe that bonga are found nowhere
else in the world, and except for small populations of them in

the eastern Indonesian islands, they are probably correct (Nooy-Palm 1979:184).

As might be expected the Toraja water buffalo is not a work animal. In many parts of the highlands, including Sesean, the task of plowing the fields is accomplished by men, who turn the earth before planting season; buffalo are rarely used for this task.[6] For most of its life the buffalo is cared for faithfully by a boy or girl whose duty it is to lead the animal around to grassy places, to bathe and scrub it, shine its horns, ride it, and generally to pamper it until it is big and beautiful enough to be used as ritual sacrifice.

Although girls or older women may sometimes guard the buffalo, men usually take responsibility for them, appraise them, stroke them, rub their genitals, and perhaps identify with them.[7] Women, for the most part, are busy with their pigs. The local *to minaa* described his children to me: One was in Kalimantan, and one in Irian Jaya. Another was in northern Sulawesi, and just one remained in Toraja. "You know him," he reminded me as he spread his arms. "He has a buffalo down there with horns as wide as my two arms can stretch."

To say that men identify with buffalo is too simple, however, for both men and women are symbolically associated with the buffalo slaughtered at their funerals, and both men and women own these animals (like any other property). The only difference between a man's and a woman's funeral is that, ideally, an extra buffalo should be sacrificed for a woman, said to be in exchange for her role as milk-providing mother. The life-sustaining role of women is thus highlighted in the context of death. Rosaldo and Atkinson (1975) posit a widespread symbolic opposition between men as life-takers (hunters and head-hunters) and women as life-givers (childbearers and cultivators). The temporary effigies constructed at Toraja funerals appear to express this opposition: females are graced with small enameled plates atop their heads; to males are fastened long swords and other warrior attributes. Yet the domains of male and female are not strictly separated in Toraja culture. Although Toraja men are slaughterers of domestic beasts (and formerly hunters of wild animals and human heads), and women of course bear children, both sexes take part in agriculture, and

women formerly cheered on their men in war.[8] Men are
strongly associated with buffalo, which are associated with
death (only at two specific occasions can a young buffalo be cut
at smoke-rising rituals). Women are strongly associated with
pigs, which although bivalent—sacrificed at rites of both life and
death—are most numerous and dramatically present at fertility-
associated rituals. Myth confirms this opposition: the mother of
Karaeng Dua' was a large white pig, whereas mythic buffalo
tend to trample and destroy the living (see pages 20 and 108).

If men and women are symbolically distinguished in this way,
then nature effaces the distinction in that both men and
women die. Death is not exclusively a male domain, and buffalo are cut for both men and women. Women own property
and desire riches as men do, and their property must be distributed and their wealth displayed. The status of both is at
stake in funerals, even if men hold center stage, cutting animals, slicing meat, and tossing it around, while women sit on
the sidelines and watch. In celebrations of fertility such as
ma'bua' the focus is on the fertile and nurturing woman in
her domains of house and kitchen. The wealth that is stressed
is the abundance of children and the great display is pigs. The
systems are complementary, for the idea of many children also
reassures Toraja that many buffalo will be cut for them at
their death.

Buffalo not only represent a kind of male identity and a
movable, visible, and classifiable sign of wealth, but they are at
the same time a standard of value. Even today, when cash is
common, rice fields are measured by the buffalo standard.
Value is based not on how many bundles of *padi* a field produces
but rather on how many buffalo were sacrificed (cut) at the funeral of the field's previous owner. For example, if Ne' Sampe
died, leaving a small field, and his sons cut three buffalo, the
field now has the value "three buffalo." Suppose that each of
Sampe's sons had cut one buffalo; each would own one-third
of the land or its produce. If one son had to pawn his share
he would receive one buffalo (or its cash equivalent) from
whomever purchased it. Some Toraja say the system works
because unlike money, which is subject to constant inflation,
buffalo remain buffalo; but these people overlook the fact

that buffalo are often bought for cash in modern times. Others argue that the value of land is always increasing when it is based on buffalo, since not only are new buffalo cut in every generation for each plot of land, but each cut buffalo means hundreds of unborn buffalo that represented unrealized wealth.[9]

Buffalo, in short, are symbols of the person, his land and ancestors, and his wealth and power. The buffalo enables people to share with others on the ritual field, to create and to sustain social connections. When buffalo are sacrificed and their meat distributed the action is no mere protein allocation. If the live animal was a convenient symbol of the person and his wealth, the slaughtered beast becomes a metaphor for the unequal division of status in society and the reciprocal ties that bind unequal statuses. The animal's various parts—head, liver, thighs, ribs—their size and shape, and the order in which they are distributed, are all infused with status-related meaning. Only the *deata* are offered a symbolically "complete" animal, as little bits of all the different body parts (as the Toraja conceive them) are arranged, along with rice, on a banana leaf for the divine feasters.[10]

## Honor and Shame

When the Toraja speak of funerals they speak not just of riches, meat, or status, but of *siri'*: honor and shame. *Siri'* is their explanation of why fights arise over meat distribution; it is their explanation, in fact, of why the system works at all: why they cut animals for their relatives, repay debts, and, at present, feel themselves caught in an endless slaughter cycle. The idioms of *siri'* and meat simultaneously describe the Toraja funeral. If one is going to a smoke-rising ritual, one says, "I am going *me'duku'*," "to get meat." If a quarrel erupts at a meat division, it is called "a meat problem," or "a problem of *siri'*." While *siri'* does appear in contexts other than meat, meat rarely is without a component of *siri'*.

In the highlands, as in lowland South Sulawesi, *siri'* has the dual aspect of honor and shame.[11] Both aspects make one human; "to know" one's *siri'* (*untandai siri'na*) is to know who one is. This is not a matter of inner subjectivity but of knowing one's "place," the recognition of self in relation to others: to those with whom one shares ancestors or *tongkonan*, to those of loftier or lesser status. *Siri'* may come to the fore in any interaction in which the relative status of two persons is uncertain, in which dignity may be asserted or shame endured. In Bugis society weddings are the prime occasions for revealing or wounding *siri'*; funerals, in the Toraja world, are dense with such possibilities.[12]

Although *siri'* may be deeply felt it is clearly defined by a public context.[13] As children become adults they acquire knowledge of social roles and hierarchies, linguistic codes, kinship relations, and avoidance patterns such as *sikasiri' datu* (mutual respect and honor) between brothers and sisters. If a child commits an outrageous social blunder people laugh, "He does not *yet* know *siri'*." If an aware adult should do so, for example by failing to show proper respect to a higher-status elder, he is condemned for not knowing *siri'*. To be without *siri'* at all is to be scarcely alive, "to have (be) a face of stone" (*ma'lindo batu*).

The most common Toraja use of the word *siri'* is in everyday social contexts in which food is shared or eaten. At meals a guest is constantly exhorted, "Don't be *ma'siri'*! Eat a lot," and he must constantly defend himself, "I'm *not* ashamed, I am eating lots!" Presumably guests do feel shame in other people's houses but must never doubt the plentiful supply of rice or the host's hospitality. To eat in a niggardly fashion is to imply that the granary might not be overflowing or its contents not generously offered. Even if one has just finished eating it is taboo not to swallow at least a few grains of rice should food be served. Sharing food is tantamount to social relations, so any situation in which such sharing is improperly conducted is conducive to shame. Conversely one may always honor another by serving food. The pervasiveness of this idiom is revealed in the standard social greeting when approaching (even if not entering) another's house: "O grandmother, is the rice cooked yet?" (*E nene', manasu moraka'?*). The friendly reply is, of course, "Yes, it's cooked!" (*manasumo!*). If by chance the visitor does want to eat and there is no rice, then both parties may be *siri'*. In general a person is ashamed to eat if others are not eating, and ashamed to be where others are eating if he himself is not.

*Siri'* may appear in numerous other social contexts. A school-teacher on Sesean gave these examples: He would be *siri'* to go to church if he were not Christian, since he would not know how to pray or to be polite, or what to do. He would be *ma'siri'* to go to market and just look around, not buying anything, for then everyone would know he had no money in his pocket. And he would be *ma'siri'* to attend a ritual if he knew no people there, for he would not know where to sit or whom to talk to, and everyone would stare. Tourists, he added, although they know no one, are not *ma'siri'* because they do not come to rituals to look for food or to ask for something. *Siri'* is thus both knowing your place and, therefore, having a part to play in a system of reciprocal exchanges—you cannot ask for something unless you first know where you stand (or sit).

Rituals, as this last example implies, are occasions when food is exchanged on a grand scale and people "ask for things" (not just from other people but from spirits and ancestors as well). They are, not surprisingly, concentrations or manifestations of *siri'*. Toraja often lament the "heaviness" of ritual obligations but say they will be *ma'siri'* if they fail to sacrifice what they can (or frequently what they cannot). At a funeral the children and grandchildren of the deceased, or those who arrange the ceremonies and contribute sacrificial animals, are called the *to ma'siri'*. One man said *siri'* was the height of his responsibilities toward his parents, expressed through his sacrifice. The sacrifice itself is called *sonda siri'na*, "the replacement for *siri'* " (toward one's parents).

Children thus fulfill their responsibilities through the funeral, and in so doing they make visible their own *siri'*, their place and honor in the group. At the same time the *siri'* of the guests and followers is at stake, displayed in formal processions offering buffalo and pigs, repaying old debts or initiating new ones. And everybody's *siri'* is at stake in the tense hours during which the meat is divided. Whether it is tossed from the center of a field or hurled down six meters from a bamboo platform, everyone hears the meat-receivers' names as they are shouted. Everyone observes the calling order, the cut of meat, and its size. In what appears to be a bewildering rush of name-calling, meat-flinging, and animated conversation, everyone attunes himself to the subtleties of what is being tossed, when, and to whom. One hears frequent whispers of *"ma'siri'*," for someone inevitably is being shamed. A meat fight may ensue, and an old man will hop around piles of cut meat, waving his knife and yelling at the meat dividers for their ignorance, oversights, or deliberate errors. In former times, people say, such events might result in murders; now the violence takes the form of words and occasional blows or throwing of meat, bones, and buffalo excrement at the offending party.[14]

That *siri'* often surfaces, sometimes explodes, at meat-distributing events is no surprise; it is, after all, what they are about. The problem is not improper meat division, because meat division in some sense is structurally improper. The criteria for determining who receives which cut of meat and when are more than complex; they often are contradictory. The contradictions inherent in the ideal and the real construction of status make its display a dynamic and sometimes violent exercise. In the past nobles might sink to poverty, gamble away their wealth, marry poorly, and slowly lose their prestigious name and *tongkonan* affiliations. Conversely slaves or poor folk might prosper, marry well, and slowly enhance their lowly name, their shabby house, their inconsequential, even tainted, genealogy. That such status changes occurred in former times is not in doubt, but it seems certain that they occurred almost imperceptibly, over generations; memories could lapse and be reconstructed. In recent decades, however, change is far more rapid as fortunes visibly wax and wane, and with them power and prestige. Genealogy and wealth, once fused in the ideal *to sugi'*, have come to be seen as conflicting sources of status, as wealth now enters from beyond the Toraja scene and diffuses rapidly throughout all levels of society. Decisions about who should receive the buffalo's hip or stomach are also decisions about human value, about ideologies that are no longer perceived as complementary but competing.

## The *Saroan*

Conceptions of family and house, blood and wealth, shame and honor underlie the complex drama of Toraja funerals. But to understand them in context we must first look at the functioning of social groups. Although the family is conceptualized in terms of *tongkonan* (the house itself and the ancestral line implied), in action it takes the form of a *saroan*. On Sesean members of a *saroan* are all ideally derived, like members of a *tongkonan*, from a common ancestor. It is said that members share not just this ancestor but "one word, one breath" (*mis-a'kada, misa' penaa*). In actuality it is quite difficult to describe the shape of a *saroan* and to distinguish it from a *tongkonan* in terms of membership. References to *saroan* in the literature reveal confusion as to whether it is a kin-based or a territorially based group;[15] but the Toraja do not define it by what it *is*, rather by what it *does*. Agus, one of my clearest informants, suggested that there were two types of *saroan*. The first, which is based on the *tongkonan* and includes all the descendants of an original ancestor, becomes the second through "a kind of metamorphosis." The second is the "village *saroan*," which anyone in the village can enter. The metamorphosis occurs through marriage, adoption, and more recently through the incorporation of such newcomers as schoolteachers or church functionaries. It seems that Agus was really describing in the first instance the ideal origin of the *saroan*, and in the second instance the ongoing process of *saroan* composition.

A look at an actual *saroan* reveals that neither territory nor kinship adequately define its shape. *Saroan* A, for example, includes twenty-two households on which I have data. Of these twelve male household heads claim active membership by virtue of their wives' ties to both the *saroan* and to village X in which it originated. Another eight men live in other villages with their wives but maintain their active ties to *saroan* A, which they inherited. Only two men who inherited membership in the *saroan* still live in village X and actively participate in the *saroan*. Another two men who live with their wives in villages where neither spouse has *saroan* ties still maintain their active role, in spite of their physical distance. All of these men (and their wives) are active in other *saroan* as well, particularly those centered in their natal (or their parents' natal) villages.

In short *saroan* membership extends beyond the immediate territorial center, and not everyone within that territory is necessarily a member. On the other hand, "other people" in the neighborhood may become active members even when their kin ties are distant or nonexistent. In this sense the *saroan* is more open than the *tongkonan*, which is impossible for outsiders to join (except to affiliate by marriage or adoption). Also, while *tongkonan* have a natural means of subdividing, as each generation builds new houses which become future *tongkonan* ("children" of the original), the *saroan* in theory is indivisible. *Saroan* fission therefore becomes a source, a focus, or an expression of social conflict, as we shall see below. But first we must examine what the *saroan* does.

In some areas of Toraja, such as Rantepao or Makale, the *saroan* once was important as an agricultural work group. In these regions fields were large and required the integrated labor of many people. A wealthy landowner was able to enlist his whole *saroan* on a certain day; the next day the group would work a different landowner's fields. Workers were not paid, people say proudly, but were fed and given a share of the produce. Curiously the root *saro* means "wages," but the pride in lack of payment comes from the feeling that *saroan* labor was based on a spirit of cooperation, the famous Indonesian *gotong royong*. One young Toraja man expressed it more bluntly: "If we don't help our neighbors now, later when we need them they won't help us. We all depend on each other." On Sesean, where smaller fields do not require a large labor force, the old *saroan* is mainly remembered in terms of such communal labor functions as house building. Here too the full participation of its members and lack of pay are stressed. Both house building and agricultural labor have declined as *saroan* functions, having been replaced by wage labor or more individual sharecropping arrangements in the case of agriculture.

In ritual life the *saroan* still fulfills a vital function. First, it is responsible for erecting all the temporary architecture required at a funeral or other rites performed by *saroan* members. It also carries out all other labor involved in preparations, from building the wooden bier for the corpse to hauling the stone that will be a monument to the deceased. At a large funeral the construction of bamboo shelters for hundreds of guests might well take several months. These tasks, however, are all secondary to what Sesean villagers consider the real importance of the *saroan*. It is a group that represents a unity, those of "one birth" (*sangdadien*); it is also the group among which meat is divided, the group that eats together.

Membership in a *saroan* is inherited by both male and female children from both parents, although a child does not become a full member until his parent dies or he himself is married. At that time he becomes entitled to receive meat at a ritual in his own name. A married woman receives meat in her husband's name, even from her own *saroan*, receiving meat in her own name only if she is widowed. Names of those who do receive are shouted from the center of a meat-dividing field or are called down from a tall bamboo platform. In exchange for a share of meat the recipient is expected to give an annual contribution of *padi* or cash, and to participate in whatever group tasks are undertaken at rituals, house building, and other labor. Finally, upon a member's death a share of all the pigs and buffalo sacrificed are given to the *saroan*, to be divided among all its members. He returns in death some of the meat that he has eaten in life.

Every person has more than one *saroan*, since at least two are inherited from each parent. As with *tongkonan* it is impossible to maintain active ties with all, a fact that Toraja acknowledge. One must balance the desire to become a well-known big man whose name is called out from many different centers, and who receives much meat, against the debts incurred through such a process. One must think especially of one's children, who ultimately will be responsible for those debts. Of Rante, for example, it was said: "He really loves to eat meat, and he does it in eight *saroan*. But when he dies his poor only son will have to slaughter eight buffalo, just to repay his father's debts!"

Some people, like Mama' Agus, have withdrawn from all but two *saroan* so that their children will not be overwhelmed with debts. "They are not even here to eat the meat; who needs the debts?" she asks. Other people are more ambivalent about the choice between meat and fame and many debts. Samaa, for example, claims that it is not so easy to withdraw. He says that he once tried, distressed by his relative poverty and what he sees as chaos in the status system. He told the leaders of one of his *saroan:* "The way the world is today, I ask you not to give me meat. I won't cut two buffalo for you when my mother dies." But they insisted that it would be taboo not to give him meat, and replied: "Never mind, it's not for that. We will give you a share anyway." Usually, Samaa notes, someone else takes the meat (he lives in Rantepao). In fact he says he would be ashamed (*ma'siri'*) not to give them the two buffalo when his mother dies.

Every *saroan* has a head, or *ambe'* ("father"), who knows each household, its composition, ancestors, wealth, and previous cutting record. The *ambe'* is a cross between a New Guinea big man and a Bugis prince. Although he must in theory be of noble blood, his acceptance in this role is largely dependent on personal qualities and his ability to maintain a strong following. There is no formal permanent office; any noble (*to makaka*) of good birth is eligible if he is clever with words, industrious, and rich. The role is gradually assumed as a man demonstrates his verbal skills in public, or his ability to attract followers when he sponsors rituals or contributes sacrificial animals to others' ceremonies. Normally, advancing age enhances the authority of an *ambe'*, but aspiring young men may play the part if they are wealthy, noble, respected, and clever. The result is that at any moment there are several *ambe'* in a *saroan*, often as many as four or five. Ideally one of these is recognized as the most important and most powerful, but the hierarchy of *ambe'*, like other kinds of hierarchy, is not always universally agreed upon. The significance of the *ambe'* and of the possible conflicts caused by their ambiguous and shifting hierarchies emerge in their ritual roles: the *ambe'* must negotiate with sponsors of a ritual on all important decisions. At a funeral, for example, the *ambe'*, *to minaa*, and relatives of the deceased must agree upon the timing, the proper number of animals to be sacrificed, and the allotment of buffalo to the various *saroan* of the deceased.

Suppose that a man named Lotong dies. Lotong belonged to two *saroan*, A and B. His residence for most of his adult life was in the village where *saroan* A was centered, and so it is in that village that the funeral will be held. The major decisions will therefore be in the hands of the *ambe'* (and *to minaa*) of *saroan* A.

Suppose further that Lotong's children agree to sacrifice a total of five buffalo. The *ambe'* will probably decide that two of these buffalo should go to *saroan* B while the other three should be given to *saroan* A. The *ambe'* of *saroan* A will then be in charge of dividing meat to members of the "home" *saroan,* while the task of dividing meat to members of *saroan* B (the "visiting" *saroan*) will belong to the *ambe'* of that group. People who, like the deceased, belong to both *saroan* will thus receive shares from two different sources. Some portion will also be reserved for guests in neither A nor B.

This simplified account barely conveys the actual complexity of such transactions. There are usually more than just two *saroan* involved, and usually a number of descendants with different loyalties and wishes; there are also, as mentioned, usually several *ambe'* who do not necessarily agree. The resolution of which groups receive how much of what variously valued buffalo (another potential problem) thus requires a great deal of finesse and maneuvering on the part of the *ambe'* and the deceased's children. At every step the individuals may choose between many options; what appears to be a cumbersome system in practice allows for tremendous fluidity, flexibility, and dynamism in social processes. On the other hand, as options increase so do the possibilities for conflicts. Even the finest balance is likely to provoke resentment or dissatisfaction on the part of some *saroan* members, between *ambe',* or among the heirs. To complicate matters still further, in addition to these transactions involving whole animals, which are called "food exchanged" or "food returned" (*kande situka', kande sulle*), there are other traditional exchanges of animal parts, such as heads or legs. "Food of the earth" (*kande padang*), for example, occurs between two *saroan* that have always made this exchange, regardless of the deceased's relationship, if any, to the receiving *saroan*. This is what the Toraja are fond of calling "the politics of meat" (*politik daging*), on a macro-level, between *tongkonan.* There is also the equally animated micro-politics of meat division to all the households within the *saroan,* the "kitchens' share" (*taa dapo'*).

The *saroan* thus regulates the circulation of meat, both within its limits and between itself and other *saroan*. Interlocking networks of meat exchange extend across a wide area. *Saroan* may be visualized as dense at the center (clustered around the *ambe'*'s house) and diminishing toward the peripheries, where they overlap with other *saroan* centers. In this system the organization of meat is inseparable from the organization of people: meat is both a political medium and, at least in part, the substance of politics itself.

On Sesean the word *saroan* is often used interchangeably with *tondok*, a highly relative term of reference to a community. *Tondok* may be as small as a single household cluster or, in recent years, as large as Tana Toraja, Indonesia, or even the planet (the *tondok* of human life). *Tondok* are more closely tied to territory than are *saroan*, but neither are defined by their boundaries. Instead they are defined at their centers by big men, or *ambe'*, the charismatic leaders who control the distribution of meat. On Sesean, where there was no supra-*saroan* political organization precolonially, the *saroan* and the *tondok* are roughly coextensive and the *ambe' saroan* are the *ambe' tondok*. Elsewhere in the highlands other levels of political organization superseded the *saroan* long before the Dutch arrived. In Sangalla', for example, in the south, highly differentiated *tongkonan* were charged with specialized diplomatic, economic, ritual, and military functions in a federation that extended to distant territories submitting to the central Sangalla' houses (Tandilangi 1975). A still more elaborate form of federation was found in Pantilang, closer to and strongly influenced by the court at Luwu, in which sixty *tongkonan* were unified within a single political framework.

On Mount Sesean, however, no comparable level of political organization emerged, and meat and politics remained fully meshed in the *saroan*. Personal power and prestige depended on how one played a lively game of meat. Even today Toraja from other regions think of Sesean as a place where men are, as Kennedy bluntly put it, "meat-mad," obsessed with debts and fond of big competitive slaughters with lively "hot" meat fights. Perhaps Sesean *is* such a place. On this mountain, meat still seems to be the essence of social, economic, political, and ritual life, condensed into a multivalent, highly manipulable symbol.

# CHAPTER 5

# Capturing the Wind

One day, when the mythical Polopadang was tending his garden, he saw a beautiful maiden stealing corn. He promptly fell in love with her, married her, and followed her to heaven, for she was a *deata*. After long trials and tribulations in his heavenly abode Polopadang decided to return to earth. As he approached his *tondok*, however, he saw smoke billowing from a sacrificial fire below, and he understood that his family on earth was performing his funeral, having given him up for dead.

The funeral is so important in Toraja life that it is held even if the person dies at sea or in a distant land. In such situations a rite known as "capturing the wind," *dipoya anginna*, is performed. Members of the family gather with the *to minaa* and climb to a mountaintop, bringing with them a sarong and a long green bamboo pole. The bamboo pole is inserted into the sarong, which is tied at one end. Holding the closed end, the relatives turn toward the south, land of the dead, and raise the cloth to the sky while the *to minaa* calls three times to the wind. As the wind comes the sarong billows out and the people quickly close the other end for a moment, before they open it to release the wind. The bamboo "corpse" and the cloth remain, to be carried home, wrapped, and provided with a proper funeral and burial.

All funerals in Toraja, however grand or simple, with or without a corpse, are intended to safely transport the soul or ghost, the *bombo*, to the next world and to free the survivors from their attachments to it. All funerals involve a liminal period of partial identification of the survivors with the corpse, and their abstention from certain life-associated foods. Funer-

als also involve a reintegration of the survivors, accomplished
by some form of sacrifice which is, whenever possible, shared
and eaten. For poor people a symbolic sacrifice will do: a
chicken egg, or even striking an empty chicken basket, a
wooden pig plate, or a pigpen. The striking sound conveys to
the gods and the ancestors the intent to eventually perform a
real sacrifice; the ghost is only angry if those who can afford to
sacrifice do not.

Although a symbolic sacrifice may satisfy the spirits, and
formerly was common for slaves or those who died in epidemics, a socially acceptable funeral must contain a genuine animal
sacrifice. A story is told of an old, poor Toraja man who one
day acquired a single buffalo. He killed himself immediately,
assured that at least this one animal would be cut and its meat
distributed at his funeral.[1] In a related story from the Philippines, Barton (1963:160) writes of an Ifugao woman who sold
herself into slavery, knowing that a relative would then perform a number of animal sacrifices: "The sacrifice of animals
and the giving of feasts is the principal outlet for the Ifugao's
pride and self-assertiveness.... It is possible, even probable,
that this poor woman sold herself in order to be able to assert
herself by means of two or three pitiful sacrifices and so
become the centre of the family's attention for a little while,
through 'sharing meat.'" Self-assertion, as Barton's comment
reveals, is a social act. In Toraja, as in Ifugao, it centers on the
act of sharing meat. A person becomes central when he gives
to others.

## The Stages of Death

Death in Toraja, as in much of Southeast Asia, is clearly a
process, not an event. When a person draws his last breath the
Toraja say, reasonably, that "his breath is no more," yet they
do not speak of him as "dead." Instead he is *to makula'*, "the hot
one," an expression suggestive of fever, anger, warfare.[2] The
body is immediately placed in a sitting position, for it is taboo
to die lying down; it is said that those not seated will be too
heavy to be carried to Puya, land of the dead. The corpse is

bathed and dressed in the finest clothes and jewelry, as if to attend a ritual, and later wrapped in cloths, with a cloth tied around the chin to close the mouth. It is then "put to sleep" in the house, either in the *sumbung* (the southernmost room) or in the *sali*, the main room, along the south wall with the head toward the west. There the corpse may remain for many months, more rarely for years, while the family begins to assemble its members and its wealth. Until the funeral actually begins the ghost, or *bombo* (which may not be mentioned), is thought to hover nearby, more troublesome then menacing.

The death ceremony begins in earnest only after its timing has been agreed upon within the family and among village leaders, and is coordinated with other local rituals and the phases of the moon. The onset of socially acknowledged death is marked by sound and sacrifice: first the intermittent striking of a gong that echoes throughout surrounding villages, preparing neighbors for the death-announcing afternoon drumbeat, described as a distinctive *ten ten pun pun*. As the drumbeat issues from the house of the deceased the relatives who have been gathering in the yard, putting finishing touches on temporary shelters or sipping coffee, climb up into the house to witness the transition of the corpse from "hot" to "dead." The surviving spouse, *to balu*, takes a tiny black chicken and wrings its neck. The chicken, said by some to be the *bombo* of the deceased, is buried under the ashes in the hearth or is dropped through a hole in the kitchen floor to the ground below. The *to balu* then performs a second rite, known as "the suicide of the cat," flinging a cat from the window of the house with the words, "Kill yourself cat, your master is dead!" Actually, when I witnessed this rite a large black cat was simply held up to the window and instructed to die. Cats are cherished in Toraja and considered the animal closest to man; this brief ritual is said to symbolize the survivors' grief and the start of mourning. Later in the day the sacrifices become slightly more substantial: a pig, called "lighting the fire," and one or two young buffalo calves, called "to cause to die together," *pa'puli*. The symbolism is again surprisingly explicit and overlaps with that of the previous series of rites: close family may not consume the meat of these buffalo, which represent the "self" or "body" (*kalena*) of the dead. With the slaughter of the buffalo, animal(s) and man "lie down together."

In the house, meanwhile, the corpse itself is moved so that it lies along the west wall of the main room, its head toward the south. It may now be properly called *to mate*, "the dead one." The reality of this condition is also signaled by the changed state of the surviving spouse.[3] From this point on the *to balu* may no longer wear clothing; he or she is simply wrapped in a loose, large cloth of any color except red (which is associated with blood and life). In the past, when men wore their hair long, a widower would tie his hair in a bun (a woman's style) and a widow would cut hers. The *to balu* must sit on the floor facing the corpse (west) and away from the sun. For several days he or she may eat no food that has been cooked or touched with fire, and for the duration of the ceremonies may eat no rice, the quintessential food of life. Bananas, and later corn and cassava, form the mainstay of the *to balu*'s diet. If there is no surviving spouse this role is filled by a substitute, a woman or young girl—formerly a close slave of the family. "She is the one who will give me water," Mama' Agus's grandmother said of a seven-year-old slave girl before she died. This girl sat by the corpse for many days, wrapped in a cloth, and in exchange was given a piece of *sawah*. The person who fills this role is known as *to ma'tongkonan*.[4] In addition many other close family members (such as siblings, children) may choose to mourn, signifying this by a band worn across their foreheads and by abstaining from rice.

On the second day of the funeral the person most closely associated with death is called: the undertaker, or *to mebalun* (literally "the one who wraps"). Rocks are thrown at his house to bring him out, and he comes to the house of the deceased. There he wraps the corpse in many layers of cloth, traditionally woven from a coarse pineapple fiber, until a long cylinder is formed. He also prepares a kind of two-dimensional effigy behind the corpse's head, a bamboo framework on which the clothing, jewelry, and betel bags of the dead are hung. With each new action another small pig is cut, singed, and made into offerings. By the end of a complete *aluk* death ritual sixty-four pigs will have been sacrificed, most of which have very little meat but are indispensable for carrying out the proper *aluk* sequences. Many of these sequences involve functions once performed by slaves. The *to ma'kuasa*, for example, are a man and woman who sit by the corpse and must eat no cooked food until a specified moment, when they plunge their hands into a cooking pot filled with steaming pig's lungs. Couples charged with holding ropes of rattan while the corpse is being lifted (*to untoe we*), a man who symbolically spears a buffalo (*to mangrok*), and even the boys who rush to collect the dying buffalo's blood (*to merara*) were, in the past, slaves.

While the *to mebalun* (undertaker) and his fellow "priest of the right," the *to minaa*, manage the details of *aluk* niceties, and a host of functionaries perform their roles, the relatives and *saroan* members who gather in the yard or house pay very little attention to them. Particularly during the first few days, when there is little meat to be divided, the atmosphere is convivial, low-key, anticipatory of more dramatic days to come. People come and go, helping with tasks, gossiping, chewing betel, and at night chanting in memory of the deceased.

Nighttime is the social high point of many ritual days. Even at the smallest, simplest funeral excitement grows as darkness falls and as otherwise indifferent neighbors wend their ways along narrow trails to partake in the atmosphere of a funereal evening. Young men and women become especially rowdy, enjoying the social opportunities afforded by the ritual gathering. But the real aficionados of the night are older men and women who know the chants. Women like to sit with the mourners around the corpse, singing dirges, telling lewd jokes, and sharing large quantities of areca nut and betel. Outside the atmosphere becomes charged with the sounds of men's voices singing *ma'badong*, the lament for the deceased. The men, clad in shorts or plaid cotton sarongs, stand in a wide circle in the yard, hands joined, swaying rhythmically and stamping their bare feet in unison. A fire burns in the center of the men's circle, where a pig is later cut, singed, and divided (with coffee) among all present. *Ma'badong* tells the story of the deceased's life, one of many times throughout the ritual that such a story will be recounted: from conception through worldly success, death, the stages of the funeral, and the journey to Puya, land of the dead.[5] Women join the men, sitting in small groups along the sidelines or around the granary, singing their own form of mourning chant (ma'londe) simultaneously. The crackling bamboo fire, the mournful harmonies, and the laughing, chanting, spitting groups of men and women, all warm and enliven the cold dark air. The voices should sound as though they are "one breath" (misa' penaa). On many such nights these sounds echo across the mountains, informing even distant households that someone's funeral is in progress.

Ritual activity begins to build toward the ninth day, called "bringing down to the rice barn," dipa'rokko alang. In the afternoon of this day a special buffalo is led into the center of the yard where it is tied to a tall stake made of bamboo and casuarina branches and hung with the horns of buffalo already sacrificed. The to minaa utters a long prayer over the buffalo, occasionally patting it on the back. This buffalo is said to transport the bombo safely to the other world; the to minaa's invocation is called "hanging on to the rope." The animal is led away, to reappear as the buffalo that guards the effigy of the dead (pa'kampa tau tau) on the final day.

The central stake is then cut down, and if the deceased is male it is reassembled to become part of the tuang tuang, a long string of incised, slender tubes of bamboo that are hung on the east side of the yard. Precise rules govern the decoration, arrangement, and numbers of the tuang tuang, which are the prerogative of high-status males, perhaps vaguely connected with headhunting in the past. According to one to minaa, tuang tuang have eyes, bones, nerves, and blood. At the conclusion of the ritual the tuang tuang are hung around the rice barn to form its "necklace." Until then, however, they are a physical link to the life history of the dead. Late in the afternoon, as the sun is setting, a group of to minaa begin a recitation of that history, known as "rocking the tuang tuang." The to minaa grasp and shake the bamboo tubes as they recount yet another version of the life and death of the deceased. If the deceased is a woman a parallel recitation occurs as the to minaa simply sit on the ground before the rice barn. The recitation occurs three times,

The corpse, a cylinder wrapped in red cloth decorated with gold stars, is moved from the house to the granary platform, surrounded by relatives and neighbors.

*To minaa* Ne' Tandi Datu pats the back of the "buffalo which guards the effigy," while exhorting the soul to hold on tight as it journeys to the land of the dead.

each said to send the *bombo* further along toward Puya, and before the final one the undertaker (*to mebalun*) gives an offering of meat and palm wine to the deceased. The drum is sounded with the "death beat," and a small procession descends from the house: a gong player, a person carrying the "provisions" of the ghost (plate, cooking pot, betel bag, umbrella), and several people carrying the corpse itself. The procession circles three times around the granary before placing the corpse on the floor beneath it. At this point the deceased has made his or her first major transition outside the house. Long into the night the *to minaa* continue to chant.

On the following day a bamboo and cloth effigy of the deceased is built in front of the granary. The effigy, or *tau tau* (*tau* = person; *tau tau* = "diminunitive person") is thought of as a receptacle for the ghost, or *bombo*. The *to mebalun* must begin its construction, although others may join in. A freshly cut bamboo pole forms the torso, through which a slender bamboo length is inserted horizontally for the shoulders. The frame is wrapped in cloths and then carefully dressed with the appropriate clothing. A male may wear a fine batik sarong from Java, with a European long-sleeved shirt (or two) under an oversized navy peacoat or a tweedy suit-jacket. Around his neck tubes of incised gold are hung, as well as invulnerability charms of boar's teeth and tusks. At his left side an ancient iron sword is fastened, and an heirloom Toraja batik is draped over his shoulder or folded across his forehead. Most spectacular is his headdress: a set of buffalo horns between which rows of old silver coins are threaded, crowned with clusters of red and green parakeet feathers or even a bird-of-paradise plume. A female is more modestly attired: sarong, lacy blouse or *kebaya*, betel pouch, wide sash of silver coins, the finest possible beads and bracelets, and a black cloth tied behind her head to form a bun, topped with a tiny white porcelain plate, a reminder of her connection to the kitchen. The faces of both male and female *tau tau* are wrapped in bright red cloth, to which are added white paper or wooden eyes. When all is in order the *to mebalun* kneels before the effigy and turns it around three times to "awaken" it, and then presents it with an offering of pork, rice, and a tiny tube of wine. Relatives now come and offer betel and tobacco, asking it for blessings and ripe old age.[6]

That afternoon all is ready for the corpse to take another step in its journey, this time visibly accompanied by the ghost in the effigy. Just before it is carried away women mourners embrace the *tau tau*, encircle it with their arms, press their faces to its blood-red face, and give a long, stylized wail. Corpse, effigy, *to balu* (suviving spouse), *tuang tuang*, spears, banners, and a set of carved wooden chickens with miniature betel bags and feathers (provisions for Puya) are then carried in a boisterous, hopping procession to the ritual field, or *rante*, which is a short distance from any settlement and is used exclusively for rituals of death. The only features of the *rante* are a ring or two of irregular, gray stone boulders, some as tall as several meters and weighing a ton or more. Each monolith is a monument to an important (noble) ancestor at whose funeral it was erected. Here the corpse is installed on a specially constructed platform that overlooks the *rante*. The *to balu* sits beside it, and the effigy is placed below it, also looking out onto the field. Spears and other paraphernalia are put in place, and a fine cock is tied to a pole or tree in the center of the field, attached to the corpse's platform by a long white cloth.

The final movements of body and *bombo* occur two days later as the corporeal remains are separated from the immaterial ghost. A buffalo, the guardian of the effigy, is sacrificed and its meat divided. The *to mebalun* is paid his wages, a gong is struck, and the caged cock is freed. As the corpse is carried away toward a grave hewn into a limestone cliff, the clothing and jewelry are stripped from the *tau tau*. In a matter of minutes all that remains on the *rante* is a green bamboo skeleton: the body has gone to its "house without smoke," its tomb; the ghost has gone south to Puya; and the living have gone home.

The stages of death conclude with quiet rituals. On the day after burial no one from the *saroan* may work in their fields or gardens. Outside the house yard a rite is held, "to sweep away the dirt" (*ussapui rumpang*): a pig is sacrificed and the *to minaa* commands all bamboo and other trees that have been cut down to grow again. A dog and chicken are also sacrificed and their blood is sprinkled around the borders of the settlement. In the house of the deceased a handful of cooked rice and pork is thrust through a hole in the *sumbung* floor, the *bombo*'s final meal. One must not look through the hole nor stick one's hand down it lest the ghost hold on. Later, or on the following day, a "smoke-rising" rite is held: a graceful altar of cut bamboo (*tadoran*) is constructed north of the granary. It is hung with sugar palm-leaf streamers and woven baskets filled with offerings of a tiny chick, cooked rice, and betel. For a moment the *to minaa* places uncooked rice on a fire burning below the offerings and then tosses it on the altar in a gesture known as *mangambok*, "to sow seed." He calls upon the *deata* to bestow blessings, and then with the help of attending children he consumes the offerings. The surviving spouse may now eat rice, and the village, house, and its inhabitants are once again *masero*, "clean, clear, pure."

## The Pig Has Eaten the Vegetables

Socially the climax of a funeral occurs on the day before the corpse is interred, the effigy dismantled, and the ghost sent to Puya. This day is simply called "the day," *allona* (also "the sun"). It is also known as the "day to receive guests," although Agus put it more pointedly when he described it as the "day to receive debts." It is the long-anticipated event which spells either glory or shame for both the sponsors of the ritual and their guests, who enter formally in processions, or *rombongan*, each from a different *saroan*. The number of *rombongan* and their participants depend on the extent of the deceased's connections: a "small person" may have just one or two short processions at his or her funeral; a "big person" may have dozens.

The men at the head of the *rombongan*, formerly slaves, lead a buffalo or two (in cases of substantial *rombongan*) and bear pigs on bamboo carrying poles. Other men follow, carrying rice baskets (only at a Christian funeral) or huge vats of sugar palm wine. Cases of beer and whiskey are common now as well. Behind these prestations come the men, in single file, beginning with the oldest and continuing in a ranked hierarchy based on age, status, and to some extent size. The irreconcilability of these ranking principles makes for a time of great confusion as a *rombongan* prepares for its formal entrance onto the ceremonial field. The same is true for the women, who follow the men. A flurry of last-minute preparations induces stage fright as jewelry is rearranged, sarongs straightened, scarves refolded, and everyone attempts to find his or her proper place in line. At one funeral I attended a friend was frantic until her father found her a hat, *ma'siri'* lest her face be seen.

A gong sounds to announce the group's arrival, and the *rombongan* enters. At a large funeral the field is encircled with temporary bamboo houses built to shelter the multitude of guests. People fill these shelters and watch appreciatively as each new group makes its dramatic entrance and proceeds to walk slowly around the field. The audience clucks approval at the girth of a buffalo, the quantities of pigs, or the composure and fine clothing of the visitors. They may also mutter disapprovingly if the buffalo seem insufficient, the pigs scrawny, or the people in disarray. The spectators watch closely for the arrival of important people whose presence identifies the group, and they may gossip and speculate on a certain pig, whose debt it is, and whether it is fitting.

The *rombongan* proceeds to a specially constructed building where men and women sit on opposite sides and a black-clad line of mourners greets them ceremoniously, offering betel nut and cigarettes. The mourners are those who feel themselves to be close family with the deceased; more distant family may also choose to join, to show their sympathy or solidarity. The betel, in the most elegant silver receptacle available, is offered first to the man and woman of highest status. This gesture used to be of utmost importance and not without its difficulties, as the presentation was often made by a young, pretty girl who did not always know whom to honor. She had to recognize the more subtle signs of status—not just seating position, but the deference of others.

Following this ceremonial greeting the members of each *rombongan* adjourn to temporary shelters where they are served coffee and cookies by the ritual's sponsors, and later on cooked rice. Much of the success of the ritual hinges not only on the public appearance of the processions but on the smooth functioning of the temporary, behind-the-scenes kitchen. For a

At an elaborate funeral hundreds of guests are housed in temporary bamboo structures. Children peer out from openings in the woven walls.

Big men await their shares of meat.

major ritual the extent of kitchen coordination may be phe-
nomenal. At a funeral I attended in Pangala' in 1978, thousands
of guests were served without apparent effort from one vast
kitchen that cooked five hundred liters of rice in a single morning. A small jeep with a wagon behind it went back and forth all
day between the spring and the kitchen, refilling three huge
drums of water. Even a smaller funeral requires considerable
coordination, as this passage from my field notes (October
1978) reveals. The funeral was held near To' Dama', and about
eight hundred guests arrived on "the day."

The cook-shack is the coolest, shadiest spot around, a large
bamboo structure walled with palm leaves. Since no one is on
display it is far more relaxed than outside: women comb each
others' hair and adjust their sarongs; children poke their hands
through the leafy walls demanding cookies. At the far end of the
shack men stand guard over four massive cauldrons of boiling
water, from which coffee is prepared in teakettles. The Protestant church women's organization contributed 200 cups and lots
of other dishes. There are three huge tins of purchased cookies,
several of sugar, and one of coffee, all contributed by the
deceased's children. About fifteen pretty girls are in charge of
carrying trays of glasses and cookies on little plates, followed by
men with pots of coffee, to serve each *rombongan*. Each time a
new group enters someone conveys its size—"make 50 coffees!"—
and in a flash everything is ready. Dishes are quickly recollected,
washed, dried.

Mama' Agus is in charge of the whole operation (Lai Sanda,
the deceased, is not a relative but she is of the same *saroan*). For
about six hours now she has sat under a leafy shelf and super-
vised, making sure no one eats too many cookies (she has eaten
nothing herself), that water is fetched, boiled, and coffee
brewed; that children are warded off; and that, somehow, the
contents of twenty large baskets of freshly cooked red and
white rice are distributed.

Pigs, which will be partially consumed with the proferred
rice, are brought by each *rombongan*, squealing and grunting
within their neatly woven palm-leaf baskets, suspended from
bamboo carrying poles. Unlike buffalo, which are led away and
tethered after circumambulating the field, pigs are simply
placed on the ground, still lashed to their poles and encased in

woven greenery. As the day wears on the field fills with pigs
and poles. Everyone knows that these pigs represent debts, and
each time a new pig is displayed a caller shouts, "Whose pig?"
and the man who bears it replies with the donor's name. "Is it a
new debt or is it old?" asks the caller. If the pig represents the
repayment of a previous debt, the bearer replies, "The pig has
eaten the vegetables!" (*mangkamo unkande utan*). If the pig is a
newly initiated exchange, a new debt, he responds, "The pig
has not yet eaten the vegetables!" A repaid debt is said to be
"clean" (*masero*), or "high status" (*to makaka*).[7]

Behind this interchange is a history of exchanges. Suppose
that Sampe brought a pig to Lolo, a pig that had already "eaten
the vegetables." It is possible that years ago, when Sampe's
mother died, Lolo had brought a pig to her funeral, in Sampe's
name. Now when Lolo is holding a funeral for *his* mother,
Sampe is compelled to return (to "cleanse") the debt. His pig in
theory should be identical in size and value to that which Lolo
had once given him. Why, however, would Lolo have given a
pig to Sampe in the first place? And what is the relationship
between Sampe, his pig, and the people in the *rombongan* that
walk behind him?

Unlike the large smoke-rising rituals such as *maro* and
*ma'bua'*, which are held by all members of a *tongkonan*, the funeral is really the responsibility of the immediate family, the
children and grandchildren of the deceased. In cases of child-
lessness adopted children usually assume this responsibility,
or siblings and siblings' children. In its simplest form this
responsibility entails the slaughter of some buffalo to be
divided among the people in the deceased's several *saroan*. The
number of buffalo depends in principle on the status of the
deceased, as well as on the financial capabilities of the children
and the agreement of *ambe'* and *to minaa*. It is also influenced by
the number of *saroan* to which meat is owed.

In addition to these basic buffalo contributed by the immediate heirs, other people also bring both buffalo and pigs. For
example, if a woman named Bua' had raised Simon's son for
several years, upon her death Simon (or his son or grandchild)
may want to slaughter a buffalo, even though there is no formal obligation. "Felt" debts are distinguished from compulsory

ones.[8] When the buffalo is brought to Bua''s funeral it must be given either in the names of all the heirs or in the name of a single person. Suppose that Simon decides to give the buffalo to Bua''s eldest son, Tandilo. This time an obligatory debt has been created: years later, if Simon's son holds a funeral for one of his parents, Tandilo must remember his obligation and bring an identical buffalo. In theory the debt ends there, but if both sides enjoy the relationship and derive some benefit from it, there will be other pretexts and opportunities for keeping the debts alive.

Essentially the same principles are at work with regard to the pigs, except that while some buffalo are not considered debts (those slaughtered directly by the children),[9] pigs are never debt-free. They may be specific repayments to specific children of the deceased, in return for the equal pig contributed by these children or their parents at a funeral of their own staging; or they may be new debts arising from a previous tie of another sort, such as adoption.

Members of a *rombongan* belong in theory to a single *saroan*, or several if groups are merged at a large funeral. In practice, stray guests who do not quite fit in may also join a group composed of their neighbors or others to whom they do have ties. They glean a sense of pride and dignity from being associated with the big man who leads the group and whose pig, in all probability, is being offered (since big men have more ties and debts than ordinary people). The followers acquire a "place," literally and figuratively: they sleep in the big man's temporary shelter, they know where to sit, and they are fed for a day. In addition to other food they eat part of the pig he brought, for half of this pig is returned to its donor, to be cooked and eaten on the spot.

The big man, for his part, encourages additions to his *rombongan*. By taking people into his charge he demonstrates his wealth, generosity, and the extent of his following, with whom he becomes "one breath, one word." He will defend their honor, their *siri'*, if it should be slighted, as they visibly enhance his own. As one big man explained to me, "On this day we feed our many people (*to budata*), and only then may be we called men." The *rombongan*, then, represents a temporary cone of power, its fluid composition revealing the flexibility, even instability, of groups and leaders. At the same time, through maneuvering in relation to competing *rombongan*, each big man engages in manipulation of his status in a wider social frame.

All debts, that is all pigs and buffalo, are carefully noted in writing. Formerly debts were simply remembered, and many Toraja still memorize them; but now writing is an additional guarantee that the debts will not be forgotten. The government collects a slaughter tax and sends an official representative to note this information too. He and a family member sit together at a table and each makes a list which specifies the name of the *rombongan* leader, its place of origin, the number of people, and for each animal the name of the recipient and its exact horn size (for buffalo) or diameter across the middle (for pigs).

## Division of a Buffalo

At various points throughout the weeks that constitute a large funeral, buffalo and pigs are cut up and their meat distributed. The climax of these distributions occurs on guest-day, simply because there are more people to receive meat, more statuses to raise or lower, more *siri'* concentrated there to boost or wound.

Even the slaughter of these animals may be filled with tension. Until the late nineteenth century buffalo were repeatedly stabbed with spears, dying slowly. This method was decried by Islamic occupiers in the 1890s and later by the Dutch. The present technique is a swift, clean cut to the jugular vein, using a long-bladed sword, or *la'bo*. When done properly, death is almost instantaneous: the animal keels over, and as blood and steam spurt forth small boys rush forward with bamboo tubes to collect the warm blood (to be used in cooking), darting around the still-kicking legs to emerge with blood-soaked arms. Sometimes, however, the buffalo proves difficult to kill. This happened at the funeral of Pong Pindan's wife (chap. 7), on a day that was particularly tense because of the presence of an unpopular government official. I was standing alongside the granary talking with Payu, the *to minaa*'s son-in-law. A buffalo

was led into the yard from a *saroan* called To' Pao, some distance
from Tondoklitak. This passage from my notes suggests how
uncomfortable a bungled slaughter may become for those in
attendance:

The buffalo's leg was tied to a post in the middle of the yard.
The *to ma'tingoro* (man who slaughters) made one slash in the
throat, but it was not deep at all. A little blood spurted. He tried
again, and again, and the crowd started shouting instructions
and warnings and the man's face tensed terribly so that he
really did look "hot." Then he gashed the rear legs deeply, so
that the animal could not run, and two other men hooked a thick
rope around the horns, and a *to mebalun* tried to restrain the
animal which kept running about and falling down, thrashing,
and getting up again. Finally, Payu was in the fray and people
yelled "give it to him"; he took his *la'bo* and with one swift blow
cut deeply into the neck and blood poured forth and the crowd
seemed to breathe a sigh of relief, although it took another five
minutes before the beast stopped heaving and making dread-
ful sounds.

The leader of the group from Pao then stood up and charged
that the buffalo did not die because of jealous magic. Payu just
muttered *pusa' ki* (roughly, "we are dizzy, lost"), but Sampe
Musu, from Tondoklitak, very articulate and confident, made a
speech that had everyone laughing (except for the people from
To' Pao), charging that if anyone had made magic the *bombo*
would have seen it and would answer for it! To this the head
from Pao retorted that the folks from Tondoklitak should give
up their hopes of getting a share of meat (*taa*); this meat is just
for us, he said, and maybe some outside visitors.

This pretty much broke up the group; a half hour after it all
started Ne' Leme had gone home. I left too, but I was told that
later the government official made a speech about how good it
was that people did not fight over meat, that this should set an
example, and that everyone is happy. (He had reason to be
happy as two pig's legs had been brought to his house earlier in
the day). I commented to Mama' Agus that the head from Pao
did not look happy; she said, right, his share was not too big
this time.

The "politics of meat" (*politik daging*), as the Toraja label such
matters, is more concretely the politics of meat division.

Depending on the occasion the meat is either distributed from the center of the yard (as above) or thrown down from a bamboo platform about seven meters high, which is erected on the *rante* or sometimes built in a sturdy old tree. The person charged with distribution is a specialist called "the divider" (*to mentaa*) and is under instructions from the *ambe'*. Meat handling is symbolically charged, whether positively or negatively: on Sesean only high-status men may have this task, while in areas such as Pantilang it is the work of those of low rank. Other men are assigned the task of hacking the recently killed animal into large sections with knives and axes. When this is done the chunks are hoisted with ropes up to the platform, where further slicers go to work. At last the divider begins to throw down pieces of meat.

With every throw the *to mentaa* shouts the name of someone in the crowd below. This is the important "naming from the center." Being named is, in a sense, being placed and having one's *siri'*, one's worth, acknowledged. As the meat thuds on the earth, usually a child runs and picks it up for the older person named. Amid much noise everyone seems to hear exactly who is called and to see exactly what size and cut of meat is thrown. On Sesean the head, heart, liver, and thighs are the most highly valued parts; this differs for other areas, but consistently all parts of the animal are assigned a value.

Ideally the first people to receive meat are the *to minaa* and then the oldest people, for age is honored after the "holding of *aluk*." However, older people are not necessarily of noble birth, nor are they always "big" in wealth. The bases of honor often do not coincide. This problem may be solved by throwing first to older people, but throwing them smaller or less-valued cuts. Alternatively the throws may come in several sets: first to all the people classed as *to makaka* (noble), beginning with the old and ending with the young, while rank within the *to makaka* category is expressed through size, cut, or number of cuts; second to commoners, again ranked by age, blood, and wealth within this class. In some areas slaves once were named from the center too, but in other areas they were simply given a share of their owners' meat, or by some accounts were permitted to grab what they could from a pile of ribs or leftovers.

Today former slaves are called from the center and often given decent cuts, innovations which some high-status Toraja refer to as "chaos." In theory the division reaches and satisfies everyone. In the words of a Sesean schoolboy who wrote an essay entitled "If I Were the Meat-Divider": "I would begin with the *to minaa* and divide until the bottom. . . . I wouldn't give anyone too little or too much, I would give the same. I would satisfy people. If children asked me [for meat], I wouldn't give; how could I give children first, old people later? Later, I would leave the yard and ask the *ambe'* if it was enough. I would be very ashamed (*ma'siri'*) if people said I didn't give." In principle meat division clearly marks who every person is in relation to the others. In practice it often demonstrates the ambiguities and contradictions in these principles.

The lack of fixed rules for determining the distribution (order, cut, and size of piece to be coordinated with age, blood, and wealth) is complicated further by a criterion which I call the "cutting history," which intersects with age, blood, and wealth, as well as temperament and acts of an individual and his genealogical predecessors. The cutting history on Sesean is a public measure of who one is, a Toraja supplement to genealogy. In fact when Toraja tell their genealogies they often include some references to what was cut for whom. Ne' Leme, Mama' Agus's older brother, claimed that as the leading big man in Tondoklitak such histories were his most important means for deciding how meat should be divided. He was proud that he remembered exactly who cut what for whom at numerous rituals in the past. He was also a good judge of who was likely to cut what in the future, based on his estimates of their character and inclinations, their previous record, the number of pigs in their pen, and the likelihood that their grandfather would die in the next few years.

Ne' Leme's calculations might run along these lines: If he cut four buffalo last year and Lalang cut only one, it is only fair that he receive more meat than Lalang at other people's ceremonies. If, however, Lalang's father is about to die, better to give Lalang a lot of meat, thereby encouraging him to cut more at the anticipated funeral. The extra meat should cause Lalang to feel both indebted and important. With his *siri'* inflated he will therefore act more like a rich big man and will cut more. Ne' Leme inadvertently outlined a model for maximizing the flow of meat (as *ambe'*) and for maximizing *siri'* and bigmanship (as Lalang the sacrificer). Had I pursued this Ne' Leme might have assured me that the *ambe''*s job must also be to limit meat and cutting, keeping both within the bounds of custom and economic feasibility.

Given the complex, overlapping, and sometimes contradictory bases for determining the distribution of meat, it is not surprising that individuals' *siri'* is often wounded at funerals. Several responses are possible if a person does feel hurt. Quiet acceptance is one, although not without some loss of status and diminished sense of self. More commonly people may bury the insult temporarily, seeking revenge at a future ceremony where it is possible to return the shame. Years later the reasons will still be remembered and understood. The most explosive response is limited to a few older men who sometimes simply lose their composure and *mangaru*: they hop in anger around the piles of meat, making speeches, shouting, or even brandishing knives and flinging meat and buffalo excrement at the crowded sidelines.

Although I never understood the dynamics of a "meat fight" while I witnessed one, Agus provided the following example. Suppose two men wanted to deflate the status of Tandi. One of them would busily flatter Tandi's son so that he would feel big and begin to demand more meat. When the son eventually demanded too much meat, the other man would chastise him publicly and cut him down to size, humiliating him and putting him (and, according to Toraja logic, his father) in his place. The problem, in short, had both nothing and everything to do with meat. The strategy was incredibly indirect and convoluted, yet the actors could read it easily. "Indeed," Agus said repeatedly, "it's all politics."

Several real meat fights occurred in April 1978. One, which I did not see but later heard about, occurred on a day when fourteen buffalo were cut. Lolo, from a village a few hours away, threw a piece of meat and bone that hit Sampe's son. Sampe, who was in the center dividing meat, strode forth, hands on his hips, and demanded to know who hit his son. As Lolo was no longer in sight Sampe merely punched the side of the house. Apparently Lolo and his parents and siblings were all very rich, but for some reason (that I could not learn) a few years previously the *saroan* in question had stopped giving meat to Lolo's mother, in spite of her long-standing ties there. Lolo was thus using this opportunity when he had been given meat to vent his anger and defend his mother's *siri'*. He shouted, "Why do you give meat to me now, when you gave nothing to my mother?" In typically indirect fashion he threw the meat not at the meat divider but at the latter's son, whose *siri'* then was defended by his father (who punched the house).

Another event around the same time had broader implications in Tondoklitak. This was a problem about cookies, but it became a pretext for a reorganization of several *saroan*. I had known for months in advance that a certain funeral was bound to be a source of conflict, as Rappang, the man in charge, happened to be an old rival of Ne' Leme's family in To' Dama'. Even their ancestors had been rivals, and Rappang's grandfather (in the To' Dama' version) was notoriously harsh and stingy. On this occasion Rappang, who was an *ambe'* in the Batukamban *saroan*, buried his mother. Years ago Mama' Agus had been furious at him, at a funeral, both for herself (feeling that her share had been ignored) and for "small people" in general. He just gave meat to those who helped him, she said. In her rage she (a tiny woman) grabbed him by his plastic raincoat and nearly toppled him, whereupon he said, "If you want to eat meat, cut your own buffalo." To this she replied by throwing a hunk of meat and some buffalo excrement, which just hit his knees. When the time came for his mother's funeral she pleaded illness, a rather transparent excuse.

Ne' Leme, on the other hand, had to go to the funeral. He spent days building shelters for the guests and attending planning sessions. Aside from general political motives in Batukamban he had a definite debt to Rappang (who was his nephew, and also a second cousin of Ne' Leme's wife). Rappang had brought a big pig when Ne' Leme's mother-in-law was buried several years before, and now Ne' Leme was to return the pig. When Ne' Leme liked people he tended to play down the obligatory nature of the debt. In this case he did not: he owed a pig.

The funeral was a large, Christian ceremony. Rappang's status was clearly high by blood (his ancestors had had slaves, and he himself was an *ambe'*), but gossip explained the funeral's size on the basis of the grandchildren's wealth and success in their work abroad. (Grandchildren's buffalo are cut in the names of their parents, from whom they eventually inherit both property and debts.) It was even said that there was little left to inherit, but since they were financially able they would have been *ma'siri'* not to cut.

The *rombongan* entered the funeral site, buffalo and pigs were noted, and by late afternoon everyone adjourned to eat. I had scarcely noticed that anything was amiss, although I was hungry (I was used to being hungry at these events since one eats only when the divisions are over). Everyone I was with, however, was not only hungry but outraged. Apparently we had not been served the customary coffee and cookies due honored guests. Worse still, no rice had been provided. As we sat on a granary people opened their own containers of cooked rice, brought in the event of an emergency such as this one. The rice was eaten with meat from half the pig that Ne' Leme had brought to his relative Rappang: the pig had eaten the vegetables, and now Ne' Leme and his followers ate half the pig. During this eating much whispering occurred, and finally I was let in on the plot: in protest against the humiliating treatment we had received, a buffalo destined to be given to our *saroan* (Tondok Doan) on the following day would be rejected.

The buffalo was to have been given as part of a standard exchange between two *saroan (panglengko)* that share family and house connections. In this case Rappang had family at both Batukamban and Tondok Doan, and it was a perfectly appropriate transaction. Two buffalo of this sort had already been given to another Tondoklitak *saroan* (Tondok Diongan). But the several *ambe'* at Tondok Doan, most notably Ne' Leme, felt slighted by Rappang's treatment and were, it seemed, delighted to have this chance to retaliate. "Who needs another debt anyway?" Ne' Leme's wife commented. Underlying the cookie talk was the sense that they had engineered a coup, for several years earlier Ne' Leme had formed his own *saroan* at Batukamban, breaking off from Rappang's. The members of the new *saroan* included those who had been slighted over cookies, but after this incident more and more people seemed to gravitate toward Ne' Leme's group, causing Rappang's own group to shrink further.

## Bringing Home the Bacon

The funeral is a stage for casting and recasting the relationships between groups, between big men and followers, and within the group. It is an intensely, at times excruciatingly, public event, and even those who stay at home or live in distant villages or towns are well aware of what transpires. The sounds of gongs and drums and chants carry messages across the mountains. People who remain at home nonetheless receive a share of meat, as informal divisions occur between family and other neighbors. Sometimes meat is sent to town, or even dried and mailed as jerky to relatives in Irian Jaya.

When the distribution of meat is finished, for most people the ceremony is over. Crowds of people begin the often long trek home. The rich and important walk empty-handed, arms swinging, while behind them walk young men (formerly slaves) hauling whole legs, thighs, or other large desirable pieces lashed to bamboo poles. Ordinary people carry their own meat if no children are available to do it for them. When funerals are in season one often sees long lines of men and women joking, gossiping, boasting, or sometimes walking quickly in silence, making their way along winding mountain trails. Most hold bloody pieces of meat wrapped in leaves or tied with grasses. Observers cannot help but note who carries what, even from a distance, and in this way the results of the day's funeral are broadcast throughout a wide region. Often we would return from a distant funeral and Mama' Agus would already know what piece we had received. As we walked our piece of meat was the object of public envy, ridicule, or simple curiosity. People would tease, "Eeeeee, you've got a lot of meat! Give me a little, o.k.?" If for some reason we were meatless the refrain

was different: "Eeeee, where is your (my) meat? You *weren't*
given any? Ohh, pity you...."

Indeed people sometimes do divide meat on the road. One
day we met a woman who we knew was a former slave of
Mama' Agus's family. She was said to be a hundred years old,
very poor and thin. She was returning from a funeral dressed
in black and almost skipping down the road, and in her hand
she held a small piece of meat. "Eee, grandchild," she exclaimed,
embracing me almost jubilantly and offering up her share of
meat, which we politely declined. I saw this woman several
times—I even saw her baptized in the Protestant church—but
only then, on the road with her meat, did she seem joyful. Only
then did she address me directly.

Ne' Lumbaa, the *to minaa*, told me a dream, and he too was
joyful in its telling. He dreamed that meat was divided and
that the pieces he was given (as he held up his hand with
fingers spread) were *ganna'*, which means both "enough"
and "complete."[10]


## Land Division

By the end of the funeral the children of the deceased have
established new reputations, positions, new degrees of *siri'*,
new cutting histories, and new debts. They spend the day after
tallying up the latter, usually exhausted and relieved to have it
over with, and ready to assess their futures. The horns from all
the cut buffalo are assembled, to be hung eventually in a row
up the center post of the carved house, visible signs of the
position of the *tongkonan* and reminders of the splendor and
sacrifice of that funeral. The more material reminder and consequence of those sacrifices is the way that land is divided.

Although some Toraja now resort to written wills or at least
verbal communications about how they wish their wealth to be
distributed, the older and more common system is based on the
number of buffalo sacrificed. As might be imagined this makes
for more than a little competition between siblings. *Aluk*
people wanted it that way, I was told, to be sure that their
children would cut enough buffalo for them to eat in Puya. The
old people, in this interpretation, felt dependent on these sacri-

fices to sustain them in the afterworld, and felt that only through a material incentive could children be induced to cut enough. Whatever the reason there certainly is an incentive toward competitive sacrifice, unless the children are more or less willing to equalize their shares. Children too young to own their own buffalo have problems, for either they acquire debts while they are still young (if an interested relative lends the child a buffalo for this purpose), or alternatively they are stripped of the basis of wealth by their own siblings. Toraja legends are filled with such happenings, with abandoned, impoverished, younger siblings driven to the forests where they suffer and eventually take revenge.[11] More commonly, in real life, the "forests" are debts in which the child grows up entangled.

But not just debts are planted; the land itself is allocated. One method of inheritance, *tekken,* involves giving a child land or other wealth during one's own lifetime. This can be done at virtually any time, for either cognatic or adopted children, and is especially common as they are growing up. It is in fact a common method of adopting a child, especially in cases of child-lessness. The implication of such adoption, with the gift of land that accompanies it, is clear: the child will sacrifice a buffalo at the adoptive parent's funeral, as well as contribute pigs to rituals held at the parent's *tongkonan.* If the latter obligation is not fulfilled the land may be withdrawn. Not to fulfill the obligation of a funeral sacrifice is considered impossible. Mama' Agus, for instance, acquired a *sawah* from Datu Allo, a childless woman married to a colonial officer under Mama' Agus's husband. "Become my child," Datu Allo said, and *tekken*-ed her a fine plot of land. Another *sawah* had been *tekken*-ed to her by a man with sons but no daughters. Curiously the man later married Mama' Agus's mother. In neither case did Mama' Agus actually live at her adoptive parents' houses for more than a day, but she cut buffalo at both their funerals. In fact she also cut a buffalo for the man's mother, perhaps because he had become her stepfather as well.

Most inheritance, however, is based on the number of buffalo cut at the funeral and not on previously bequeathed land. The competition this may engender has led to corpse stealing in the past. According to a rather incredible (but believed) story, in the 1950s the funeral of Rante Allo was scheduled to take place in Tikala. Most of the family wealth, as well as the houses of her grandchildren, were concentrated there. In another village, however, Rante Allo also had five stepchildren from her husband's previous marriage, one of whom was married to a government official. They conspired to hold the ritual in their own village, where they could sacrifice the majority of buffalo and so obtain more meat, prestige, and land. They managed to steal the corpse from its Tikala house and began the funeral in secret, calling the Tikala relatives only when the buffalo were ready to be cut. Predictably the grandchildren were outraged and refused to attend. Ten buffalo, already slaughtered, just rotted. The *ambe'* from Tikala said, "Eat your buffalo, you don't respect us. Your hearts are rotten!" In spite of their slaughtered buffalo the conspiring adopted children failed to win their stepmother's land.

Even a properly conducted funeral may become quite complicated. Ne' Tumba', Mama' Agus's aunt, divided her gold but not her land before she died. In spite of her three marriages Tumba' had no children of her own, and the recipients of her wealth were therefore her siblings and their children. Fourteen buffalo were cut at her funeral: four by one set of five nieces and nephews (they should have cut five, but were unable); five by Mama' Agus and her siblings (who formed another niece-nephew set of five); one by another nephew; one by a sister; one by a brother; and two by two adopted children of another brother. In addition two former slaves each cut a buffalo to assert their connection, although they received no land in return.

More than ten years later, in 1978, one of the adopted children of Tumba''s brother decided that she was entitled to land worth three buffalo, in spite of the fact that she had cut only one buffalo at Tumba''s funeral. During a heated family conference that went on for hours in the midday sun, she dredged up every ritual in her past to prove her extensive sacrifices and demanded to know whether she was not part of the "blood bones," *rarabuku*. The others assured her that she was but agreed that she could not have this extra land. In fact, some pointed out, she never should have received a thing, for her adoptive father had long ago gambled away his (and hence her) share. They had given her land worth one buffalo in spite of this, and now, they said indignantly, "She wants to be like us! It cannot be."

The meetings at which disputes such as these are resolved are called *kombongan*. *Kombong* means "to gather into a unity," "to form." Gold dust, for example, is *dikombong*, "to become gold." A stand of bamboo trees owned by the *tongkonan* is also called *kombongan*. The purpose of forming all the disparate persons in a family or group into a wider unity is explicit at dispute-settling *kombongan*, and everyone with an interest may attend and speak their mind. The *ambe'* and other big men usually play the leading roles, but many others talk as well. The *kombongan* is an animated public forum for voicing and resolving grievances: fines are set for divorces, the causes of epidemics are determined, or, as in many cases like this one, it is a medium for working through the conflicts engendered by and reflected in the inheritance process.

## Reversals, Tricksters, and Greedy Grandmothers

Actual funerals have great potential for conflict: in their performance (the immediate "politics of meat"), in their legacy of indebtedness, and particularly in matters of inheritance, where disputes may persist unresolved for decades, growing more complicated with every death. Like magnifying mirrors myths reflect and exaggerate the conflicts and central preoccupations of the Toraja funeral. Shame and the necessity for splendid sacrifice produce a family not united but torn apart; and a mother's body not honored by men but trampled on by buffalo. The stories reveal the wishes, fears, and competitive hostilities that lie just below the surface of real funerals.

One of these legends is a particular version of the tale of Lando Rundun ("Long Hair"). In a popular Sesean myth Lando Rundun, an extraordinarily beautiful Toraja woman, marries a Bugis (Bone) man when he discovers one of her mile-long hairs floating downriver in a golden grapefruit. The version of the myth that concerns us here, however, comes from Pantilang, geographically midway between Luwu and Sesean.

Lando Rundun's mother dies on Sesean, her birthplace. She and her siblings begin the two-day walk across the mountains from Pantilang, where they live, to Sesean. They arrive dressed in shabby rags and empty-handed. The Sesean side of the family is aghast to see them, and for an entire week they torment the new arrivals day and night with songs of scorn and ridicule about their wretched clothes and impoverished state. At last it is guest day, and to the shock and shame of the Sesean family a vast procession arrives from Pantilang, bringing with them not just several, but hundreds of every named variety of buffalo. The *siri'*, both honor and shame, is utterly reversed in this stunning defeat of the Sesean branch of Lando Rundun's *rarabuku*.

If this story represents competition between two branches of the family, a more thoroughly self-indulgent use of the funeral is typical of Dana', the Toraja trickster. We have already encountered Dana': he told the residents of Palopo that the *datu's* mother-in-law was a pig, and he also induced the *datu* to give birth to *padi* and then stole the seeds. In another episode Dana''s mother dies and he places her body along a buffalo path where she is trampled by scores of buffalo. Accusing the rich buffalo owners of murdering his mother, he demands that all their buffalo be sacrificed for her. In this way he provides an enormous funeral for his (mutilated) mother.

The Toraja find this story riotously funny, as they find most Dana' stories. Dana' has the knowledge of a marginal man, and his outrageous tricks act out a burlesque of all that is central to Toraja thought, feeling, and action. Dana' resorts to such tactics because he is a poor man, a small man. He lacks status by blood, and in some regions he is said to be a slave; he lacks status by wealth; and in most versions he also lacks a home. By all accounts he is a wanderer. He is, however, clever and a wily trickster. Like tricksters everywhere Dana' has a voracious appetite (Radin 1972), which in its Toraja guise is mostly geared toward meat. He knows how to scare the guests at rituals and make them run, leaving the meat behind for his total consumption. He never works hard or sacrifices for his share. Reciprocity is not his way; he gets but never gives.

Dana' appears in an interesting asocial aspect in an episode from Pantilang, where he is explicitly a slave. At a ritual, as meat is being divided from the center, he calls out: "Where's Dana''s share? *That's* Dana''s share. The ears for my ears, so I may hear my orders." He continues: "That's not enough! The legs for my legs, the wages of my walking," and so on through arms, shoulders, until he has named every part of the animal. He so completely identifies himself with it that the meat dividers are tricked into giving him the entire buffalo, on the grounds that only then could he function as a whole person to serve the others. "If not, nothing else will happen on the earth," he threatens. Mocking the foundations of the social order, Dana' frightens big men with their dependence upon the small, and the small man becomes the whole.

The same motif, without Dana''s rationale, is found in some versions of the story of Toraja's greedy grandmother, Indo' Orro Orro. If Dana' represents a rootless, wandering, hungry, tricking male figure, Indo' Orro Orro is a female figure even more strikingly outside society. In fact she is not clearly human, for she sometimes eats, or tries to eat, other humans. She inhabits the forest and has very long breasts covered with thorns that she uses as weapons, flinging them back over her shoulders to attack. She has a mouth so large that when she laughs it opens to cover her eyes and her entire face.

This mouth not only hides her face but it devours things. In a popular tale two siblings are stranded in the forest, searching for food after their wicked stepmother has fed them human excrement disguised as rice. They manage to kill a wild pig but first must cook it. They are forced to ask for fire from Indo' Orro Orro. She insists on following them to the pig roast (in exchange for the fire?) in spite of their pretense that they merely want to cook some porcupine or grasshoppers. After the pig is roasted they cut it up. The older child says, "O, Indo' Orro Orro, give a leg to my younger sibling." She replies, "Then you will crave legs." The child says, "Give him the ear." Indo' Orro Orro says, "Then you will be all ears." The child asks for the liver and she replies, "You will lust after liver." Thereupon Indo' Orro Orro "divides" it all to herself, saying, "The share for my legs, the share for my arms, for my ears, for my head," and so on.

In the end the children retrieve the meat from Indo' Orro
Orro through tricks of their own and are reincorporated into
society by finding their real mother and by sharing food. Inter-
estingly this food is rice, not meat. As strangers they are first
offered "pig rice" (vegetables) in exchange for delousing their
mother's hair. At the moment of recognition real rice is forth-
coming. Rice, of course, is also subject to manipulation, as
when excrement is disguised as rice by the stepmother. And
rice may be more or less aristocratic, on a scale from "fine"
(*halusu*) to "coarse" (*kasara'*), or it may be wrapped in special
banana-leaf packages suitable for nobles or the gods. Unlike
meat, however, rice cannot be divided into distinctive parts of
a (former) whole to express both differences and social com-
plementarity. In rituals of planting and harvesting rice is
associated with community and the spirit world in their regenerative aspects. To a great extent in the realm of women, who
spoon the rice out from their places at the hearth, rice is profoundly linked to life and is opposed to death.

## Rice and Unity

Meat and funerals are not wholly divisive, nor are rice
and rice rituals wholly unifying. They are, rather, at different
ends of a continuum. Rice rituals merely highlight and more
sharply focus the ideals of unity or community which, although expressed at the funeral, are overshadowed there by
other themes.

The end of the death season and the beginning of the agricultural year are marked by *medatu* in September (when Toraja
formerly brought tribute to Luwu's *datu* and in exchange
received blessings on their rice seeds). Related families in a
house yard prepare their seed and offer chickens in the house,
yard, spring, and field, accompanied by *to minaa's* prayers. Only
*aluk* people still perform this rite, which is clearly an offering to
*deata*. The seed is then soaked, dried, and scattered in its
seedbeds. *Piong* is prepared everywhere: sticky rice cooked
inside a bamboo tube set directly on the fire. It forms both
offerings to gods and treats for all the family, guests, and mul-
titudes of children who go from place to place receiving it.

Although one may be given a larger or a smaller piece, *piong* is basically statusless. One simply peels back the bamboo strips like a banana and eats. Few people bother to notice the size of the piece or the color of the rice, for it is invariably welcomed and consumed at once with pleasure, and shared with whomever might be present. The only animals sacrificed at *medatu* are chicks, often so tiny that their meat is inconsequential. As long as the *to minaa* receives the head, and everyone else a nibble, the distribution does not become a real concern.

Nine months later, in June, the fields have turned a golden yellow with ripe rice. This is the hungriest time, just before harvest. It is also the only time I heard Toraja say, "Our land is beautiful, the fields are beautiful, our hearts (*penaa*) are happy to see them." According to *aluk* the fields may not be harvested until a symbolic harvest is first carried out and shared. A few ripe ears from each person's fields are cut, brought home, boiled in the unhusked state, then sun-dried, husked, and cooked again. This rite is like the Christian New Year, said *to minaa* Lumbaa, for Toraja begin to eat rice again. Although each household conducts this rite separately, part of the fun is that children go from house to house asking for rice, calling out, "Is it cooked yet?" It is a sort of social free-for-all, and there is food for everyone. It is also the only occasion upon which women invoke the gods and the ancestors, silently blessing the hearth by touching a feather dabbed in chicken blood to each essential part: clay pots, fire rocks, storage racks, serving spoons.

The following day is called *menammu*. On this day the community emerges, explicitly and visibly, as a *saroan*. A single pig is slaughtered, toward which each household must promise to contribute a certain number of bundles of new *padi*, or in recent years cash. This contribution is taken as a sign of a household's (kitchen's) membership for the coming year, and a piece of fat is given to the donor. Most of the cut-up pig is placed on an intricate green offering of palm leaves and bamboo, later to be divided among officiants at the ritual: *to minaa*, the male "earth mother" (*indo' padang*), "he who chases away mice," and others who are said to "guard the taboos."[12] These officiants abstain from eating "death meat" (meat associated with a funeral) for the duration of the growing season; now they may eat large chunks of pork. The rest of the group gives up a larger share to the officiants, accepting only tiny pieces of fat.

The fat provokes much laughter. There is nothing wrong with fat; in fact it is highly desirable. But this fat is cut into many cubes from the ring of fat that encircles the pig's neck. It is, I was told, divided equally among all. In Toraja terms it is "equal" in that everyone receives some amusing little cubes, but some people receive more equal cubes than others. A piece of fat usually corresponds to ten bundles of *padi*, so if a person contributes twenty bundles, he receives two pieces. Rich people may promise fifty or sixty bundles, thereby receiving five or six pieces. There is an air of great seriousness to this whole affair, as a man jots down a list of members and their shares; but at the same time the scene is slightly comical. It's just playing, people say, it's just for ceremony, for form: it's "just *aluk*." They recognize, however, that the form has meaning even if there is not much to eat. Through this simple ring of fat they affirm their place in the *saroan*, not just as members but as members of a certain rank. They also promise that in the coming year they will do whatever the *saroan* does (participate in its rituals), and of course they have the promise that they will eat with the *saroan* whenever anything is done, whenever meat is divided.

In some areas of Toraja the women most visibly express the unity of the *saroan* at *menammu*. While men are busy cutting up the pig and making offerings, a woman from each household (kitchen) brings to the ceremony a sooty clay cooking pot filled with newly harvested rice. A man goes from woman to woman, holding a woven tray on which he collects spoonfuls of rice from every pot, combining the rice of all the kitchens. This rice is then put in a large basket and from the mixture all the people present are served. The *saroan*, at this one meal, has become a single household, a single kitchen, sharing from a single pot. Even this meal, however, is not without distinctions: the order in which rice is served, its quantity and color, and the little packages of sticky rice all still inform everyone who one is.

*Menammu*, the moment at which the unity of the group is made most visible, may also be its most vulnerable moment, as a splinter group may choose not to attend and to hold *menammu* on its own. Even if nothing so drastic occurs it may provoke uneasiness as each person affirms his place and responsibilities within the group. Tensions and confusions that have simmered throughout the year may rise to the surface at *menammu*, as they did in Tondoklitak in 1978. The problems surrounding that harvest ritual may serve as an introduction to the history of this village on Sesean.

The major conflict in 1978 concerned religion, for no one was sure whether or not Christians should participate in *menammu*, or what the church itself should do. There were three options for Christians: to attend the ceremony (where the *deata* would be fed); to contribute *padi* for the pig; or to refrain from doing anything. Most people chose the middle road, since to refrain completely was tantamount to social withdrawal. Some Christians attended and risked accusations that they were merely seeking meat. Almost everyone, *aluk* people included, seemed troubled by the lack of a clear alternative. The problem was aggravated by the failure of the established Protestant church, for the third consecutive year, to hold a Christian "thanksgiving" equivalent of *menammu* at which a pig is cut and divided among the congregation. Protestants spoke unhappily of disorder and corruption in their church and were wary of the growing strength of the Pentecostals, who did perform a well-attended "thanksgiving" at a small settlement high up the mountain slope. The Pentecostal church had been active in the area only since the early 1970s. It appealed, however, to many Protestants who found Pentecostal curing powers stronger, as well as to poorer people who were told that one could still be a good Pentecostal without large animal sacrifices. The Pentecostal ceremony signified another step in the shift of religious power away from the established, more upper-class Protestant church.

On another level *menammu* in Tondoklitak in 1978 was disturbing because it reminded people of the split that had occurred within a major local *saroan* (chap. 6). The whole situation was further complicated by the death of Tandi Bua', the twenty-two-year-old son of an important couple in the village. Tandi Bua' had been welcomed home several months before with a Christian "thanksgiving" (in fact intended to reconcile two feuding factions of his family). He had worked for several years in Ujung Pandang on a public works' project, where he was, as his father later put it, "paid in cold rice." His untimely death had been foreshadowed at his welcome ceremony by a bad omen in the pig's bile, something I learned only after he was thrown from his motorcycle. Tandi Bua' had been startled, people said, by a *deata* which appeared out of a rock in the shape of a horse. In the shock of the death of this handsome, intelligent, and well-liked youth, many devout Christians suddenly and openly began to speak of bile omens and *deata* as though both were accepted facts of life.

Tandi Bua''s death was even more distressing because it coincided with the beginning of the harvest. For both Christian and *aluk* Toraja the separation between death and the rice harvest had to be maintained. Although his grandparents wanted his body returned to Toraja, feeling that even two buffalo sacrificed in the city would not equal one in Toraja, in the end the whole family went to Ujung Pandang. Tandi Bua' was buried there, with one buffalo cut and a procession of two hundred cars and motorcycles. The reason given was that his body could not be brought back to Toraja while rice was being harvested. Some people felt this simply was not true, but no one seemed to know for sure. Doubts were expressed about the *to minaa*'s wisdom.

Aside from these doubts and the surfacing of a complex interplay of Christian and *aluk* thoughts and feelings, the effects of Tandi Bua''s death were felt in the delay of the harvest and its ceremonies. The community awaited the return of the family from the city so that it could *menammu* together. Not only the immediate family but the space around it was considered polluted by the death, and everyone in theory had to wait. But the *padi* was ripe and a prolonged delay would ruin it, so some, like a schoolteacher on the slope, disregarded the prohibition altogether. When the teacher later called his neighbors to his house for a Christian thanksgiving, however, some refused to attend, believing that in mixing life and death the teacher had ignored his obligations to the community.

These events reverberated in the village, and what emerged

from *menammu* was less a sense of regenerative oneness than a sense of loss and opposition: *aluk* animists opposed to Christians, Protestants opposed to Pentecostals, villagers opposed to outsiders (like the teacher), urban opposed to rural rituals, *saroan* opposed to *saroan*. To understand how these (and more) confusions came to be, I turn in the next chapter to the history of the small settlement called To' Dama'.

# CHAPTER 6

# Change at To' Dama'

To' Dama', "the place of dammar," was a creation of the colonial era: a novel cluster of households wedged between two revered *tongkonan* with mythic pasts. Less than a kilometer to the northwest stood Polotondok; two kilometers to the east was the great house of Batukamban. Between the two, in the years prior to Dutch rule, only two features distinguished the landscape that is now To' Dama': a market, or *tammuan* ("meeting place"), and a ceremonial field and spring. In the interplay between the new village of To' Dama' and the traditional settlements that surround it there is a drama of adaptation as well as alienation, of desired change as well as loss. The story that follows is culled from many stories told by Mama' Agus, her brothers, and other people of To' Dama'.

## A Meeting Place

Throughout the highlands a series of overlapping six-day market cycles operates, as it did in the precolonial era. One of the major markets in the northern region in precolonial days was To' Dama'. At an altitude of 1,400 meters on Mount Sesean, To' Dama' was strategically located between the Rantepao valley to the south and the more rugged, partially forested country to the north and west. The lower altitudes were rich in rice land and close to the source of fruits and vegetables that grew plentifully in warmer terrain; the upper altitudes, poor in rice, produced coffee and forest products such as rattan and dammar (resin). Trade in the fragrant resin, essential for lighting prior to the introduction of kerosene, gave its name to "the place of dammar." At this market a lively barter occurred in products from the forests and the lowlands. There, in the late nineteenth century, slave trade was carried on as well.

The second special feature of the landscape between Polotondok and Batukamban was a wide field, just above what is now the main gravel road. This sacred field, or *kalaparan*, was the arena for smoke-rising rituals such as *maro* and *ma'bua'*. Local lore recounts that there the first *maro* ritual in all of Toraja was performed, as well as a *ma'bua'*, celebrated hundreds of years ago by the great *tongkonan* Polotondok. As proof, a tall old sandalwood tree grows in the center of the field, alongside which is buried a stone mortar, a foot or more in diameter. The *kalaparan* was associated with an exquisite spring which flowed about a hundred meters below it, where people washed and dressed in fine clothes and ornaments to prepare for celebrations. The spring, still beautiful and clear today, was surrounded by red-leaved cordyline and other sacred red and yellow flowers. All this was viewed as testimony to the powers of the water source and of the *deata* which inhabited it, said to appear in the form of a giant snake.

To' Dama' was thus a meeting place, both sacred and economic. Living places were elsewhere: scattered in the landscape, clusters of three or four houses were well hidden under massive stands of cultivated bamboo. Population was sparse, however, and within an hour's walk there were no more than five houses which could be called *banua kabusungan*, powerful or sacred houses that had performed *ma'bua'*. Of these five, Polotondok and Batukamban were among the strongest, and for this story the most important, for a union between them produced the family which founded and now inhabits To' Dama'.

Polotondok was a great house to behold, and even its several granaries were unusual. One was supported by twelve columns instead of the customary six, cut from the smooth, cylindrical trunks of the *bangga* palm. Smaller houses stood beside it, and at the rear and around the sides were cruder wood or bamboo shelters housing the family's many slaves. In Mama' Agus's childhood the yard was always bustling and wonderfully alive, filled with people working, children playing, cocks crowing, pigs running underfoot.

Legends about Polotondok abound. Some say that the building itself had walked from its original setting in Kesu, far down Mount Sesean and south of Rantepao, an area rich in fertile *sawah*. Others claim that it originated from the north, the wilder Seko country where Toraja men sought dammar in the forest and traded warily with strangers who were feared for their magic. No doubt both legends reflect historical truth, as people from the richer south must have slowly pushed northward, opening new land, while people from the north must have intermarried with the more settled rice growers on Sesean. Whatever its origins the house was protected by two snakes that curled around it and a casuarina (*buangin*) tree that grew beside it, so tall that it was visible from the Rantepao valley. When the area was attacked from Pangala' by Pong Tiku's men, all the houses burned except for Polotondok and its granaries, protected by water which came forth from its walls.

Like Polotondok, Batukamban and its surrounding settlement were known for invulnerability. Here the entire settlement, or *tondok*, was said to have been encircled by an enormous protective snake that tied its head to its tail at the village gate. Batukamban remained unscathed during the years of civil wars, the only major *tondok* in the area to do so. Remains of walled stone fortifications were used again as hiding places during the Japanese occupation and are still visible.

At some time in the early 1880s a marriage occurred between these two houses. Ne' Tandi Allo, a *to minaa* from Polotondok descended from a long line of *to minaa*, married a Batukamban woman named Ne' Lale. Both were of undisputedly high (*to makaka*) status. In fact Ne' Lale, as Mama' Agus remembers her, always had so many people taking care of her that she could do very little for herself and grew to be a frail, gentle, and very helpless old woman. Eight children were born to this distinguished couple, two of whom (To Napa and To Pare) were to become important *to minaa*, one of them (To Pare) a leading *ambe'* as well. Both are still remembered by their descendants, as well as others, as charismatic ancestors. In this sense the marriage of Ne' Tandi Allo and Ne' Lale was a clear success. Their children played important social roles and helped to forge an alliance between the two houses, Polotondok and Batukamban.

In other ways, however, their marriage was seen as less successful: their many children produced few grandchildren who enhanced the "family bamboo clump" by marrying between traditional illustrious houses. The youngest son died as a childless youth, poisoned by a jealous lover. The second son produced many descendants, but a number of them are said to be "mad" and he himself remains an incorrigible gambler. To Pare, the next son, remained childless in spite of fame, power, and many wives. He too was quite a gambler, which served to diminish his houses' former wealth. Even To Napa, the beloved blind *to minaa,* left few direct descendants. His only child, a daughter, married a Chinese man, and one of his two grandchildren did the same. The eldest son had no children, and little is remembered of his story.

In addition to their five sons, Tandi Allo and Lale had three daughters; Ne' Lale remarried after Tandi Allo's death and had still another daughter. Of these four girls three married Dutch or German men, allying themselves with a power (at that time) more impressive than an ancient snake-guarded *tongkonan,* but in the long run they failed to consolidate a house alliance in any traditional or enduring sense. One of the daughters, Tumba' (whose problematic inheritance we learned of in chapter 5) was married three times, twice to Dutch husbands and once to a German, but she never had children. She did, however, manage to found the settlement of To' Dama', largely through her own initiative. Another daughter, Tampang, married a German named Mareks, a man whom Mama' Agus grew to adore. They had five children, but all left for Holland at the end of World War II, during which they had been interred as Dutch colonials. Between then and 1978, when Mama' Agus received a printed notice of her aunt Tampang's death in Delft, virtually all contact with Toraja had been severed. The marriage of Ne' Lale's ninth child, her daughter Nipi, led to only slight continuity: Nipi's short-lived marriage to a German geologist produced three children, two daughters and a son. The daughters disappeared, as did their father, presumably in Europe. Only the son, Wym, remained in Indonesia, rediscovering his elderly mother in the early 1970s after he had worked for many years in Jakarta and as a pearl fisher along the central Sulawesi coast. Wym moved to Rantepao with his wife, a Chinese woman from southeastern Sulawesi. Ne' Nipi, his mother, never remarried.

The only daughter of Tandi Allo and Lale to marry a Toraja man was Mama' Agus's own mother, Paretasik. Even she married unconventionally, falling in love with a high noble from Pantilang who was passing through the Batukamban area trading water buffalo. This wandering trader, Sobu'tu, asked her for some powdered lime and persuaded her to come with him to Pantilang, in spite of the objections of her father, who protested, "What night-bird is this, that my child brings?" Although there had been no previous family connection, and although Pantilang was a good three days' walk from Batukamban, the marriage provided a valuable link to the greater wealth and more elevated status of Pantilang's nobility. This was the case in spite of the fact that Paretasik maintained but distant connections to her husband (she was not his only wife) or with Pantilang society (throughout the marriage they rarely lived together). She did give birth to five children of high blood, however, and in 1978 four of them lived in or near To' Dama'.

### Founding a Village

The Dutch, arriving in the Sa'dan highlands in 1906, appreciated the strategic location of To' Dama' and established a military outpost there to use in their forays against Pong Tiku's northern fortresses. When the fighting was over they built a large wooden guest house on a field near the sacred spring. Here Dutch troops stayed when necessary, or local officials might tether their horses and spend the night, a way station on their patrol of the hinterlands.

The nearest settlement to To' Dama' at that time was Polotondok. One of the Dutchmen who found his way there was a sargeant who asked Tumba', then a young Toraja girl, to be his wife. Tumba' agreed, and although her parents "were not afraid," as Mama' Agus puts it, her mother, Ne' Lale, did sit sadly looking at the stars and saying, "My poor child, you will no longer see our sky." In fact Tumba' saw quite a few sky-scapes in her life, for the sargeant took her to Java (Jakarta, Bandung, Jogjakarta). He drank heavily, and after ten years she left him to return to Sulawesi and marry a Dutch engineer working in the mines at Suroaco (site of the present-day Inco nickel mine). When he too decided to leave for Java she said, "I've had enough of Java!" and chose to remain in Palopo with her sister Tampang and Tampang's German husband, Mareks. About this time a stranded young German sailor, Emil, arrived at her uncle's house in Palopo, and Tumba' married for the third time. They moved to Masamba, north of the city, and began to raise ducks, selling the eggs at an army dormitory and becoming rich enough to buy an automobile. They drove the car, carrying wood, to Palopo, selling the wood along the road and transport-ing passengers as well. Business expanded and they moved to Palopo, managing, among other enterprises, a brick factory, an auto repair shop, and a cattle farm. They even had an ice cream tub; Mama' Agus's younger brother, Gessong, fondly recalls his boyhood job of churning the ingredients. In spite of these worldly successes Emil drank a great deal and was a terrible spendthrift, and many times Tumba' would assault him with a mattress beater, shouting, "Rotten *Balanda!* You work so hard for your money and then you throw it out!"

Tumba' left both Emil and urban life in the early 1930s, returning to the highlands with her nephew Gessong. In con-trast to her gambling brothers and drinking husbands, Tumba' had good practical sense and an eye for the business possibili-ties of To' Dama'. There, on a high, rounded volcanic rock she built a small house of bamboo. In those days, apparently, it was still easy to attract workers if you were "respected," and Tumba' had no trouble finding laborers eager to build her house in exchange for the meals she provided. From this spot she began a small business, selling rice, coffee, and sugar. Sev-eral other relatives moved in, eventually including her brother, the *to minaa* To Napa, and her younger half-sister, Nipi.

In the mid-1930s another nephew moved to To' Dama'. He was the eldest son of Tumba''s sister Paretasik, a youth in his twenties known as Tandi Allo (after his revered grandfather), later to become Ne' Leme. Like others in his family the young

Tandi Allo had already lived a fairly complicated and unconventional life, moving between his mother's villages of Batukamban and Polotondok; his high-ranking father's village at Pantilang; his uncle Mareks's European household in Palopo; and, on his own, working as a truck driver in the remote province of Kendari, on the southeastern leg of Celebes. There he was married to a Sesean woman of commoner status. Following an accident in his truck he divorced his wife and returned to Sesean, whereupon he married a woman whom many saw as the perfect choice—Ne' Tato, a granddaughter of none other than Pong Tiku from Pangala', who was also related through maternal links to the *tongkonan* at Batukamban. This marriage thus fulfilled the ideal of "returning to the house" (*sulle langan banua*). It brought a daughter back within her mother's territory and it meant an expansion of influence, as Ne' Leme and his family now had a close connection to Pong Tiku's important houses in Pangala'.

Ne' Leme was as industrious and clever as his aunt Tumba', and he immediately bought the land just below her house from people up the mountain who needed cash to pay their taxes. The land, then planted in cassava and coffee trees, bordered a road-in-progress, a trail that the Dutch were expanding in order to connect Rantepao with the north. Here Ne' Leme built a house, a wooden frame raised on large, neatly chiseled stones. Neither Toraja nor Bugis in shape, it imitated the form of the nearby Dutch guest house. With wooden shutters on its many windows and a front door facing west, it was a radical departure from the virtually windowless *tongkonan* that invariably faced north.

Ne' Leme began to cultivate his rice fields (inherited from his maternal *tongkonan*), to plant new coffee trees, and to trade in coffee, rattan, and whatever else made for lively business. He had just a bit of education (having been among those hidden in the early years from school recruiters, although he did attend school for about a year) and a great deal of business sense and other talents. A skilled craftsman, he carved implements and hardwood furniture, and he invented new styles of rattan basketry, which he sold to a Chinese trader. Across the road from his house he set up a warehouse where traders from northern

Tanta Tumba' (*left*), the founder of To' Dama', in Java (1920s). Archival reproduction by C. Zerner.

Om Mareks, Tanta Polina, and three of their daughters. This and the following three photographs were taken in Palopo in the 1920s by a Japanese photographer and saved by Mama' Agus. Archival reproductions by C. Zerner.

Ne' Nipi with one of her daughters.

Ne' Leme posing on a bicycle.

Mama' Agus (with braid) surrounded by her Palopo cousins.

Ne' Nipi. Photograph by Jean-Luc André.

Ne' Leme. Photograph by C. Zerner.

Mama' Agus in To' Dama'. Photograph by C. Zerner.

villages could bring their goods, which he would purchase and then transport by horse to Rantepao. In 1978 he still had the scale he had used in his business, a beautiful instrument with an ebony bar and brass attachments, made in Java, that he had bought in Palopo from the Dutch. Ne' Leme's wife was also hardworking as well as wealthy and endowed with many slaves. Together they began to accumulate numerous pigs and buffalo. They built a large and finely decorated granary by their house, along the roadside facing south; it is as traditional in appearance and orientation as their house is novel.

In addition to boasting grandparents of renown, Ne' Leme also valued the high *puang* status he had inherited paternally. *Puang* such as his father's family were treated in Pantilang with a fear, trembling, and respect unknown in the Sesean area. His father's *tongkonan* in Pantilang was made entirely of fragrant sandalwood. Slaves could not set foot in it but had to cook in the bamboo kitchen below. During the several boyhood years that Tandi Allo spent in this house he must have acquired an understanding of his own high status, tempered by a sense of relativity based on the contrast between the Pantilang hierarchy and the more easygoing society of Mount Sesean. His perspective on cultural differences could only have expanded during several later years spent in the Palopo household of his uncle Mareks. He emerged from all this with confidence, modesty, and a sense of humor about who he was and what status was all about. He opted for To' Dama', perhaps because it was midway between the hierarchy of Pantilang and the looseness of the Palopo Dutch. As a new village it was a sort of frontier: geographically between his two old houses, culturally undefined. But the options were there, and the new road being built by the Dutch suggested a future that would lead somewhere.

Over the years Ne' Leme built up his position in the surrounding area, contributing many pigs and buffalo at rituals and creating a wide net of debt relationships at numerous houses, until he was recognized as a significant *ambe'*. In his practical way he suggested the marriage of his younger sister, then called Laba, to a man well known in the Toraja highlands: Kombonglangi', head of the district of Tikala. Although Kombonglangi' was already married to a Tikala woman, and po-

lygamy was unusual in this part of Toraja, presumably there
was political justification for this second marriage. The district
head was in need of a northern power base in addition to his
native center at Tikala, just north of Rantepao where Mount
Sesean begins to rise, so the marriage was in the interest of
both families. Ne' Leme would acquire a brother-in-law who
was the most powerful colonial officer in the most populous
district, and Kombonglangi' would acquire a wife (and brother-
in-law) belonging to the local, traditionally powerful houses.

For Laba, who was later to become Mama' Agus, these political needs were not particularly impressive. As a young girl
she had often shown her independent spirit. Once, she laugh-
ingly recalls, she impulsively jumped off a boat into the sea,
although she could not swim, and had to be rescued by a strong
Papuan sailor. And she loved to play mischievously at forbidden games such as "marriage," which in its Toraja variant entails
acting out the "funeral" of a spouse, thereby transgressing
some strictly held taboos. She was less than ten years old when
she left the highlands to live with her aunt Nipi and Nipi's
German husband, the geologist. These were eye-opening years,
as her uncle's geological surveys took them all over central and
southeastern Celebes. For weeks they would hike through the
jungle, and the young Laba would be carried on a platform like
a little princess. They met peoples who spoke strange languages, wore strange clothing, and did memorable circle
dances. They saw great gatherings of monkeys in the jungle[1]
and the vast calm lake at Suroaco. At other times they traveled
for months by boat around the islands and peninsulas of southeastern Celebes, where people lived in stilted houses in the sea.
There, Mama' Agus now recalls, the people were truly "wild"
(lampung): they wore no clothing, ate raw fish, and had never
seen such things as the soap and mirrors that this expe-
dition brought.

After several years of such adventures Laba was adopted by
her other aunt, Tampang, who had acquired the Europeanized
name Polina and the Dutch title Tanta (aunt). Polina was married to Om (uncle) Mareks, who was something of an adven-
turer himself. The details of his life are not clear, but he seems
to have been orphaned when quite young, in his native Ger-

many, and to have run away with a school friend to Holland and then to Singapore, sweeping floors and peeling potatoes on a steamship. Eventually be became a mercenary in the Dutch army; he fought in the Boxer Rebellion in China, and then for several years in Lombok and Aceh. In 1906 he landed with the Dutch troops in Palopo. There he met and married Polina, who was living with her sister Nipi, and took charge of a water-works project in the city. At first he and Polina were childless and they adopted Laba (Mama' Agus) as their daughter. It may have been at this point that Mama' Agus acquired her "Dutch" name, Lies. Several months later Polina became pregnant, but Mama' Agus remained with their family for many years. Once, she remembers, someone asked her *Balanda* uncle, "Why is your child black?" and Polina replied, "This isn't Holland, you know, it's Indonesia, and so children here are black!"

The years of late childhood and adolescence spent in Palopo were special, happy years for Mama' Agus. Much of her time was devoted to caring for her five younger cousins, all of whom slept in a long row of beds in a single room, "like a hotel." She was very fond of *Om* Mareks, who in spite of his handlebar mustache, his fierce eyes, and his nickname "Dutch Devil" (*Balanda setan*) was a kind, generous man. She was equally fond of her aunt, who taught her how to bake cakes, set tables, embroider delicate cloths, and dressed her in prim white skirts, anklets, and mary jane shoes. The Palopo world was filled with potted plants, tricycles, and Sunday church pic-nics, in the midst of a waning Islamic kingdom. Here Mama' Agus learned to speak Bugis as well as some Dutch. She wit-nessed the ceremonialism surrounding the court at Luwu, including the *datu*'s annual bath, with the same great curiosity as the (more frequent) brawls of beer-drinking *Balanda*. Like her aunts she was attracted to European men and had a brief romance with a Dutch major, who would take her for wild motorcycle rides along the shore, or to the movies. Her heart was broken, however, when she learned that he had been visit-ing Toraja prostitutes in Palopo. For a time she also was quite close to a Dutch woman doctor, following her around and learning how to treat and bandage wounds, and the doctor offered to take her to Holland to study medicine. Mama' Agus wanted very much to do this, but she asked her own mother first, who just cried and hugged her, saying, "My only daughter, how can you go away?" "That's my fate," Mama' Agus added wryly in telling this story, "illiterate, but lots of talk!"

At some time during the Palopo years Kombonglangi' came to the city and met the young Mama' Agus. Eight years later, during the Japanese occupation, he proposed marriage. She refused, not relishing the prospect of being a second wife to an older man (he was in his forties) with a large stomach. The Japanese years were difficult, however, and eventually she consented to marry him if the Japanese should lose. During this time her closest family, Polina, Mareks, and all their children, were interned in camps scattered throughout the province. She managed to see her uncle in a Pare Pare camp, although she could not speak to him; later he was moved to a freezing cold camp in western Toraja. Soon after she learned this the Australians entered Makassar and released those interned. Mama' Agus went to the city as quickly as she could, where she was reunited briefly with Mareks, Polina, and their children. Things had changed, however, and they said to her, "It's not our world now" (*tannia linota totemo*) Perhaps knowing that their future in Indonesia was not bright, they encouraged her to decide about marriage. Under pressure from her parents in Toraja as well, Mama' Agus finally said yes to Kombonglangi'. She left Makassar and returned to the Toraja mountains, and for all practical purposes to a Toraja life. Her old world had fallen to pieces. Shortly thereafter Mareks, Polina, and their five children left by boat for Holland.

Mama' Agus, who must have been in her early thirties, was married to Kombonglangi' ("sky-gatherer") in Tumba''s little bamboo house on the rock in To' Dama'. During the war the Japanese had completed the road, even holding a ribbon-cutting ceremony, although there were few vehicles that might use it at the time (nor was there any fuel). When the war was over the logical spot for the district head's house was by the roadside, opposite Ne' Leme's house. There Kombonglangi' built another, larger wooden house in the Dutch-Leme style, with no expenses spared. He even included an outhouse in the back, and a huge stone vat was hauled up the mountainside to serve as a washing tub. A long kitchen was set up to provide for veritable banquets for the many guests the new couple could expect to entertain as government officials. What Mama' Agus liked best were the flowers planted in the front yard and those lining a stone path that led to the front door: dahlias, pink roses, and special mulberry bushes from Makassar. This modern, tin-roofed house was made to run efficiently with the labor of many (former) slaves and other followers.

To' Dama' burgeoned as a minor economic and political center, and other relatives began to move there. Papa'na Anis, a younger brother of Ne' Leme and Mama' Agus, married a Sesean woman and built a bamboo house along the road in 1954. A few years later he added a small shop, or *warung*, in front, selling hot coffee and packaged goods like sugar, noodles, matches, and kerosene. Papa'na Anis also introduced packaged cigarettes and has been doing a thriving business in clove cigarettes (*kretek*) ever since.

By the 1950s, then, a new village had been formed, located between two prominent old ones and drawing a Toraja family that was Dutch-influenced, largely Christian, and at the same time traditionally respectable, with an added measure of high status from its Pantilang ancestry. The appearance of the village was radically new. Instead of hiding under the bamboo it boldly straddled two sides of a wide road. Some of its houses did not even face north, and their simple, undecorated surfaces with wide windows were in striking contrast to the ornately incised, windowless traditional house. Around Mama' Agus's house sacred red-leaved cordyline plants were interspersed with the Dutch flowers her husband had imported from Makassar.

New also were the institutional buildings, church and clinic (the latter in the former Dutch guest house), and the commercial flavor of both Papa'na Anis's *warung* and Tumba''s house on the rock. The lively market was gone, however, having never recovered from the economic contraction during the Japanese occupation when there was little to trade. Even in 1978 there was an "empty" day, with no market in the six-day market week, a day once named "To' Dama'." The small church building was not the only sign of religious change: the sacred-

ness of the smoke-rising ritual field, the *kalaparan*, was challenged by an immense wooden Bugis-style house that rose on
its northern end. The schoolteacher, who had no close family
ties in To' Dama', had built this house in blithe defiance of traditional prohibitions and the sentiments of Christians and
animists alike.

In spite of these innovations, in other ways To' Dama' was a
perfectly traditional settlement. With the exception of the
schoolteacher all of its residents were close relatives: three
siblings and several maternal aunts and uncles, among them
To Napa, the *to minaa* who provided a religious (*aluk*) vitality in
the same community that housed the Protestant church. As in
more classically constructed settlements this group within the
*rarabuku* was able to maintain close interrelationships and to
reach important decisions, about land or ritual or other *tongkonan* matters, among themselves. Because of their proximity to
two ancestral houses allegiances were easily maintained and
expressed through the give-and-take of meat in the *saroan*. For
the ambitious, such as Ne' Leme, this provided the opportunity
to rise as an *ambe'*. The location also ensured proximity to most
of the family's *sawah* (except for that in Pantilang); although
To' Dama' did have a commercial side its economic base was
still the land. Most of this land had been inherited from family
members at Batukamban and Polotondok, and some had been
acquired less directly, for example by adoption. All of it,
throughout the 1950s, was largely worked, planted, and harvested by sharecroppers and by slaves.

## Further Changes

The turbulence of the 1950s left the Sesean area relatively
unscathed, in part because the disparities here were not so
great as elsewhere. There were few landowners who could
claim to own more than a few hectares of land, and few people
who owned literally none at all. Still this decade did witness the
emergence of new relationships between those who held the
land and those who worked it. With the independence of
Indonesia finally achieved the word "slave," or *kaunan* (and with
it the institution), was to be abolished in Toraja. Eventually not

just the name but the relationship itself began to change. The trusted laborer who was paid in kind and fed (call him slave, follower, or sharecropper) was gradually replaced by the wage laborer as cash became more available, more useful, more desirable. Along with the growth of the cash economy the institutions of church and school began to transform the relationships between high and low, rich and poor.

Schools did not begin propitiously on Mount Sesean. The first three-year school in this area was opened by the Dutch mission in 1914, near the *tongkonan* Polotondok. In 1917, a year also memorable for the murder of the missionary van de Loosdrecht on Sesean's lower slopes, a Menadonese teacher, angry at a student for stealing fish (so the story goes), hit him between the eyes with a plate. The student died, the teacher fled on horseback, and the school was closed.[2] Another school was not opened in the area until 1947, when a three-year public school (SR) was established on the original school site. Accessible and open to all (unlike the elite schools of the colonial era), this school marked the beginning of a spurt in populist education at Tondoklitak, which was paralleled elsewhere in the highlands. In 1957 a middle school (SMP) was built by the Protestant church on the same site, and in 1963 the initial public school became a six-year school. A government school ("Presidential Instructions," or INPRES, funded from Jakarta) was created in 1975, making Tondoklitak a minor hub for primary education.

Among other subjects the schools taught religion, and education, not surprisingly, was closely tied to Christian conversions. Patterns of religious change on Sesean were similar to those in other parts of the highlands: minimal interest during the colonial period with more massive baptisms occurring only in the late 1950s. The exception to this pattern was the small enclave of Christians in To' Dama', thanks to the arrival of Tumba' and her family from Palopo in the 1930s. Prior to this only six households had been baptized in the entire Tondoklitak area. Although Tumba', Ne' Leme, Mama' Agus, and the rest of this contingent were perhaps more thoroughly Christianized than most, having lived in European households within Islamic cities, their impact upon their neighbors was slight. Between 1949 and 1952 a small wave of conversions (forty to fifty people) accompanied the construction of a new church building. Major conversions did not take place, however, until 1958–60, when another two hundred people joined the church. This movement parallels the trend throughout the highlands, in response to Islamic guerrilla activity on the peripheries of Toraja and to the more immediate presence of Andi Sose's troops in 1958. After Sose's defeat the appeal of a religion that could provide an identity opposed to Islam (a more worldly and "legitimate" religion than "animism") began to have more force. Conveniently, the Protestant church simplified the conversion process at this time, eliminating previously required years of study. In Tondoklitak the church-sponsored junior high school, opened in 1957, also contributed to the new wave of interest in religious conversion.

We have already seen how Christianity entailed (or was supposed to entail) the renunciation of such basic commitments as "feeding the ancestors," as well as almost the whole smoke-rising side of ritual life. The philosophy of the new church also had serious social implications: how could the fundamental Toraja principles of hierarchy and status be reconciled with the new equality of all mankind in the eyes of God? This problem bothered the mission representatives from the beginning; van de Loosdrecht found himself in serious trouble when he began to address such questions. In 1950 anthropologist Kennedy (1953:189) wondered about this too, but his elite informants assured him that things were one way (egalitarian) in religious affairs and another way in the mundane social world: "I think there is trouble brewing here," he added. "Education is dynamite. . . . Christianity can be dynamite too."

In To' Dama' and the surrounding areas the Protestant church grew, but not explosively. In fact its current membership is not much greater now than the three hundred who were registered members in 1958. Most of its egalitarian issues remained largely theoretical: its doors were open to all, including slaves, but this did not eradicate a quickly imposed seating hierarchy from front to back (or, for that matter, on the church council, which is composed of big men). Ideas do brew, however, sometimes in reaction to the church, and by 1978 the Protestant church in To' Dama' was often accused of being a haven for the rich, scorning the poor or poorly dressed. A Pentecostal church, established in the early 1970s some distance up the mountain, attempted to draw its congregation from those poor or the disenchanted. Even the Protestant minister preached the importance of love rather than rank in marriage, to a rather unpersuaded audience in 1978, and he baptized an old former slave, the undertaker's grandchild, and a host of other people, old and young, of high status.

One of the changes that Christianity's more egalitarian ideology made possible was the gradual opening of ritual competition to all. One no longer had to be a nobleman to be buried with a lavish funeral replete with scores of slaughtered buffalo and pigs. At a proper Christian funeral a wealth of *aluk* detail would be eliminated, including the rites attendant upon the slaughter of sixty-four tiny pigs, which involve more food for the *deata* than for human guests. There would be no feeding of the soul, no effigy, no invocations to the spirits. Nor would there be a need for the many *aluk* ritual officiants, from the *to minaa* and *to mebalun* to the slaves with specialized roles. But while Toraja Christianity simplified the form of ritual it did not reduce the important act of sacrifice and all that it implies: the network of debts, gifts of meat, and demonstrations of one's wealth and greatness. Christians of any status could participate to their utmost in such demonstrations.

## Beyond the Highlands

According to government statistics in 1977 more than two-thirds of the population of five thousand in the village of Sesean Suloara were registered as "still *aluk*," as opposed to those who were "already Christian." Such figures are deceptive, however, for they do not reflect the skewed age distribution: many of the "still *aluk*" group are in fact the very old or the not-yet-baptized very young; Toraja in the middle age group are rapidly converting. Particularly as schooling becomes more pervasive the social pressure on children to convert is strong. Kalua, the thirteen-year-old daughter of a very conservative *to minaa*, told me wistfully of the fun she had when she went to church on Christmas Day with her school friends to eat little cakes (*ma'deppa*). She was the only non-Christian in her class.

In school children are taught to feel disdain for their parents' backward ways and for the "irrationality" of a "not-yet religion" that worships "demons" (*setan*). Christianity, on the other hand, is clearly associated with "modernity." The fact that sermons are read from a book contributes to this connection. "Our book is in our breath, our stomach," the old *to minaa* Tandi Datu told me proudly, but the younger generation is not impressed. For a complex set of reasons this generation is not only rapidly converting to Christianity but also rapidly leaving Tana Toraja. Religious change facilitates out-migration; migration, in turn, promotes further religious change. In some ways it even necessitates it, for it is impossible to live abroad and still adhere to *aluk*. At the same time migration is closely tied to economic necessities, and in turn has generated unprecedented economic changes.

Migration, or *merantau*, is probably the single most dramatic fact of social life in villages such as To' Dama' today. *Merantau* is an Indonesian word which is classically defined as "to go abroad; to leave one's home area (especially of Minangkabaus); to sail along the reaches of a river; to wander about; to take a trip; to emigrate" (Echols and Shadily 1961:292). As this definition suggests *merantau* is not a particularly recent phenomenon elsewhere in Indonesia: the Minangkabau of West Sumatra are famous for their propensity to send young men abroad in search of worldly wisdom and experience as well as wealth (Kato 1982). Closer to home Bugis men have a centuries-old history of long-distance trade and travel by small sailing boats (Lineton 1975a).[3]

For the Toraja, however, there are no historical precedents for extensive migration, nor are there traditions that view the prospect of distant travel with relish. On the contrary, highlanders traditionally shunned unnecessary movement, preferring to stay close to their significant centers: the *tongkonan*, the place of the umbilical cords. Rituals reinforced the centripetal tendencies of Toraja life by periodically reconcentrating dispersed family members at the center, and kinship ideally did the same, as preferred marriage, "returned to the house" (*sulle langan banua*). The extensive travels of Mama' Agus, her brother, and her aunts were all unusual. Indeed even her father's trip to Mount Sesean, all the way from Pantilang, strikes Mama' Agus as odd, for in those days, "when the world was still dark," people simply did not travel, and certainly did not marry, so far away. A centripetal, homeward-bound orientation is expressed in the Toraja term for *merantau: ma'lemba kalando*, roughly "the long haul." *Ma'lemba* means to carry something lashed to a bamboo pole across one's shoulder, and it evokes an image of a man returning from the fields with newly-cut *padi*, bringing home the life-sustaining harvest.[4]

In spite of this centripetal preference historically Toraja did sometimes travel. Thousands of highlanders captured as slaves were sold in the lowlands at the end of the nineteenth and the beginning of the twentieth centuries, although these were surely unwilling travelers. A small number of men went to the forests of Rongkong or Malili seeking dammar (resin), or north to Galumpang and Seko where they traded for *ikat* cloths and iron. Others went east to Palopo, on the Gulf of Bone, either for trade or to present occasional tribute to Luwu's ruler in exchange for blessings on their rice seed. Trips such as these, which had the purpose of bringing something of value from the outside back to the highlands, were considered dangerous. Unknown spirits lurked in the forest and "other people" might indulge in harmful magic against strangers. To ensure a safe return a small clump of earth was taken from the houseyard and carried with the traveler.

During the colonial period there were some changes in the patterns of mobility. In the 1930s, for example, several thousand young Toraja men and women migrated to Makassar and elsewhere, seeking work and cash to pay their families' taxes in the aftermath of the Great Depression (Bigalke 1981:254). Kennedy (1953:27) noted that in 1949 there were several hundred prostitutes in Makassar, and he was told that many of them were Toraja. On the whole, however, he was impressed by the provincialism of the Toraja, especially in contrast to the Bugis, a quality he attributed to the lack of both movies and travel or knowledge of the world beyond the village. In a settlement about five kilometers from Rantepao, for example, he estimated that 80 percent of the women and 20 percent of the men had never visited the capital Makale (less than twenty kilometers away), that less than 5 percent of the villagers had ever left the district, and that far less than 1 percent had ever left the island. "No one from this kampong [village] has ever left Indonesia. There are few opportunities for leaving the community, little money, and little knowledge of the outside world. Usually they never even think of it, and few of them have any desire to leave" (1953:178).

Had Kennedy lived to visit Mount Sesean in 1978 he would not have recognized Toraja "provincialism." In To' Dama' and surrounding Tondoklitak the new out-migration was a dominant theme in daily conversation, and recent history tended to be seen in two broad divisions—before and since *merantau* (migration). Personal history was also seen in a new way: as part of the expected life cycle almost everyone would go to school (and perhaps high school, although not always), convert to Christianity, and then head as soon as possible for Kalimantan, Sabah (East Malaysia, just north of Kalimantan on Borneo), or even more distant Irian Jaya. There young men would find work with timber corporations, felling trees, driving tractors, or as mechanics, while women would typically become cooks and housekeepers for foreign or wealthy families. Those who did not follow this route were often children of Dutch-influenced, more prosperous families, who went instead to universities in Ujung Pandang or Jakarta. In a small survey of forty households in Tondoklitak, less than a third of 149 people between the ages of fifteen and thirty-five lived in the village in 1978, while almost 60 percent lived outside Tana Toraja altogether, mostly in Kalimantan and in Sulawesi's cities. Eighty percent of this sample had lived on the *rantau* for more than a year at some time during the previous ten years, and of the 20 percent who had returned, more than half had plans to leave again.

One of the striking facts about this migration is its recent advent; in Tondoklitak the first migrants are said to have left only in 1967. The reasons for this timing, as well as for its upsurge, are well understood by many villagers. Until 1965 South Sulawesi was still racked by rebellion, and travel was

The coffee factory on Mount Sesean is opened ceremonially as an official from Ujung Pandang cuts a ribbon before an audience of Japanese, Toraja, and other South Sulawesian guests.

Schoolchildren in To' Dama': an orchestra of bamboo horns along the road.

difficult and dangerous. After 1965 peace not only returned to the province but President Suharto opened Jakarta's doors to foreign investment. Multinational corporations quickly became established in Kalimantan and elsewhere, seeking to exploit the archipelago's rich tropical forests and oil resources. Until this time young Toraja had found themselves in villages with little to do, in spite of primary and sometimes secondary education, Indonesian literacy, and some technical skills. Pressure on agricultural land was intense, and few other sources of income were locally available. In Tondoklitak a small, Japanese-owned coffee-processing factory opened in 1977, and even then it could offer steady employment to just a few. When job opportunities arose in Kalimantan word traveled fast. In the roadside *warung* at To' Dama' news and gossip were exchanged and the attractions of *rantau* life described. Young men and women began to leave, sailing across the Makassar Straits. If they were pushed by population pressure and lack of opportunity at home, they were equally pulled by the lure of good work and money abroad.

The migrants' purpose is often expressed as "looking for money" (*undaka' ringgi'*). What is also attractive, especially for many poor and low-status migrants, is the potential to convert money into symbolic capital: new status in the Toraja highlands. The stigma of inherited low status is less visible far from home, but most migrants do not stay away indefinitely. Nor are they satisfied with buying blue jeans, gold watches, and giant radios, although these certainly are desired, acquired, and proudly displayed on trips home. Most migrants send home gifts whenever possible: teapots, fine cloths, and especially money, which is used in building bigger and better houses. The house remains, as it was traditionally, an important representation of the family's worth and history. Still none of these signs are real substitutes for the ultimate demonstration of honor and value (*siri'*) through providing and dividing meat on the ritual field.

When a close relative dies, then, most migrants try to come home to organize or at least to attend the mortuary ceremony. For such events no expense is spared, including costly round-trip transportation by small plane, slow boat, and bus for whole contingents of relatives and their children. Few would miss the chance to affirm, or perhaps create anew, their status. For families of poor or low-status migrants the wealth acquired in Balikpapan or Tarakan provides a chance to sponsor funerals far in excess of what was formerly allowed by *aluk*, when a slave, for example, could at most cut a single, plain, gray buffalo. Today such families, returning from abroad with pockets bulging ("lots of money," people now say, instead of "lots of buffalo"), perform the most elaborate, seven-night funerals, sacrificing dozens of expensive buffalo. Ironically such sacrifices no longer ensure the heirs a sizable inheritance, for families of poor people or former slaves usually have little "old wealth" to bequeath. Cash may be converted into buffalo and prestige, but not into the land that once sustained both that prestige and future wealth.

If the economic gains of the nouveaux riches (*orang kaya baru*; known in acronymical Indonesian as *OKB*) make such performances possible, their legitimacy (or lack of it) is tied to religious and social issues that have not yet been sorted out in Tana Toraja. The fact is that almost all migrants are Christian. In my Tondoklitak sample the only non-Christians were several women who had married Bugis or Javanese men and had become Muslims like their husbands. All the migrants had had at least a few years of schooling. On both dimensions this group contrasted with those who had never left the village, of whom several had no education whatsoever and some retained their *aluk* religious affiliation. The popularity of Christianity abroad is not difficult to understand: it is clearly associated with the modern, multiethnic, multicultural worlds of Balikpapan boomtowns, or kitchens with tupperware and dishwashers, worlds in which everyone can claim a well-established religion. Besides, *aluk* is simply not viable in a distant land, for it cannot be practiced without practitioners and without the social community in which it makes sense. It is not spiritual meditation or communication between men and gods, but a system of action that requires priests of the left and right (*to minaa* and *to mebalun*) and a host of other ritual functionaries, many of whom formerly would have been slaves. Social acts, namely rituals, are the lifeblood of *aluk*, a reality acknowledged by

Toraja migrants. "What if I should die in Kalimantan?" I often heard. "Better a proper Christian ceremony than a partial *aluk* one."

Among the implications of this increasing Christianization (as migration continues, so too does the conversion process) is the peculiar position in which many find themselves in relation to their parents, or grandparents, who may still adhere to *aluk*. This emerges upon death, for custom dictates that a funeral be performed in accordance with the deceased's religious preference. Sometimes a last-minute conversion may occasion family feuds, as in one case when a Catholic son and a Protestant son could not agree on what their father had decided to become in his last days. More often the situation is that Christian children become immersed in a fully *aluk* ritual. The paradox, as we shall see in the next chapter, is that the elaborate funerals now performed by wealthy, low-status Christian children for their *aluk* parents would have been impossible according to the precolonial rules of *aluk*.

Status, in short, is in flux, and to add to these changes the *rantau* (migration) has facilitated formerly forbidden marriages. Traditionally women were strictly forbidden to marry down, and a union between a slave man and noble woman was punishable by death or banishment. On the *rantau*, however, women are as numerous as men; in fact more women than men had migrated from Tondoklitak. Many migrants are single when they leave Toraja and meet spouses abroad. Often these spouses are from totally different parts of Tana Toraja, and sometimes the status discrepancies are very upsetting to the couple's parents. In Tondoklitak the son and daughter of an important *ambe'* each married a descendant of their own family's former slaves, a fact that the *ambe'* would not reveal to me. The son left Toraja in 1972 and had not returned in 1978; the daughter came home once, but her husband remained in Irian Jaya where he works on ships and is rumored to be rich. Beyond these mixed marriages there are also marriages to foreigners; Tondoklitak women have met and married Bugis, Javanese, Chinese, and Filipino men within the last ten years.

For all the flexibility and mobility of the Toraja in recent years there is still a strong identification, perhaps stronger now that migration is in full swing, with being Toraja. There is, of course, utility to being "invisible," as revealed in a story told of a former slave who found a good job at Inco, the Canadian nickel mine in central Sulawesi, by informing the boss that he was a close relative of a high Toraja *puang* (noble). Impressed, the boss hired him, only to discover later that the man was indeed related to his *puang*, but as his slave. The migrant had exploited the Toraja euphemism "child" (i.e., slave), and the boss, too far from Toraja to know the difference or even greatly care, fell for the ploy (Bigalke 1978, personal communication). By contrast, the difficulties of life abroad are revealed in a story about a Toraja man in Ujung Pandang who sat in a *warung* waiting for coffee. Annoyed by the length of the wait he called to the owner and challenged him, "Don't you know who I am? I just cut sixty buffalo for my father!" The Bugis *warung* owner apparently just eyed him and replied, "You fool" (Bigalke 1978, personal communication). This story is no doubt apocryphal, since no Toraja would reasonably expect to impress a Bugis with his lavish sacrifices. Nonetheless, the fact that it is told reveals the Toraja migrants' awareness of their otherness abroad. Their consistent interest in ritual at home is one way of retaining a vital link to their Torajaness and asserting it to a community that comprehends it. As one Toraja man told me, *siri'* is only visible at home: "We have value only if others value us." Wherever his eight children journeyed in their inevitable *rantau*, he smiled, they would always come home.

For those who remain at home in the villages the *rantau* produces other kinds of difficulties. Culturally, older people experience themselves as left behind, unable to keep pace with the mobile generation's understanding of the world, of fashion, of money, of pop music, and of English. Many parents who can afford it try to compensate by visiting their children for several months at a time, sometimes traveling to distant corners of Sulawesi, Java, Kalimantan, and Irian Jaya. But in addition to their parents the youth have also left behind a growing labor shortage. If the *rantau* began as a response to insufficient land and work, it has created a situation, at least in Tondoklitak, of diminishing labor to work the fabulously terraced rice fields on

Sesean. Only eight percent of the fifteen- to thirty-five-year-olds I surveyed functioned actively in agricultural labor. Everyone knows that if the *sawah* walls and irrigation systems fall into disrepair, rebuilding them will be a long and costly process. But, people say, who wants to work backbreaking jobs in the fields for little pay when there is easy money to be made across the sea. In 1978 Ne' Gessong, Mama' Agus's younger brother, hung about the *warung* for days, in despair, for he could find no one to weed his *sawah*, a task too big for one man alone. Finally he found and paid a laborer. His most steady worker is an eighty-year-old former slave of his wife's family; while loyal, the man cannot possibly help Ne' Gessong for many more years. Ne' Gessong himself is almost sixty and has few options. His five daughters all became or married school-teachers, of which he is quite proud. His wife is said to be daft, and his adopted sons have either stolen his land or become vagabonds. Eventually Ne' Gessong's daughters probably will hire laborers, if they can be found, or sell the land. Meanwhile he and his contemporaries reminisce about the old days when fields swarmed with people whom you could order here and there, this way and that. "We used to have a lot of people," Ne' Gessong says. "It was not lonely then."

### A *Saroan* Divides

Looking back over the history of To' Dama' it is clear that its distinctive origins did not separate it from the broad transformations that occurred on surrounding Mount Sesean and throughout the Toraja highlands. Schools, Christianity, and most recently the economic tapping of Kalimantan by multinationals, have generated deep challenges to the older social order. The challenges, however, continue to operate according to "traditional" cultural forms: rituals, *saroan*, and their most expressive acts, meat divisions.

*Saroan*, as we saw in chapter 4, are like interlocking circles. Any individual, depending on birth, marriage residence, and other choices, has a distinctive set of *saroan* to which he owes allegiance and from which he receives meat. As I began to understand this I realized that Mama' Agus and her brother Ne'

Leme claimed membership in different primary *saroan*. For Mama' Agus her most important tie was with a *saroan* called Tondok Diongan (literally "Lower Village"), centered in the old house of Polotondok. Ne' Leme, on the other hand, was affiliated with Tondok Doan ("Upper Village"), centered in a house perhaps one hundred meters above Tondok Diongan. They shared other *saroan*, such as the one at Batukamban, but this split so close to home made me curious.

It was difficult for me to learn the story of this split, since ideally *saroan* should never split. When a *saroan* is formed a pig is sacrificed and an oath is spoken by the *to minaa*, cursing those who might leave it at a future time. In the early twentieth century Tondoklitak seems to have been composed of eight *saroan*, with clearly defined relations as allies in war, exchange partners in meat or livestock transactions, and observers of the same taboos. Such relations were called "reciprocal honor/ shame" (*sikasiri'*). In those days, people now say, "we were not all divided up; we were one word, one breath." By most accounts serious segmentation in *saroan* began in this area in the 1940s and 1950s when there were too many people, not enough meat, and power struggles among the various *ambe'*. Since the *saroan* exists to divide meat, an overcrowded *saroan* cannot supply its members adequately if, for example, a single buffalo is sacrificed. Hence power struggles occur, since power is largely the power to divide meat, the source of most *ambe'* arguments.

The split between the original *saroan* Tondok Diongan and Tondok Doan seems to have occurred during the 1950s. A trivial incident precipitated it: the mother of an *ambe'* from Tondok Diongan stole some rice seedlings from the field of a rich Tondok Doan man. At that point Tondok Doan was simply a wealthy *tongkonan*, but the rich man accused the old woman of lacking *siri'*, and he formed the breakaway *saroan*. Underlying this quarrel was the problem of too many frustrated big men in the old *saroan*. At the harvest ritual, *menammu*, which followed this break the lines were drawn: the rich man and his friends and followers held their own rite with their own pig.

Among those attending the rite of the new *saroan* was Ne'

Leme, whose motives were unclear. He smiles now and insists that "*saroan* are according to your pleasure, not like *tongkonan,* which you cannot chose." Other people point out that if he simply wanted power he already had it in his original *saroan,* where his ancestors' ties were strong and clear. There were, however, other reasons for his shift, in particular his ties to a man at Doan who adopted him and from whom he had inherited great wealth. Also his wife's important family had connections there, and he may have been pressured by her side of the family. In addition to these motivations (which others assigned to him) it is also possible that Ne' Leme was attuned to changes that were taking place in To' Dama' and throughout the highlands. A distinctive attitude and style characterize the new *saroan,* of which he is now considered the "top" *ambe'.* In Ne' Leme's words, "All the meat is given to the rich at Tondok Diongan; they are greedy and expect lots. But I don't need a big share. What about the poor who get nothing? Better to make the division more equal, and then, if still nothing is left over for the poor, what can you do?" Needless to say Ne' Leme always receives a substantial share of meat, but that his description is not sheer distortion is confirmed by those in other *saroan.* Mama' Agus, who believes firmly in keeping her membership in her ancestral *saroan* at Tondok Diongan, nonetheless agrees with her brother. It is true, she says, that "the division at the old *saroan* ignores the common people in favor of the rich. The new group is much fairer."

Tondok Doan began as seventy households, now boasts two hundred, and supposedly is growing still. In fact, although this is difficult to confirm, it does seem to provide more room for social mobility. At least several people of low birth are clearly active members of Tondok Doan: one is the daughter of a former slave of Mama' Agus's grandmother, who decades ago sat by Ne' Lale's corpse as the substitute for the widower; another is Pong Pindan, the former undertaker.

# CHAPTER 7

# The Undertaker Becomes a Big Man

The first man I photographed in To' Dama', I later discovered, was the former undertaker, the "priest of the left." In the photograph there is a strange quality to his penetrating eyes, his lined face, his head wrapped in a thick white turban—so strange, in fact, that everyone in the village who saw it did a kind of double take and some exclaimed, "Why it's Pong Pindan! Just like a ghost (*bombo*)!" Others said, "Why it's the *to mebalun*!" What they clearly had forgotten was that several years before, this man had undergone a ritual purification to sever himself from his previous state and work. In his new, cleansed state he could no longer be called *to mebalun* but was Pong Pindan, a name roughly translated as "Mr. Clean Plate" (*pindan* is a white ceramic dish).[1]

Clean or not, Pong Pindan still made people think of ghosts. The photograph shows him in the dark of night, surrounded by an assortment of mourners, their faces partly hidden by the turbans wrapped around their heads, their eyes reflecting the camera's flash. These are the villagers, mostly women, who habitually gather to sing mourning chants (*tukang ma'londe*). People of To' Dama' seemed both attracted to and repulsed by the rather ghoulish atmosphere projected by the photograph.

I thus learned about the *to mebalun*, the key actor not only in funerals but in *ma'nene'*, a ceremony performed at the close of the funeral season in honor of all ancestors. Traditionally the role of *to mebalun* is inherited, and children of *to mebalun* families inevitably marry children of other *to mebalun* families. As a ritual practitioner the *to mebalun* embodies fundamental contradictions: he is rich but low; he is indispensable but tainted by the corruption of death and decay. The *to mebalun* is the focus of

Pong Pindan (*center*) and mourners at a funeral.

At the funeral of Pong Pindan's wife, *to minaa* Ne' Tandi Datu chants her life story in the rain.

ambivalence, of the desire both to maintain the tie between the living and the dead and to be rid of the deceased altogether.[2] He is the traditional mediator and from this role derives his riches and his power.

The *to mebalun* and his family have always been subject to numerous strict taboos. Their house must be a certain distance from other people's houses. They must have their own water source and cannot use the springs that are used by others. They are not allowed to work in anyone's fields, although they may own small plots of land themselves, to be worked only by members of their family. They cannot set foot in other people's houses, or even in the yards of those houses, though they might sometimes ask for *padi* by leaving their basket on a rich man's granary, slipping away unseen until the basket has been filled. Other people cannot and will not approach the *to mebalun's* house except to call him in time of death. Even then his house is not entered: rocks are thrown at it to announce the need. It is a grave insult to call an ordinary person a *to mebalun*. A thirteen-year-old boy in To' Dama' horrified the neighbors when he yelled "*to mebalun*" at his mother.

In the event of a death one has no choice but to call the *to mebalun*. He emerges from his house and is then free to come and go in the yard and the house of the deceased, which is already contaminated by death. His task is to prepare the deceased for burial. He seldom speaks but prepares small offerings of pork and palm wine for the deceased. He later brings the body fluids, which have been collected in a bamboo tube, to the grave, along with such provisions as the deceased's umbrella and a portion of an iron cooking pot. He begins to make the *tau tau*, the effigy of the dead person, and later feeds it and turns it to the west, the direction of death. Finally, when all is done, he is paid an ample wage. Depending on the lavishness of the funeral he may receive a buffalo or more. Sometimes he bickers silently, refusing the wage offered, while the family reluctantly adds more coins to the pile until at last it satisfies him. He pockets the money (or *padi*, in former days) and the family breathes a collective sigh of relief: the debt to death is finished, and the body, amid shouts and gongs and chanting, is carried to its cliff-side grave.

The *to mebalun's* wealth reflects not his landholdings, which are small, but his wages as a ritual specialist. He is necessary: people inevitably die and their survivors must pay him for his services; the demand (until recently) was never low. He exercises a peculiar power at a funeral. As one Toraja explained, "He is the government (*pemerintah*) now. Until we pay him, and he accepts our offer, life cannot resume as usual. We are in his power."

The particular power of the *to mebalun*, and the ambivalence with which he is viewed, emerge vividly in the *ma'nene'* ceremony. His central role in this ritual is perhaps related to its transitional character. Just as the *to mebalun* personally bridges the living and the dead by caring for the deceased's corporeal remains and the spirit's bodily needs,[3] *ma'nene'* is a rite that links and separates the ritual cycles of death and regeneration. For although Toraja divide the ritual cycle into smoke-rising rites of fertility, agriculture, and household, and smoke-descending rites of death, *ma'nene'* defies such classification. Agus suggested that *ma'nene'* might be 70 percent smoke-descending, since it occurs at the very end of the death rites phase; but another man thought it might be smoke-rising, since blessings are requested from the ancestors. Mama' Agus said, "It's hard to say: there is happiness, there is sadness. It's related to the ancestors, but you are not allowed to shed tears."

*Ma'nene'* is usually held in August, after the community's dead have been buried and before planting rituals have begun, and it only takes place in a particular area every five to ten years. At that time all *aluk* persons, no matter how poor, must participate. For days preceding the *ma'nene'* that occurred at To' Dama' in the summer of 1978, minibuses filled with squealing pigs drove up from Rantepao and the *warung* were busy selling betel and tobacco for use in offerings.

The first notable event in the ceremony is the sacrifice of a small buffalo for those ancestors who were previously buried without such a sacrifice. If a single buffalo is cut for the whole *saroan*, everyone in that *saroan* with such an ancestor will give money to the buffalo's owner. The purpose of the money, one man explained, is "so the ancestors will bless us, will give us health, wealth (*ringgit*), buffalo, rice fields, cassava, even skill in school. We ask and ask for everything, we say 'bless us with riches,' and we give the ancestors betel and cash. If you don't put down money, you don't get blessed."

On the following day the cliff-side graves are opened, inspected, cleaned, and repaired. If necessary corpses are rewrapped by family members, and sculpted effigies that stand on ledges before the graves are dressed in new, fresh clothing.[4] Ancestors may also be relocated at this time if a gravesite is in dispute or only "borrowed," or if the spot is plagued by bumblebees. For several days the graves remain open and people bring offerings of betel and place them in old wooden dishes at the foot of the cliffs. Some Christians bring real or paper flowers, in unusual defiance of the teachings of the Protestant church.

The climax of ma'nene' is called "to feed" (ma'pakande), when buffalo are sacrificed for high-ranking ancestors. The buffalo meat is known as "full, healthy padi" (pare lapu), signifying, it is said, a pretty girl, happiness, or good rice. A final offering is given to the ancestors: buffalo meat and pork roasted in bamboo tubes; an egg; red, black, and white rice; and a slender tube filled with sticky rice. A small sum of money is included in a basket which the to mebalun must stroke with his palm. As he draws his hand across the basket he scoops up the coins, a silent gesture referred to as his prayer, or imbo.[5] The remainder of the offering is taken to the graves, where the ancestors are called upon to eat and to replace the small gift with many times more food for the living. The graves are then shut.

At midday everyone gathers at the edge of the rante, a field usually reserved for funerals, which is ringed with stone menhirs, monuments to important ancestors. Each family clusters on its own mat to prepare an offering basket for the to mebalun, exactly like that already given to the ancestors. The to mebalun moves from mat to mat across the field, a small crowd following him and pressing around him to witness each transaction. Again he must touch the basket with his palm and take the money (and the rice and meat). Or he may simply refuse to do so, sitting in stubborn silence while the family adds more money to the pile. He may also walk away from a mat without accepting anything, as old people run after him to drag him back and toss in a few more coins, until at last he stuffs the money into his betel pouch or plastic bag. The rates vary: at least one thousand rupiah for the recently deceased, a lesser sum for those who died long ago. In spite of the fairly standard rates, however, the game of payment may be prolonged and continue for as much as half an hour at a single mat, with much joking to ease the strain.

Although eventually the *to mebalun* always accepts the money, and the family always manages to find enough extra money tucked away to appease him, the tension between the *to mebalun*'s refusal of the offering and the family's resistance to paying more seems to be an essential element in the drama. The outcome is never in doubt, but the encounter is repeatedly played out as though it were. The event replicates the ritual of paying the undertaker at funerals where, although the stakes are higher (perhaps forty thousand rupiah at a major ceremony), the structure of pay-off and resistance is the same. At *ma'nene'*, as at the funeral, the undertaker is ironically referred to as the "government," the "head."

It is not surprising that the ambivalent attitude toward the undertaker surfaces in disputes over money, for wealth is not merely useful or desirable but is traditionally a sign of spiritual potency and the gods' blessings. Socially and spiritually the undertaker's wealth poses a contradiction: how can he be blessed and potent, how can he be of lofty status? The contradiction is particularly striking if we realize that the *to mebalun* embodies not only (in some sense) death but also greed. Structurally he is forced into dependence on others: he owns little land of his own, and even what he does own is polluted. He is forced to take, not to give. This is emphasized in both the funeral and *ma'nene'* through the structure of the pay-off, where his actions seem to reflect greed par excellence. Toraja confirm this interpretation; they often say, "He gets a lot of meat and money!" with a mixture of envy and disgust. Although wealth is desired and strived for, greed is strongly condemned. The rich man ideally holds ceremonies and distributes his wealth, thereby raising his status, but the *to mebalun* traditionally has no possible means of doing so. He simply accumulates riches unto himself. Thus we might imagine that people see in him some of their own base impulses, and try to resist them.

Through their final payment to the undertaker Toraja acknowledge the strength of those impulses but temporarily rid themselves of their influence, while at the same time they convert the potential burden of the ancestors, who may harass the living, into blessings.

Hours later, as the *to mebalun* nears the last mats, interest in him tapers off and shifts to the center of the field where a kickfight, *sisemba'*, is beginning. In this sport men and boys of all ages race across the field in rows, holding hands, shouting, and kicking whomever lunges toward them. The idiom of the game is "heat" (*malassu*) and its gesture, aside from kicking, is *mangaru*, to hop up and down in anger or a warlike challenge. It is as though the payment to the undertaker, and to death's domination, allows a hot eruption in the form of a great variety of named kicks, releasing the energy of a new phase in the ritual cycle, one on the side of life and regeneration.

## "Mr. Clean Plate"

The present Pong Pindan of To' Dama' had been the local *to mebalun* until about 1971. For forty or more years he had buried the parents, grandparents, sisters, and brothers of people throughout the area. He was of course from a long line of *to mebalun*. Born about two hours' walk over the mountain, he had married the daughter of a To' Dama' *to mebalun* and moved to her house. He was surely competent and reputedly clairvoyant, his piercing eyes said to be capable of seeing *bombo* in this world. But he eventually decided to undergo a ritual cleansing and thus put an end to his lucrative career.

I had learned that to cleanse himself Pong Pindan performed a ceremony at which a pig was sacrificed and a *to minaa* was present. Supposedly he was thereafter freed from the taboos of *to mebalun*-ship. Nonetheless one sensed that the stigma of his previous role survived. On a map-making walk my guide anxiously bypassed the small trail that led to Pong Pindan's house. One morning, months later, as we climbed that trail, I had my doubts that what I was doing was permissible. We were not invited to enter the house, a disappointment in terms of my curiosity but a relief for my sense of social norms and pollution fears. We sat instead on the granary and talked with Pong Pindan's wife, an old, thin woman named Pare, and a son. Later someone said with evident relief, "It's good you did not go inside the house; Pare has tuberculosis." When she died six months later I was told that she had beriberi.

Nene' Pare would not tell me much about her family; she simply said her ancestors were all dead. All but one of her nine children had left home, for which she felt much bitterness. And her husband's siblings' children no longer visited either. Why? "We have no rice," she said. We were sitting beneath her rice barn and the pen was full of pigs, but I let the comment pass. "They just don't come," she repeated, "unless there is a need. There's a lot of rice where they live in Pangala'." At no time in the conversation did she mention that one son-in-law was then a working *to mebalun* in the area.

Nene' Pare died, and late in July her funeral took place. Against the backdrop of Pong Pindan's former traditional and ambivalent role the funeral was rather startling. Indeed it was confusing and unsettling to many people in To' Dama'. To those Toraja of high status whose wealth was waning the event was truly distressing. Yet the funeral was conducted with no complications. Unlike the Javanese funeral of young Paidjan described by Geertz (1973:142–69), which failed because its central form (the *slametan,* or communal feast) remained unchanged, the funeral of Pong Pindan's wife was at least a partially effective ritual act. Blind to changing social patterns in an urban context, the funeral in Java proceeded to everyone's distress "against the grain of social equilibrium" (1973:168). If Nene' Pare's funeral in Toraja was successful, it was because it shifted kaleidoscopically with that grain. While maintaining its traditional form it made clear an image of emerging social reality, an image that some people would have preferred not to have seen.

In the past, when the undertaker's riches were the wages of his work with death, he was as dependent on the community as the community was on him. Modern Christian funerals, however, do not use *to mebalun,* and unemployed undertakers are usually happy to find work for cash elsewhere in Sulawesi or in Kalimantan. Away from home they convert to Christianity

and live in relative anonymity and prosperity. Like other
migrants, however, they too feel the need to return to Toraja
for important ceremonies. "Self-worth," reflected Pak Sarira,
"is only there if other people see it. Through rituals it is made
visible." At the funeral of Pong Pindan's wife the former
undertaker's family displayed its new *rantau* wealth and sacrificed and distributed it in an attempt to transform that wealth
into worth.

All of Pong Pindan's scattered children returned home for
the funeral. The oldest was a middle-aged woman who had
married a Javanese soldier during the Japanese occupation.
They now lived in an Islamic area on the southwestern coast of
Sulawesi. Lolo, the oldest son, wore shoulder-length hair, tight
jeans, and a big watch. He was remarkably gruff and aggres-
sive: he walked uninvited into our house, demanded photographs, and addressed me as *iko,* the informal (and in this case
inappropriate) term for "you." Lolo was truly marginal: he had
joined an Islamic rebellion in Mamasa (west of Tana Toraja)
and married a Mamasa woman. When she died he sought jobs
in the forests of Kalimantan, but more generally he was
thought to be a vagabond. A third child, a daughter, lived in
Menado (northern Sulawesi) with her husband, a carpenter.
Another lived in Ujung Pandang where her husband (also from
a *to mebalun* family) was studying urban planning. A son came
from Islamic Bone where he was stationed in the army, having
previously been in Menado and East Timor. The youngest
brother, a gentle-looking man in his late twenties, came from
Tarakan in Kalimantan where he raised and sold vegetables.

Only three children had remained in Toraja: one daughter
still living in her mother's house in To' Dama'; another living
with a relative down the mountain; and a third having married
the practicing *to mebalun* in a nearby village. None of these three
had converted to Christianity, but all the children who had left
the highlands were now Christians, with the exception of the
first daughter who became a Muslim, like her Javanese husband. The child of the youngest brother in fact was baptized in
the To' Dama' church during his visit to Toraja. For all of them
Christianity and mobility obviously offered a way out, an
escape from the lifelong stigma of being undertaker's children

and from the work of death. In Bone or Kalimantan no one
need know who they are. Nonetheless they all returned for
this funeral, having by no means sacrificed their Toraja identity. Through their return they attempted to recreate that
identity in more acceptable, even desirable form. In providing
an expensive and elaborate funeral for their mother they
hoped to "make themselves big" and begin to shake off the
pollution which attached to their undertaker history.

In theory Pong Pindan's wife should never have had an elaborate funeral. A simple ceremony, lasting no more than a single
day, would have been her due, with at most the slaughter of a
single, plain buffalo. But her children were now capable of
providing an expensive funeral, thanks to their education,
employment, or military careers. They decided, and the leaders
of the community agreed, that the highest level of mortuary
ritual could be performed, lasting several weeks and entailing
the sacrifice of thirteen buffalo and dozens of pigs. Although
many of the sponsors were Christian, Nene' Pare herself still
"fed the ancestors," and so the form of the ritual would follow
the finely detailed structure of a traditional *aluk* funeral.

Pong Pindan belonged to Ne' Leme's relatively new *saroan*,
Tondok Doan. Over the years he had managed to accumulate
enough wealth so that by 1978 he was already considered, by
Ne' Leme at any rate, to be an *ambe'*, and he was high on the
priority list for meat division. In fact Ne' Leme liked to minimize Pong Pindan's *to mebalun* history to such an extent that he
introduced him to me, and addressed him publicly, as Ne' Balo,
a name and title (Ne') that implied a good deal more respect and
admiration than the appellation "Pong Pindan."

So the stage was set for Pare to be buried in style. I was not
aware of any disagreement among the *ambe'*, but there was
murmuring and disapproval, and some disbelief was voiced in
daily conversations. As the time approached for the funeral
people began to say, "Really this cannot be." But then they
added, "These days, anything goes. Besides, the *to minaa* and
the *ambe'* just want more meat to eat." It even was discovered
that according to strict custom Pong Pindan had never been
thoroughly cleansed. He had, its seems, performed a lesser
form of smoke-rising ritual, but he had never held the highest

Bamboo, bright red cloth, a satiny jacket, and strings of silver coins: the effigy of Pong Pindan's wife, a tiny enameled plate atop her head.

One of innumerable lively moments at the funeral of Pong Pindan's wife.

rite, *ma'bua'*. Purists argued that a *to mebalun* was still polluted until the *ma'bua'* was performed, or at least until he gave a pig to another of his houses which did hold such a ritual. In the coffee shop along the road some Christians said in frustration, "Had the *to minaa* To Napa been alive, this never could have happened."

Resigned to the event the villagers came to the funeral, whatever their convictions. It was a bizarre conglomeration of people, for relatives appeared from every part of Toraja and all of them were related to the *to mebalun*. It was for the traditionally minded person a concentration of pollution, yet one at which the normal populace were obligingly present, where they mingled hesitantly and received their due. As the Toraja rarely lose their sense of humor, they dealt with what must have been unusual discomfort by joking openly about who was and was not an undertaker, and where to find someone to wrap the corpse, a task not proper for a close family member to perform.

The funeral itself was much like any other. For days and nights the intricate steps went on: a chick's neck was twisted, a cat was symbolically thrown from the window, buffalo and pigs were slaughtered, and meat, as always, was divided in complex ways and argued over. As usual the village head demanded a "development" thigh, which everyone knew went into his own cooking pot. Several long afternoons were spent in debates about the funeral's timing (it interfered with Indonesian independence day), the penning of pigs (a "modernizing" move), and whether the rich men (*to sugi'*) from the other *saroan* had contributed their proper share to the new teacher's house-building. I took many photographs and was constantly asked to give them away. By night the usual chanting was overpowered by exquisite bamboo flute music, an art form centered in a district with a large *to mebalun* population. The *to minaa* adjusted his recitation of the deceased's life story to include, in sacred speech, the cleansing of Pong Pindan as he (and by implication his wife) turned from west to east, from death to life. The guest day, as might have been expected, was not a major event. Only two *saroan* entered in procession, bringing a few medium-sized pigs. But a substantial number of buffalo were slaughtered by the returning children, and everyone knew that no expense had been spared. Even a group of about twenty French tourists found their way to this rather off-the-road spot, where they handed out Gauloise cigarettes and gaped at the spectacle, understanding little of what they saw.

The funeral, then, was remarkable only for its cast of characters. There was no crisis comparable to the delay Geertz describes in Paidjan's Javanese burial, occasioned by an Islamic official's refusal to officiate at a non-Islamic funeral. Still to almost everyone in Tondoklitak the funeral of Pong Pindan's wife represented a strange turn of events. The whole community was sharing in the former undertaker's wealth and meat. And in a talkative culture the person who was once formally without a voice was now moving into the role of public speaker. People often comment on the to mebalun's lack of words: he feeds the spirit and the effigy in silence, he "prays" in silence with a gesture of his palm, and even his stubborn bargaining is silent. In this he contrasts strikingly with the loquacious to minaa, who uses poetic speech to communicate with gods and spirits, and with the ambe', who uses skillful ordinary speech to move people in the everyday social world. Pong Pindan was gradually assuming the role of ambe', although the effectiveness of his words remained to be seen.

For many people this funeral represented proof that the world was not as it once was; that ceremonies did not always restore things to their proper places, or as Malinowski (1954:53) thought, assure "the victory of tradition." One could, in short, buy status. "Pong Pindan is trying to make himself big," said Mama' Agus. "He is becoming a noble by buying his position. But he will not forget that he is just a 'small man' (to bitti'). People don't forget. Their names don't disappear." Yet Mama' Agus is aware of the gradual disappearance of her own family's name. Years ago her grandmother Ne' Lale was honored and respected like a raja and buried with a splendid ceremony. "Now," Mama' Agus mused, "we no longer have value worth even half a cent. Our power, our 'umbrella-dom,' is gone."

# CHAPTER 8

# "Our Umbrella-dom Has Disappeared"

*Kapayungan,* a rather untranslatable expression that I gloss as "power," is a form of the root *payung,* "umbrella." The Toraja dictionary defines *kapayungan* as "glory, grandeur, magnificence" (Tammu and van der Veen 1972:396). In the sense in which Mama' Agus uses it, "umbrella-dom," it suggests both godliness (looking up; in Luwu umbrellas symbolize divine status) and sheltering protectiveness (looking down).

Events such as the funeral of Pong Pindan's wife make it clear that the old umbrella-dom, if not fully gone, is certainly folding. During the summer of 1978 three or four other funerals of a similar if less striking nature were conducted on the mountainside. Yet while funerals were the major expression of these changes they were not the only ones. On the same mountain slope in the previous six or seven years numerous houses had performed *maro* or *ma'bua',* houses which by genealogical criteria had no right to do so. In the fall of 1978 seven houses united to hold a *maro* in the smoke-rising field above To' Dama''s road. The extraordinary number of participating houses was said to be the result of the families' plans to convert to Christianity after first achieving the highest possible status within *aluk.* In spite of the proliferation of such rituals it was often commented that they lack the powers they once had in the days when men in trance could cut off their own heads and dance.

Accompanying the talk about declining potency (of men and *deata*) are tales about former slaves. These stories, which are told by high-status Toraja, seem to confirm that in spite of signs to the contrary ancestral rank still matters in the world.

Many of the stories and their interpretations are based on the concept of *mabusung:* offenses to those of higher status, both human and divine. The worldly symptom of *mabusung* is illness, especially a gravely swollen stomach, or sometimes death.[1] If the signs of *mabusung* do not appear, however, men may intervene to correct an inappropriate relationship between high and low, especially between slaves and their masters. This is done through a gesture—a hair is pulled from a person's arm—and a spoken curse. The curse charges the slave and his descendants to die, if he truly is a slave, or to live and prosper, if he truly is not.

In one of these stories a slave of Mama' Agus's family refused to carry something and then denied being a slave. An uncle went to him, pulled out an arm hair, and uttered the curse. Everyone in the slave's family died except for one man, who came to To' Dama' and declared that he was still a slave. He is now said to be as old as the hills and still strong. In the early 1970s his house was planning to hold *ma'bua'* and he came to To' Dama' requesting *padi*. "How is it that you are going to *ma'bua','*" the family challenged, "and yet you come asking for *padi* as a slave would? You are already rich!" The man who told me this story added, "It's just like all those people who show up here at harvest time and ask for rice, admitting their slave-ness to get food, but not to work." In Mama' Agus's version of this event the slave replied that he needed more rice to feed the large family of "mothers and fathers" from To' Dama' that would attend the ritual. "But if you are needy, why *ma'bua'*?" she persisted. "It's not me," he replied. "My kids ordered me to." His children had all been on the *rantau,* and now they wanted to become big men. In spite of their ambivalence all family members from To' Dama' did give this man some *padi*. The one uncle who attended was presented with an entire buffalo leg as a sign that he was still honored (*kasirisan*).

A second story concerns a household cluster just down the road from To' Dama', where a wealthy *to makaka* had a *kaunan* whose son joined the army. When the son wanted to marry, his prospective bride's parents insisted on proof of his high status. To this end the *to makaka* rode on horseback to the bride's village, where he claimed that his former slave's son was in fact his own child. He made this false claim because he feared the army man's reprisals, a point that seemed so obvious to the narrator of this story that he did not mention it until I asked about it. Years later a member of the *to makaka*'s family was in the marketplace and saw the former slave's brother wearing much gold jewelry. The *to makaka* sneered at him, saying loudly, "Perhaps you have forgotten your *puang* (owner)!" When word of this encounter reached the army man he began to feel as if his "hands were iron," and he wanted to kill the old *to makaka* family. He called a public meeting (*kombongan*) to which a very old slave was summoned to testify to the army man's ancestry. Terrified (probably quite wisely), the old slave claimed to forget; in fact he was both *ma'siri'* toward the *puang* and frightened of the army. With the meeting at a stalemate it was decided to remove a hair from the former slave's arm and speak the curse. Since then members of his family have been consistently dying, one notable victim being the only person killed in the collapse of a crowded Rantepao pool hall. As a result of the proof supplied by the curse the names of this slave family and their ancestors have been carved on the front of the *puang*'s *tongkonan*. It is clear, said an educated young man, that the soldier was wrong; he was in truth a slave, and his death illustrates the "law of karma" (*hukum karma*).

This story was related to me by a number of high-status people and had made a deep impression on them, for it was interpreted to reveal the power of *mabusung* (or, in its Sanskritized version, karma) in the face of apparently insurmountable obstacles: wealth and the military. The financial success of the former slave's family is flaunted in the quantities of gold jewelry worn to market. Fear of the army motivates even the *puang*, who lied to the parents of the desired bride. And the old slave, torn between fears of powers old and new, resorts to silence. The death of numerous family members is seen as vindication of the old powers, and the slaves' names are inscribed conspicuously on their owner's house, a brazen act in postindependence Indonesia, where the word "slave" is rarely uttered publicly.

The story is reassuring to the disappointed nobility, validating a worldview often belied by the egalitarian rhetoric of

Christianity and by pressures from the government to elimi-
nate both the practice and the mention of slavery. For many
people there is a genuine conflict between older status values
and the new ideologies. For example, the sympathy that Mama'
Agus usually expresses for "small people" (*to bitti'*) probably
arises from an interplay between her partly Dutch-Christian
upbringing, her grandmother's reputation as having been kind
to slaves, her early adoption by a slave family that she thought
of as her own, the Jimmy Carter-inspired Indonesian talk of
"fundamental human rights," and what she views as her own
present poverty. At the same time, however, her identity is
deeply rooted in her superior genealogical position. Her self-
conscious embarrassment about the status system vanished
dramatically when she proudly explained how she simply *had* to
sit on the front of the granary platform, the highest-status
seat at an important funeral.

Other people continue openly to espouse the old system, if in
novel ways. There is, for instance, a fifty-year-old schoolteacher in Rantepao who said: "No one willingly freed the
slaves after independence; it was the slaves themselves who
took their freedom. They went to school, went away, and
earned money, while we sat quietly and knew it was *mabusung*."
This teacher saw slavery as compatible with humanitarianism,
the second of the government's "Five Principles" (*Pancasila*). As
humans we respect each other, the teacher explained, so as
nobility we must treat our slaves with decency, and they in
turn must honor us.

Over the past thirty years fewer and fewer former slaves
have accepted the schoolteacher's remarks. In 1950 the begin-
nings of such changes were already discernible to Kennedy
(1953:163), who wrote: "Social classes have not changed much
in the last years. But today slaves are not quite so humble. For
example, previously, if a master said to a slave, 'Come to work
tomorrow,' there would be no question that the slave would
come. Now, if the slave does not want to, he will usually make
an excuse." Today only *kaunan* who are in their seventies or
eighties "admit" (*mangaku*) their slave status. There is, for
instance, one-hundred-year-old Pare Baru, who is said to have
asked: "Will it be washed with cool water, and disappear?"

(referring to her slave status). Mama' Agus, when caught off guard, will say that this is a "good attitude," but at another moment she will show pity for the old men and women who bow and scrape and shrink in the presence of high-status people, "like cats soaked in hot water." But she adds realistically, "It's just the old people who follow those old customs. The young no longer need us, they can seek their living elsewhere. Even the *to mebalun* no longer needs us."

One alternative mode of seeking a living is to join the national army. At least a part of people's resentment of the military (voiced quietly of course) stems from the fact that the composition of the army crosses status lines. There some Toraja "small men" have found careers, cash, and power. And attitudes toward the military are closely tied to attitudes toward the government. In many Toraja areas former nobles now hold official power; elsewhere, including on Sesean, this is not the case.

The village head on Sesean in 1978 was in fact a man of moderate birth, neither high nor low. But he had become a paratrooper in the 1950s and in the early 1970s became the government village head. He made no secret of his wealth: his enormous wooden house was surrounded by a wide field on which many buffalo grazed; he rode a big motorcycle, wore huge gold rings on his fingers, and sported the latest Western fashions from Rantepao, including a Russian fur cap. His wealth, it was well known, came not merely from his salary but from his power over meat.

Not surprisingly it was in the realm of meat that conflicts between the local government and indigenous politics surfaced. For every animal ritually slaughtered the village head was entitled to a portion of the slaughter tax. But in addition, through persuasion, coercion, and various other methods, he often obtained whole buffalo in the name of local development projects. It was agreed that most of these animals contributed to his private development as an even bigger man. "He eats us to the bone," people said. Rituals almost always had a day or two, or at least several hours, devoted to battles, mostly losing ones, against his demands for meat. Even these were fought, in part, in the old idiom of *siri'*. One of his offensive acts, for

instance, was to address Ne' Leme publicly as *iko*, the disrepect-
ful "you." For this Ne' Leme vowed never to speak to him
again. Another time he demanded a second chicken leg (the
losing bird's leg at a cockfight is given to an important person).
Ne' Leme, who was expecting to receive this leg, flushed red
and glowered silently.

In the context of a discussion about this village head Mama'
Agus commented, "Our umbrella-dom is gone." If it is gone (or
going) on a village-political level, it is also waning personally
for people like Mama' Agus. As she said, the little people no
longer need the big ones. Equally revealing is her thought that
her own family's value now is not worth half a cent. Social
value has begun to be reckoned in money, and the problem of
money versus blood is overwhelming for those like Mama'
Agus who are not tied into the cash economy. In 1978 her
oldest son Agus found his first job with a pepper export firm in
Ujung Pandang, and in 1979 he transferred to a job in Makale.
He will probably continue to send his mother a little money on
a regular basis, enabling her to buy sugar, matches, kerosene,
and coffee, and to pay necessary wages to the men who cut
firewood or repair the pigpen. Leny, her second child, lives in
Jakarta and has infrequent contact with Toraja. Ruben, the
youngest son, in 1978 was still a student in a prestigious and
expensive university program in Ujung Pandang. Five years
later he moved to Irian Jaya, employed by the agricultural
office there. Encouraged to enter college, these young people
did not consider taking the lucrative labor or service jobs
accepted by so many lower-status Toraja of their generation.

In short Mama' Agus will probably have enough cash to get
by, but she is surrounded by people with visibly growing riches
whose many children hold high-paying jobs in Nonokan or
Tawao. The money is sent home and is turned into bigger,
better, Bugis-style houses, radios, watches, and fancy clothes.
Signs of wealth appeared all over To' Dama' in the two years I
lived there, years which saw the growth of three new bamboo
*warung* by the roadside, two new granaries, and two large
Bugis-style houses. The owners of this new wealth are often
families whose status by birth is insignificant. Inevitably these
signs evoke some jealousy from Mama' Agus as she recalls her

own former wealth, which seems to have declined quickly after her husband's death and his exhausting, expensive funeral. Her mother died several years later and she too was buried with a major ceremony. Mama' Agus thinks that people then began to cheat her out of her land and *padi*. As a single woman she felt defenseless, and she sees herself as too generous, too good at incurring debts (by lending), and too patient to demand their repayment. She now finds herself reduced to subsistence living, needing cash to pay for labor and other essentials that were once available to her in abundance as a result of her status.

Mama' Agus's solution has been to try to withdraw from the ritual whirl while still holding on to values, particularly concerning blood, ancestors, and power, which no longer seem to have great force in Toraja society. She now accepts meat only at two *saroan*, asserting that her children can do well without the debts incurred at all the others. "Big deal," she says, "if I don't have a giant funeral. Let them bury me in a cardboard soap box, without ado." Yet her ties with her two *saroan* are tremendously important to her. Even though she feels that one of the *ambe'* is a coarse, disrespectful man, she would not consider switching to her older brother's splinter *saroan*. "Yes, it is heavy, but after all it's my ancestors' house. I cannot leave it."

If Mama' Agus has felt the need to withdraw from ritual and social involvements, tending to her pig garden but letting the rosebushes and orchids around the house grow wild, her brother across the road has taken a very different tack. Ne' Leme remains an active man at seventy-two, building fences, harvesting coffee beans, inspecting irrigation channels, and most of all engaging in local politics and astutely gearing his actions to the changing times. Not that he has renounced the older values: his pride in his own birth and his wife's is undiminished, but this merely strengthens his power that is also based on recent wealth and clever cutting and meat distribution. His children are not all successful: a son is a playboy-gambler; a daughter eloped with a brilliant but irresponsible schoolteacher; another son works in Palopo for a foreign development project. Ironically the most prestigious job is held by a son who is a public prosecutor in Irian Jaya and is married to a woman with some slave ancestry. This marriage occasioned a major family dispute, but after many years Ne' Leme was reconciled to it and a ceremony was held in the To' Dama' church to reunite the family. Ne' Leme now accepts his children's many paths, and as they have all produced grandchildren he is happily assured of many descendants, or *lolo tau*, even if they are not centered in To' Dama' or the highlands. His focus, unlike his sister's, is on the present and the future; for Mama' Agus the past and the world outside her own are almost more engaging.

Raised in many ways as a marginal person, and having seen numerous styles of being in the world, Mama' Agus has a sense of humor and a sensitivity about her present situation which transforms what might be bitterness and alienation into a kind of self-reflective irony. It was perhaps these qualities that enabled her to welcome me, a stranger, into her house, her life, her history. She sensed the remarkable nature of her experiences, lived simultaneously in the thick of events—the girl whose mother was chosen as *Tumbang*, the highest role in the ritual *ma'bua'*; the wife of the district head—and on the margins—the privileged niece in her German uncle's fine stone house; the girl too sheltered to learn to read but too modern to know by heart the geneaologies and myths and poems she loved. Aware of this, she cultivated her contacts with the "outside," with Europe and America, and so it was no accident that I discovered her. Yet much of our communication and mutual understanding was not about the "outside" but about the Toraja culture of her early childhood, a culture distant from us all.

# CHAPTER 9

# The Ritual Dilemma

Ritual has become problematic, not only in To' Dama' but throughout the highlands. It presents at once a personal and a cultural dilemma. For some, such as Mama' Agus and other fading nobles, it is a reminder of lost wealth and status; for others, such as teachers versed in the language of development, it represents a frustrating obstacle to *modernisasi,* sapping precious resources and energy. For a few, such as Ne' Leme, it is a familiar game that can be strategically manipulated, bending with the changing winds yet still a guarantee of old pride and position. For low-status migrants, such as the *to mebalun's* children, ritual is a familiar game to be played in new ways, a stepping-stone toward previously undreamed-of rank; for high-status migrants it frequently has become a wildly inflated competition. For Protestants, Catholics, Seventh Day Adventists, and *aluk* adherents alike, it has served to highlight both religious differences and their syncretic accommodations. To some extent, of course, ritual always must have been a fact with which Toraja had to deal. But in recent decades the shared understandings that once informed ritual—about blood, wealth, prestige, and power; about gods, ghosts, and men— have become less shared, less understood.

Paradoxically the rumblings of ritual doubt have been paralleled by a ritual renaissance of sorts, as performances increase in size and frequency, and by the emergence of a self-conscious Toraja cultural identity, increasingly defined in terms of ritual.[1] Indonesian nationhood, youthful migration, and international tourism have forced a radical expansion of the Toraja world and a coming to terms with what it means to be Toraja. Rituals,

especially funerals, have come to occupy a central place in the
construction of that identity. Migrants sponsor funerals, affirming their links to home, and foreign tourists, for their own
reasons, come to see them. At the same time, for most Toraja
ritual remains bound to identity in an older sense: the person
and his worth are validated through sacrifice, that vivid and
visible link to the ancestors and to living kinsmen and followers.

While Mama' Agus has withdrawn into the village, her three
children, like many of their contemporaries, are forging lives
elsewhere. Agus, who was thirty in 1978, is a handsome, trim,
soft-spoken but intense young man. Of all his siblings only he
expresses a deep personal and intellectual commitment to
Toraja. Unlike his younger brother, Ruben, he is not embarrassed by his culture's deities and rituals but finds them fascinating as an ideological system with structural oppositions and
neatly ordered hierarchies. He is intrigued as well by the politics of meat, and he usually manages the family's ritual affairs,
traveling to distant villages to obtain repayment on old buffalo
or to negotiate new debts. He is at the same time commited to
change. After studying accounting in Ujung Pandang and
working briefly at a pepper export firm, he returned to Makale
to take a job with a new family planning program, something
that clearly goes against the traditional ideal of many children.

Leny, his younger sister, grew up like her mother with a
fascination for the outside world. I never met Leny, who lived
in Jakarta during my fieldwork and returned for a visit only
after I had left. She worked as a pharmacist, and her husband, a
very high-status (unrelated) young Toraja from Sangalla' (the
south), was studying government and diplomacy. He had ambi-
tions to go abroad, to Paris or perhaps to New York, which
quietly worried Mama' Agus, who even then missed her
daughter very much. In fact they did travel far from Indonesia
after 1978: Leny's husband was posted initially to Papua New
Guinea and then to Helsinki. Leny seems to have maintained
her distance all along: when she got married, for example, the
wedding was held secretly in Jakarta, depriving the Toraja families on both sides of the chance to prepare a marriage feast and
to sacrifice many pigs. Her husband's family in Sangalla' was
not at all pleased with this, but Mama' Agus claims to have

been delighted to have been spared a new round of debts.

Finally there is Ruben, twenty-five years old, with long black hair, flashing eyes, a bright smile, and a heart set on his image of modernity: Elvis Presley, motorcycles, and Christianity. He would like to thoroughly reject the village and its ways, although he studied agriculture at the university in Ujung Pandang. He is an ardent Protestant who feels that the fatal flaw of *aluk* is to feed false gods or satans; he does not want to cut at rituals, although he proudly remembers how much meat he used to get as a child with an important father. And he wants to marry a woman outside his family, because he wants to improve the gene pool, having learned how marriage between close kin may have deleterious effects on the offspring. He thinks he might even marry a Chinese woman, and adds, moreover, that his current Chinese girlfriend is very rich.

Ruben's attitudes are not uncommon. One day I met a young man of about twenty as he was returning from *ma'nene'*, the *aluk* ceremony in honor of the ancestors. He lived in Ujung Pandang but was in Tana Toraja for the funeral of a grandparent, and he had come up the mountainside to watch the kickfight that is the climax of *ma'nene'*. He told me how he wanted to marry a French or American girl, to save a lot and become rich. "We Toraja just accumulate things in order to destroy them," he explained. "You never can get rich that way. If you marry a Toraja girl, you must always think of her grandparents, and the buffalo that you will someday cut for them." The curious thing about this fantasy is the youth's lack of concern for *siri'*—it does not matter to him that he cannot enhance his name through sacrifice and meat divisions; it is sufficient that his wife be wealthy and that they hold onto that wealth. Accumulation rather than distribution has become the goal, a *to sugi'* of a different ilk.

For many people of an older generation, however, *siri'*—honor as well as shame—remains a powerful motivation in both ritual and everyday life. For the generation raised in the late colonial era, now in their forties and fifties, *siri'* is also a problematic issue that is debated by people of high status, wealth, and education. In different ways the ritual dilemma may also be acute for former slaves and other poor Toraja who

are caught in an escalating competition and often find their
newly acquired wealth leveled by an afternoon of buffalo
slaughter. It is difficult to say whether such people find the
symbolism of ritual investment entrapping as well as attractive;
their voices have been largely silent, with some recent exceptions encouraged by the Catholic church (see appendix A).

One of the most outspoken high-status critics of the ritual
system is Pak Lande. A prominent Christian politician, a leader
in the Protestant church, and the director of a Rantepao high
school, Pak Lande created a stir throughout the region at the
funeral of his father, who had been the first native Protestant
evangelist in the highlands. At this funeral, held in the mid-
1970s, Pak Lande turned away scores of buffalo that guests
tried to bring, insisting that contributions should be directed
toward irrigation, schools, and other village development projects. Traditionally a great funeral should have been held for a
man of his father's status, and some members of his family
were infuriated at the turn of events. Since then several
important Christians have died in Rantepao and their funerals
have followed this minimal model. For most Toraja, however,
this is simply not an option. Pak Lande himself admits that his
decision was accepted only because his parents and ancestors
had sacrificed and given so much to everyone in the past.
Without such ancestors, Pak Lande said, "you must cut, thanks
to that distinctively Toraja form of shame or siri'. If you don't,
people say 'the fire is extinguished,' or 'the mat has been rolled
up.' You no longer have a right or a place to sit upon the
granary. Other people sit there."

Pak Lande, in turning away the buffalo offered, cancelled all
the debts (there may have been several hundred) that others
owed to his father. Such a move is possible for very few people,
for the cancellation of debts is virtually the cancellation of
social relations in a system that still depends heavily on
exchanges of meat and animals to link groups and individuals.
Also most people in Toraja are still intensely concerned with
where they sit and whether "other people" sit there. Lande's
place is so well established in urban, nontraditional "seats" that
he has less investment in and no doubts about his prominent

seat in front of the granary. For others, like Mama' Agus, that once-certain place on the mat is much more tenuous, and the social and emotional stakes in it are far greater.

## Return of the Flying Dutchman

While Pak Lande argues for the reduction of ritual extravaganzas and a deemphasis on *siri'* he also promotes, as a hotel manager, the newest movement into the highlands that encourages these extravaganzas. Tourism in 1978 was barely lapping at the edges of To' Dama'. It was, however, very much on people's minds, and when some French visitors appeared at the funeral of Pong Pindan's wife it was no great surprise. For a moment, at least, Tondoklitak had become a dot on the international map.

Indonesia officially embraced tourism in 1969 when Jakarta's first Five-Year Plan recommended it as a strategy to increase the flow of Western capital. The second Five-Year Plan, in 1974, concentrated on the expansion of tourism into more remote provinces, including South Sulawesi (Crystal 1977). In fact tourists had already begun to venture into the highlands in 1971. By 1972 several hundred foreign visitors witnessed a major performance of *ma'nene'*, honoring *aluk* ancestors, in Pangala'. Still more attended the much publicized funeral of the man reputed to have been the last great southern *puang* of "pure" noble blood: Puang Laso' Rinding of Sangalla'. This ceremony also drew a British film crew, financed by Ringo Starr (of Beatles fame). The death feast of the ninety-year-old Puang thus became the first media event to reach Europe from the highlands, via French, Swiss, and Belgian television. The event was also recorded in print: the first bilingual (Indonesian/English) summary of Toraja ritual and history was published in Ujung Pandang in 1972, in memory of the Puang.[2] In the same year *National Geographic* discovered "a people so genial ... that even their funeral rites are more joyous than somber" (Meyer 1972: 793–94).

Tourism grew rapidly in spite of rugged travel conditions from Ujung Pandang and the simple accommodations in the Toraja towns. Tana Toraja, known by its acronym Tator, began to be billed as an alternative to Bali for tried and true tourists, just as beautiful and more exotic, remote, and primitive. In 1975 as many as ten thousand tourists visited the regency (Crystal 1977:111); four years later, according to an improbably high estimate in the newspaper *Kompas* (1980), twenty-five thousand tourists visited South Sulawesi, most of whom went to Tator. During 1977 and 1978 hotels and souvenir shops sprang up all over Rantepao, and in the peak months of July and August the streets of the towns were dense with Westerners. Village boys carved miniature Toraja houses for sale to tourists,[3] and the more enterprising hired themselves out as guides. The sleepy transportation industry began to boom and minibuses proliferated. An airstrip was under construction, designed to allow direct access to the highlands from Ujung Pandang and possibly from Bali.[4] Fears were expressed that the area was simply not equipped to handle the potential influx of flying foreigners. In a touch of surely unintentional irony the landing strip was christened "Pong Tiku Airport," a tribute to the Toraja big man who fought fiercely against Dutch troops in 1906.

To date the airport remains unutilized, but this does not appear to have stopped the flow of primarily French, German, Swiss, and Australian tourists. Tator has also recaptured the interest of the North American media and tourist industry within the last few years. In 1981 "Sulawesi—Far from the Tourist Path" was featured in *The Boston Globe* (Lieberman 1981), and an article in the *San Francisco Examiner and Chronicle*, "In Indonesia, There's Life after Death" (Godwin 1981), included tips on how to behave respectfully at funerals. In early 1982 no less a guide than Clifford Geertz led a luxury American cruise ship tour on a one-day visit to the "land of heavenly kings." The group visited "a fascinating people who practice unique burial rituals, create beautiful artworks, and build striking, intricately carved houses," according to the American Museum of National History brochure (1982). The Sierra Club, the Harvard Alumni Association, Society Expeditions, and numerous small travel groups have recently added Toraja to their itineraries. In travel appeals the exotic houses and rituals of these off-the-beaten-track natives are invoked to excite the Western imagination.[5]

Conveniently for the tourist industry the returning migrants of the 1970s were generating more ritual activity precisely at the time when travel agents sought to promote the area's ritual attractions. Paradoxically, however, the returning migrants who sponsored rituals had usually converted to Christianity, while tourist agencies chose to stress Toraja ritual and religion "of the ancestors." It would not, after all, be easy to entice European travelers with promises of Calvinist or Catholic mortuary rites.[6] The lure is the chance to see the exotic, the Other. Typically visitors arrive in organized tours and spend a day or two in Toraja, during which time they are shepherded around to funerals, grave sites, souvenir shops, and Chinese restaurants.

The problem is that the tourist trade thrives on images of paganism that many Toraja rejected long ago and increasingly reject with the rising Christianity fostered by migration. It is perhaps not surprising, then, that the growth of tourism has coincided with a movement to reinstate, rationalize, and revitalize Toraja *aluk*. One of the leaders of this movement, Pak Kila', argues that tourism and *aluk* should nourish each other: tourism will bring not only sorely needed economic growth to Tana Toraja but a renewed pride in *aluk* rituals and heritage as essential aspects of Toraja culture and identity. *Aluk* will continue to draw tourists.

Pak Kila' is a Sesean man, proud of his descent from a long line of *to minaa*. He is one of a small number of highly educated and articulate men of his generation (he is about fifty) to profess adherence to *aluk*, and he was instrumental in Jakarta's recognition in 1969 of *aluk* as an official "sect" of Hindu-Dharma, a category that includes Balinese religion as well. From Jakarta's perspective this legitimation fit nicely with New Order policies, ranging from the containment of orthodox Islam and the support of socially conservative sectors, to the campaign for tourist development that began with the Five-Year Plan of 1969. From the Toraja point of view "feeding the ancestors" (*pa'kandean nene'*) and the myriad rituals that this entails now constitute a religion with a name: *alukta*, or in its longer version, *aluk to dolo*, "the *aluk* of the ancestors."

Pak Kila', who has held several important political positions in Tana Toraja (including head of the tourism office), views Jakarta's support as essential for the survival of *aluk*. The national Ministry of Religion has provided an official who handles the needs of the Toraja *aluk* constituency and who shares the title of dharma minister with a *to minaa* in the regency Department of Religion. Kila' also hopes to obtain government funds to support the teaching of *aluk* in the villages, along with the other official religions that are taught in school. He is eager to preserve and translate ritual speech, of which he is a keen interpreter, and to develop a program to support and "train" *to minaa*.[7]

This movement depends on literacy and bureaucracies, and Pak Kila''s office periodically issues written statements on matters ranging from birth control (showing how it does not conflict with *aluk*) to the problem of animal sacrifice (distinguishing Christian "social" sacrifice from *aluk* sacrifice to the gods). These documents stress that *aluk* adherents worship not rocks and trees but God in three forms (a trinity of Puang Matua, *deata*, and *nene'*), which happen to find their temple in those rocks and trees. Toraja religion, in other words, is in harmony with the monotheistic principles of the nation.

The effects of Pak Kila''s imaginative attempts to legitimize and revitalize *aluk* and to restore the prestige and social functions of the *to minaa* remain to be seen. The incongruities that result from the use of *aluk* by Christian entrepreneurs are far more obvious: *aluk* is now promoted as an image through which the outside world can perceive and come to know the Toraja. A wealthy, educated, and well-established Protestant, for example, ran one of Rantepao's oldest (early 1970s) and most successful hotels. In 1978 she celebrated the completion of the first guest house in the countryside in her own village, a few kilometers from Rantepao. Built in the form of a traditional *tongkonan*, the house stood on piles with an arched roof and exterior walls incised with traditional patterns. Guests were invited to sleep on the floor on woven mats, to get a feeling of Toraja life. The hotel was inaugurated with a ceremony, *aluk* in form, traditionally held to bless a new *tongkonan*. The owner was determined to provide an "authentic" ceremony for her tourist-guests: she bought and sacrificed numerous large pigs and even hired a flute player and a *to minaa*. Another would-be entrepreneur was less polished in his scheme to capitalize on *aluk*. He planned to build a guest house on Mount Sesean where visitors would be entertained by hired groups singing funeral laments. Both Christian and *aluk* villagers were appalled that such chants, appropriate only on the occasion of a death or funeral, might be sung at any time to unsuspecting strangers.

*Aluk*, in short, is no longer that comprehensive view of the world and how to act within it that Dutch missionaries encountered early in this century. "The *to minaa* have lost the ear of God (Puang Matua)," the Protestant minister told the congregation at To' Dama', and many Toraja would agree. For other, older villagers the gods of *aluk* are still pervasive and its rituals unquestioned, although such people often convert to Christianity just before they die. For men such as Pak Kila' it is worth a serious effort to rekindle and appreciate the poetry and power of ancestral *aluk* for its own sake, for the Toraja who have not yet realized what they are losing and for the rest of the interested world. Others in Tator, especially the recent entrepreneurs, view *aluk* largely as a tourist lure, an image of Toraja's uniqueness.

Tourism apparently is adding fuel (and occasional sparks) to an already raging competitive fire. Elaborate funerals sponsored by members of the old nobility, both Christian and *aluk*, have increased at an extraordinary rate. One such funeral occurred in September 1977 at Langda, a village not far from Rantepao, for an *aluk* man reputed to have been among the richest in the regency. Reports were that between forty and seventy buffalo were sacrificed, many of great value. One enormous castrated buffalo alone was worth 1 million rupiah (U.S. $2,500), and the cost of temporary visitors' housing was said to be 3 million rupiah (U.S. $7,500). Hundreds of foreign tourists joined the throngs of guests, as did British, French, and German television crews.

A still more lavish funeral was held near Rantepao the following year. Ne' Atta', a wealthy Protestant, was feasted and interred at a reported cost of 90 million rupiah (U.S. $225,000). The visitors included an entire procession from Jakarta of foreign embassy officials' wives, clad in sarongs and bamboo sunhats. A carved wooden effigy of the deceased was defended by the family as a "portrait," although the mission had long ago banned the use of effigies at Christian ceremonies. Nationally publicized and criticized for its extravagance (see appendix B), Ne' Atta''s funeral also came under local fire from Christian leaders who labeled it an irreligious spectacle (*tontonan*) performed for the pleasure of foreign guests and Jakarta dignitaries (Kompas 1978). Other prominent Toraja figures defended the whole affair, suggesting that Westerners seek to discover in Toraja the mysticism that they have lost (Tempo 1978:27). The extent to which such arguments may be carried is revealed in this passage from my journal: "In the minibus to Makale, a man in his thirties, clearly a 'big man,' struck up a conversation on 'caste' (*kasta*). He said that if Toraja did not maintain their 'caste' differences there would be no flood of tourists to see rituals. No one would be interested if the Toraja weren't 'feudal' (*feodal*): there's nicer scenery in Bandung!"

The Toraja themselves remain intensely interested. When Ne' Palimbong, a wealthy, noble Christian died in Pangala', his funeral was less extraordinary for its cost (about U.S. $125,000) than for its cast of characters. The ritual was managed primarily by the old man's son, a retired major from Ujung Pandang who owned a rice mill, a clove plantation, and a small hotel. The young Palimbong also had a reputation for great generosity and a vast network of connections in the business, military, government, and professional worlds. On guest day rumors spread that the Bugis governor of South Sulawesi would attend (he did), as well as a sacrificial elephant and lion (they did not).

At the funeral of Ne' Palimbong the presence or absence of tourists made little difference: attention was riveted on the guests of honor, the big men of Sulawesian power. In smaller, more remote villages, however, the core of any ritual remains

the "family bamboo clump," and the presence of foreign guests
is far more striking. It is common on Mount Sesean, especially
in the summer months that coincide with the peak funeral
season, for a group of ten to twenty pale Europeans to appear
suddenly in the midst of a ritual field strewn with buffalo meat
and blood. They may appear awkward or be dressed inappro-
priately, but the fact remains that marvelously rich, well-fed
white people have traveled thousands of miles and spent mil-
lions of rupiah to attend the death feast of some obscure vil-
lager's grandfather. The tourists use their expensive cameras
to photograph events they do not understand, not knowing
what is Christian and what is *aluk,* who is a noble and who, as
at Tondoklitak, is a former undertaker. Still by their sheer
presence they charge the ritual with importance in a world that
extends far beyond the edges of the mountain hamlet. Once
powerful in colonial times, the *Balanda* returns, honoring (if
unintentionally) Toraja ancestors. The ritual field becomes
what it ideally is: the center of the social universe, drawing
prestigious visitors from afar.

# Epilogue

To Napa, the old blind priest of Mount Sesean, lived to be nearly one hundred. When he died in the early 1970s he was one of the last Toraja men to wear his long hair wrapped around his head. He was also the last *to minaa* on Mount Sesean to possess the knowledge of myth, genealogy, and sacred speech that distinguished a "true" *to minaa,* and perhaps was the last *to minaa* with the powers to drive mice away from the fields, to help women in childbirth, or to foresee the future. In his old age he was often borne in a sedan chair along steep mountain trails so that he might officiate at *aluk* rituals in distant valleys.

Shortly before his death To Napa converted to Christianity. His reasons, people say, were two: he did not want to separate from his children, who were already Christian; and he knew that upon his death there would be no more *to minaa* who could perform an *aluk* funeral in its fullness. For at this ritual the *to minaa* must chant for days and nights, addressing ancestors and spirits, retelling the history of the deceased: from conception in the mother's womb, through actions in this world and in the next. To Napa knew that the beauty, order, perfection, and completeness of this sacred narrative would vanish when he died. He thus opted for a simple but complete funeral in modern Christian form, acknowledging with this act the changed times. To Napa believed so deeply in the powers of his *aluk* that paradoxically he comprehended, accepted, and participated in its demise.

# Notes

### Chapter 1. Introduction

1. Wallace originally drew his famous line dividing Indic and Australian fauna to the island's west. Fifty years later he moved the line to the east of Celebes. See Whitmore (1981) for a discussion of Wallace's fascination with the island and for the paleogeography of the area.

2. See Errington (1983) for an interpretation of Bugis conceptions of hierarchy and potency in traditional Luwu, a former kingdom on the Gulf of Bone.

3. *Inflasi* is not a uniquely Toraja complaint. The Bugis, for example, speak of *inflasi Andi,* referring to the widespread, uncontrolled use of that formerly restricted noble title. On the eastern island of Lombok *inflasi Tuan Guru* ("teacher inflation") is used to describe the popularity of orthodox Islamic teachers, who are commoners and who attract wide followings that threaten the position of the old, rather weak nobility (Ecklund 1977).

4. At the time of my research primary written sources included Crystal (1970, 1974), Harahap (1952), and a series of articles by Koubi, Nooy-Palm, and Tandilangi in *Archipel* (1975). Kennedy's (1953) posthumously published field notes contain a wealth of information and provocative insights, and Wilcox (1949) offers a sensitive, novelistic account of his experiences in the highlands. A marvelous dictionary by Tammu and van der Veen (1972) treats ritual as well as everyday language, and two of van der Veen's (1965, 1966) monumental translations of ritual texts are available in English. Dutch accounts, especially Kruyt and Kruyt (1922) and Kruyt (1923–24), are dense with material about an earlier period. The definitive compilation of Toraja-related works published before 1978 remains Nooy-Palm's (1978) annotated bibliography. Since then major studies of Toraja culture have been published by Nooy-Palm (1979) and

Koubi (1982). The latter is a particularly rich source of ritual oratory texts. Shinji Yamashita, Elizabeth Coville, and other anthropologists have recently undertaken research in the highlands, and we can look forward to a new generation of writing about Toraja.

## Chapter 2. The Historical Context

1. All myths and stories cited are versions recounted to me during fieldwork, unless otherwise specified. There are several published sources of Toraja stories, including Radjab (1950), Adriani et al. (1916), Nooy-Palm (1979), and Koubi (1982).

2. The image is derived from Anderson's (1972:22) classic interpretation of the Javanese idea of power and the ordered polity as "a cone of light cast downwards," the radiance diminishing with greater distance from the center.

3. The history of coffee and slaves that follows is based on Bigalke's (1981) study of Toraja social history, in which extensive Dutch archival material is elegantly integrated with field interviews. My debt to Bigalke's important work should be evident throughout this chapter, and again in Chapter 6. I am grateful to him for generously sharing his thoughts and critical insights, both in the field and after, and for answering the wry query of his Bugis colleague, who upon learning of his plans to write a history of the Toraja asked: "Oh, do they have one?" (Bigalke 1981:5).

4. The growing trade in highland slaves may also have been tied to a decline in lowland warfare, which decreased the supply of lowland captives (Bigalke 1981:79). It has been suggested as well that the sale of slaves was a useful source of cash for lowland nobles, many of whom had become addicted to the opium introduced by the Dutch (Andi Anton 1977, personal communication).

5. This intriguing line, *kena kena to Balanda*, is often sung by children who (at least in the presence of American *Balanda*) seem to spontaneously form a circle and erupt into a frenzied, almost taunting, laughing chant. More formally it is also sung at the *maro* ritual (see chap. 3) by a whirl of running, jumping boys with leafy garlands on their heads who precede the *bate*, a ceremonial bamboo pole that is carried in procession to a ritual field where trance will occur. All this makes it even more unfortunate that it is a difficult phrase to translate, but people's different interpretations are nonetheless revealing. Aside from the two possibilities mentioned in the text some people say that the "original" line is *tigena gena*, meaning "to come all at once in a horde," as the Dutch indeed arrived. See Volkman (1980).

6. Neither term had such resonances in the northern Rantepao area, but the Dutch were not linguistically sophisticated at this early stage.

7. An elaboration of the meanings of *aluk* would require a chapter in itself. In English literature it is sometimes translated as "the way," and *aluk to dolo* as "the ways of the ancestors" (Crystal 1970). Although *aluk* implies the myriad spirits that inhabit the cosmos, and the ancestors whose genealogies stretch back into the heavens, it is far more focused on action. In some regions it is close to the word *gau'* ("act"); in Pantilang the Indonesian word *kebudayaan*, "culture," is translated *gau'*. In Luwu the generic name for ceremonies is *gau*, or "what is done" (Errington 1983:563). On Sesean the reply to "what is done?" (*apa di pogau'*) at any ritual or ritual stage is usually simply "chickens," "pigs," or "buffalo" (are "done," that is sacrificed). The sacrifice is the essence of what we translate as "culture." Until I understood this I was often baffled by the set response of people who reeled off lists of rituals and what was sacrificed at each the moment they heard that I was studying "culture."

There is yet another sense of *aluk* that is sometimes interpreted as "symbolic action." When, for example, a tiny piece of fat is distributed to everyone at a harvest ritual, people laugh and say, "It's not to eat, it's just *aluk* (*alukna bang*)" (see chap. 5). Or when an empty pigpen is struck at a funeral of a poor person or a slave, in lieu of a real sacrifice, this too is "just *aluk*." This was a common usage on Sesean, although Elizabeth Coville (1983, personal communication) reports that villagers in Awan, west of Tondoklitak, often oppose *aluk* to "just play."

8. For a fuller account of early mission history and its political implications see Bigalke's (1981) suspenseful chapter 6.

9. About 10 percent of the population of Tana Toraja is today Islamic, concentrated in the towns and southern regions. There were no Muslims in the To' Dama' area. Many Toraja Muslims are descendants of Bugis traders who settled around larger markets beginning in the late nineteenth century, trading coffee, slaves, and cloth (Bigalke 1981:40). Such men often married local highland women and practiced a flexible, "accommodationist" Islam, participating in Toraja ritual, sharing buffalo meat, and even contributing pigs (ibid., 206). By the 1930s there were several thousand Muslims in Makale and Rantepao, including Bugis (ibid., 209). The growth of Muhammidiyah (reformist Islam) in the mid-1930s may have been a setback for the growth of Islam, which became more militant and separate from the Toraja community at large. At the same time growing ethnic

consciousness may have narrowed tolerance for identifiably Bugis traits such as Islam (ibid., 212–13). By 1952 the effects of the Islamization of Kahar Mudzakkar's guerrilla struggle were clearly felt, as both Christian and *aluk* Toraja were attacked, their villages burned, their families killed or forced to convert, their pigs and pigsties destroyed. By 1953 the number of refugees from the guerrillas in the Toraja towns had swelled to 20,000 (ibid., 423). In some areas Christian conversions were massive: in September 1953, 3,486 baptisms occurred in Buakayu, and 3,369 in Bittuang; in Rembon, 3,000 persons were baptized in one October week, while 252 baptisms took place in Mengkendek in just two days (ibid., 433).

From 1950 to 1965 growth in the Protestant church (Gereja Toraja) was 10 percent annually, or from 23,000 to 90,000 (ibid., 434). During this period the church also asserted its political strength as parties had begun to form and maneuver in the years after independence. In the 1955 national election the Protestant party Parkindo won fifteen of twenty seats in the legislative assembly, or DPRD (Crystal 1974:141). The remaining seats were divided between Masjumi (reformist Islamic party), PNI (Indonesian Nationalist party), the Catholic party, and the PKI (Communist party). The Parkindo victory represented among other things the end of power of the high southern nobility for the next two decades, in favor of the educated, Protestant, slightly lesser elite. This pattern began to change only in Suharto's "New Order" Indonesia after 1965 when socially conservative sectors regained power under the aegis of GOLKAR, the government organ. By the 1971 election the old southern nobility, supported by GOLKAR, was back in office (ibid., 144). In the 1977 election GOLKAR received approximately 97 percent of the Toraja vote.

### Chapter 3. The Pregnant House

1. The system of adoption is a complicated, flexible one that may establish links between otherwise unrelated families or strengthen links between related branches or houses. It ranges from the formal adoption ceremony described in the text, known as *anak dibuang tama tambuk* ("child thrown into the stomach"), to a more common mode not marked by a ceremony, known as *disarak* ("separated"), to a still more casual practice called *diruru* ("found"). Whatever the mode it is usual for the child (or young adult) to be given a piece of *sawah* (*ditekken*) as well as the responsibility for sacrificing livestock at the adoptive parents' funerals. Most Toraja seem to have been adopted at

least once, and virtually all adults have adopted children of their own. Among Mama' Agus's adopted children, for example, are a girl whom Mama' Agus's husband cured of a serious illness and two babies whom he helped to deliver; a niece whom Mama' Agus "requested" of her brother before she had natural children of her own; a cousin who lived with Mama' Agus while attending school; and Limbong, the niece who lived with her during our stay, an abused child adopted long ago. High-status children are frequently adopted by lower-status families, who may benefit both socially and materially from such connections. Agus, for example, was adopted by a man who received rice from Agus's family for over a year and can safely antici-pate that Agus will slaughter a buffalo at his funeral.

2.  Compare this to Errington's (1983:551) description of childbirth in Luwu, where formerly a coconut was bonked on the floor near the infant's head to protect it from future shocks and loss of conscious-ness, a practice now thought unnecessary since babies hear loud noises such as radios. The great concern with cutting the umbilical cord is interpreted as a concern with possible loss of *sumange'* (Bugis), "life-energy," that is but tenuously attached at the newborn's navel. Here, as elsewhere, the Toraja concept of "breath" (*penaa*) closely parallels the Bugis-Luwu concept of *sumange'*.

3.  The more stratified the area the closer the preferred marriages among the nobility. In southern Toraja, and in some areas around Rantepao as well, first and second cousin marriages are permissible and desirable for the nobility although prohibited for slaves and commoners. The same pattern holds for the Bugis, for whom close cousin marriages at noble levels are considerably more important.

4.  The significance of the *maro* ritual, its states of trance, and espe-cially the potency of heirloom iron swords are discussed in Zerner (1981). In southern Toraja a related ritual of trance is known as *ma'bugi'*. Crystal and Yamashita (1982) describe two versions of *ma'bugi'* and analyze it as a ritual of healing and purification.

5.  The *bate*, or bamboo tower, may be interpreted as a "tree of desire," bending and swaying toward the source of the family's wants throughout the known world. See Zerner and Volkman (in press) for an interpretation of a *maro* ritual text that has this movement as its central theme. The lines quoted here are taken from our translation in that paper, where the original Toraja text is given in full.

6.  For a systematic treatment of related Bugis conceptions of houses, persons, polities, and navels, see Errington (1978, 1983). To date such an analysis has not been performed on the Toraja house. Here I note just a few points on house-body imagery. As in Luwu houses and

persons have "navels" (*posi'*) in their centers, and it is at the "navel post" (*a'riri posi'*) that the Toraja fertility effigy of *ma'bua'* is installed. Houses, like persons, also have apertures; women of childbearing age should not sit in doorways lest they have trouble giving birth. Both house and body are adorned with *sura'*, carvings or tattoos (the latter are no longer used) that enhance the exterior (especially the front or "face") and express status and ritual history.

The symbolism of the granary should also be noted: it plays an important intermediary role in the transition of the deceased from house to grave (as in the transition of rice from being grown to being consumed; see Coville 1983). And it too is adorned, in this case following a major funeral when it is wrapped in a "necklace" (*dipamanikan*) of incised bamboo tubes, associated with males and headhunting (see chap. 5). In contrast to the enduring house and granary many Toraja architectural forms are intentionally temporary. See Zerner (1983) for a discussion of the rich symbolism of the ephemeral architecture of both smoke-rising and smoke-descending rituals.

## Chapter 4. Status, Shame, and the Politics of Meat

1. The term "slave" is questioned by Bigalke (1981:88), who observes that the "system looks more like a grid of statuses ranging from a kind of exalted serf (kaunan bulaan) at one extreme, tied to the communal land; to pawn (kaunan indan); to client (kaunan mengkaranduk), forced to seek the support of a patron for protection; to abject client or slave (kaunan tai manuk), who came closest to being property, worked under coercion (the imminent threat of sale), and probably remained outside the master's kinship group." Bigalke is quite right to point out these gradations, as well as to note that distinctions in the north were not always so finely drawn. I use the word "slave" both to avoid the cumbersome terminology of "exalted serf," "abject client," and so on, and to follow Toraja usage which, at least in the north, tends to conflate all these categories in speech as simply *kaunan*.

2. During her early childhood years Mama' Agus believed that she was a *kaunan*, and she was often sent to her natural mother's house to ask for rice or betel, not knowing her true origins. Her brothers used to tease and torment her as a slave. Now she prefers to think of her adoptive parents as commoners, and she is proud to tell of her adoptive father's military prowess.

3. This version of Pong Pa'pak was told by *to minaa* Ne' Lumbaa.

4. In positing the inseparability of wealth and spiritual and worldly

power the Toraja resemble many of the hill tribes of mainland Southeast Asia. The Ao Naga of Burma, for example, link "innate prosperity" with rich men; while the Lamet of northern Laos use a single term, *hrkiak*, to encompass the qualities of the wealthy— strength, courage, and "badness" (Kirsch 1973:13). "Badness" is reminiscent of the Toraja expression "hardness" (*ma'karra'*), which is rendered into Indonesian as "supernatural power" (*kesaktian*). This is suggestive of concerns for invulnerability and impenetrability found throughout Southeast Asia, including neighboring Luwu. In Luwu, however, connections between riches and potency are downplayed in favor of the intangible energy (*sumange'*) that suffuses the world and is especially concentrated in the ruler (Errington 1983). This is not to suggest that Luwu's rulers were not wealthy, for they were, but rather to point to a different conceptualization of their power, at least from the nobles' point of view.

5. The recently introduced, larger, white-haired, so-called English pigs (*bai Anggarisi*) are said not to require cooked food. Might this be a new category of "other pigs"?

6. Kennedy (1953) was struck by the lack of animal labor in the fields around Rantepao. On Sesean, one reason for this is that many fields are simply too small or steep to permit a plow, but this does not hold true throughout the highlands.

7. It could also be said that men identify with their cocks, as in Bali (Geertz 1973). Much of the Toraja male's energy, however, is also absorbed by caring for his buffalo. If cocks on some level may symbolize pure animal fury and violence, as Geertz suggests, buffalo are a symbol of property and power, the stable bases of society. But they at the same time symbolize the divisiveness of meat and its distribution, the relationships between leaders and followers. Like cocks, they too are put to fight, but their lumbering, uninspired locking of horns or thrashing of heads, until the more timid partner runs away, seems more a comic parody than a serious display of fighting spirit. In a funeral the buffalo fight (between those buffalo of children of the deceased that will be sacrificed) is usually followed by a human (all male) kickfight.

8. Toraja women sometimes slaughter chickens (although never pigs or buffalo), and men sometimes plant gardens, particularly corn or cassava (for human consumption), as well as cash crops such as cabbage. Cassava gardens for pigs are almost exclusively a woman's province.

9. Compare the situation described by Labby (1976:18) on the island of Yap, where land's social value is based on the ancestors'

investment of labor: "it was they who had made the land what it was, had developed its resources, built its gardens, its taro patches, and its fishing equipment, and it was they who had earned for it the social position that its occupants represented." Land in Yap is culturally transformed and defined by the labor of the ancestors, as are the people who live from that land. In Toraja the process is similar, except that ritual and sacrifice are the primary terms of transformation and definition.

10. Nooy-Palm (1979:206) observes that the exception to this total offering is the shoulder blade, which is absent for unexplained reasons.

11. Working in Luwu, Errington (1977) has emphasized the importance of *siri'* in its two senses in Bugis conceptions of person and polity. For a discussion of *siri'* in Makassarese society see Chabot (1960).

12. Bugis weddings and their ramifications, especially in terms of "social location," are described and analyzed by Millar (1981, 1983).

13. Most private emotional states are described by the word *penaa*, "breath." When our *penaa* is gone we die. But it gives us more than organic life: it is the locus of most feelings. (The stomach, *tambuk*, is another locus.) *Penaa* is usually translated into Indonesian as *hati* ("liver"; usually translated into English as "heart"). *Penaa* is said to be hurt, happy, big, small, dark, light, trembling, and so on. Only rarely does one say, "My *penaa* is ashamed"; more commonly one says, "I am ashamed."

14. Such behavior contrasts dramatically with that expected of a Bugis whose *siri'* had been wounded. For a Bugis this explosiveness would be interpreted as a loss of control and self-respect, entailing a loss of *siri'* (Andi Anton 1977, personal communication).

15. See Hamdan (1976), who cites conflicting statements on the *saroan* by Kennedy (1953) and Ihromi (1975).

## Chapter 5. Capturing the Wind

1. This probably apocryphal story was related by a Bugis friend. Suicide is considered a "bad death" among the Toraja.

2. Heat (*makula'* or *malassu*), with its fiery associations, is often opposed to *sakke* (coolness, cool water, health, blessings, purity). Following through on this opposition Yamashita (1981) suggests that the mortuary ritual process may be interpreted as the "cooling" or "purification" of the "hot" dead. He points to other "hot," warlike motifs throughout the funeral (cockfighting, buffalo-fighting, war

dances, and, formerly, headhunting), and notes that the highest form of funeral is known as *dirapa'i*, or "making peace."

3. Identification of the surviving spouse with the deceased is still more striking among the Berawan of Borneo, whose mortuary rituals are described by Metcalf (1982:104): "The widow's ordeal in the house of mats is such as to make her into a kind of corpse. She is given filthy clothes to wear. In the heat of the day, she sweats profusely in the stifling confines of her mat prison, a wetness not unlike that overtaking the corpse.... She is forbidden the company of other people, just as is the dead man's soul.... The same applies with equal force to a widower. The spouse is made to share as much as possible of the fate of the deceased, precisely so that he or she will not in actuality have to share that fate."

4. This expression for a substitute mourner is derived from the root *tongkon*, "to sit," especially "to sit in mourning at a funeral." The fact that *to ma'tongkonan*, literally "those who share an ancestral house," are in practice those who sit together in mourning is simply underscored by this individual's ritual role and title.

5. See van der Veen (1966) for discussion of various forms of *ma'badong* and translations of the chants. *Ma'badong* and other dance forms are also described in Holt (1939).

6. A fuller discussion of spirit effigies is found in Volkman (1979a).

7. Yamashita (1981) calls attention to the centrality of *masero* in Toraja thought, which implies not only a paid debt but "clean" (clean water, for example), "clear" (a cloudless sky), "pure" (unmixed blood or ancestry), and "purified" (cleansed of ritual pollution). The implications of a paid debt, a pig that "has eaten the vegetables," are thus far broader than simply satisfying economic obligations.

8. The line is not always clearly drawn. There is no Toraja ideal of a purely altruistic act of giving (much to the Catholic missionaries' frustration). Mauss's (1967) assertion that all prestations, however voluntary or disinterested they might appear, are in fact obligatory and interested is commonsense wisdom to Toraja.

9. In another sense they are debts: they repay children's gratitude toward their parents, and in exchange for them the children inherit land proportional to their sacrifice. These buffalo also repay debts to the *saroan* as a whole. When Toraja say these buffalo do not represent debts they refer to the specific sense of a debt between two living individuals.

10. The context and implications of this dream are interesting. On the morning of the previous day Ne' Lumbaa had performed a preharvest rite in his house, where we were staying. He slit the throat of

a beautiful white chicken and recited an *imbo*, or prayer, over offerings of meat, blood, rice, and betel on banana leaves. The *imbo* called
upon all the *deata* within the house and fields; the *deata* on the earth
(*lino*), below the earth, and in the sky; and all the ancestors, as well as
Pong Tulak Padang, who supports the earth, and Puang Matua,
"because he created everything in the world." The prayer lasted over
half an hour and was followed by a second *imbo* that was very short
because, as Ne' Lumbaa explained, by then the *deata* have arrived and
"we just say, 'eat, it's cooked!' " The next morning he performed only
the second, brief *imbo*, saying that our good sleep and dreams of the
night before meant that the spirits were already near and need only
be invited to eat. He had dreamed of sufficient meat divided; his wife
had dreamed that Charles photographed the sun.

11. A classic story in this vein is that of Pong Bulu Pala ("hairy
palm of the hand"), who as a boy is killed in the forest by his father.
He is restored to life by a magical cock and acquires more riches than
he might desire. Revenge on his family takes the form of excrement
from his countless buffalo that floats downriver from the forest to
his natal village, poisoning the land and nearly causing starvation
among the villagers. Reversals of food (meat or rice) and excrement
are a common theme in Toraja stories.

12. The role of the most important of these "smoke-rising" officiants is explored by Coville (1982) in her study of the *indo' padang*, the
male "mother of the land." This person is subject to numerous taboos
involving interruptions of growth or disruptions of order: he may
not cut his hair, chop wood, drink roasted coffee, retrace his steps to
retrieve something, or mix different vegetables in a common pot.
Coville suggests that he may be seen as the inverse of the widow/er
(*to balu*) who takes on stringent prohibitions because of her/his close
contact with polluting death, while the *indo' padang* is subject to
equally strong taboos because of his close association with growth
and his vulnerability to defilement. As Coville has noted rice ritual is
as subtle and important as mortuary ritual. It is difficult to observe,
however, without an intact *aluk* community.

### Chapter 6. Change at To' Dama'

1. Mama' Agus's description of this monkey community is a fascinating reflection on Toraja conceptions of social life: "There were
hundreds of them, like a *kombongan* (gathering), and all had brought
food—berries, cassava, and other things as well. They sat around in a

circle on the forest floor and the 'boss' sat in a tall tree. He had a 'spokesman' (*jurubicara*) who shut up the monkeys if they made trouble or began to fight. He had them all bring their food into the center pile. Then about ten monkeys distributed the food, giving a few grains of corn to the young, until it was given out to every monkey."

2. An alternative school was opened several kilometers away in To' Hiasa, not the easiest walk for an unmotivated child. Mission sources attribute the closing of the Tondoklitak school to the fact that the lowland teachers complained about the cold (Bigalke 1981:478); but ironically the site to which the school was moved is equally cold.

3. Lineton (1975a, 1975b) suggests that the effects of Bugis migration from Wajo (South Sulawesi) may be ultimately conservative, as low nobles and wealthy commoners who might otherwise challenge the entrenched high nobility are drawn abroad. Kato (1982) examines the relationship between Minangkabau migration and the persistence of matriliny in the West Sumatran Minangkabau homeland. Siegel (1969) discusses a striking, all-male form of *merantau* from Aceh (North Sumatra).

4. Other expressions include: *male lako padang*, "to go to the land"; *male lako tondokna tau*, "to go to the country of the (other) people"; and *male mambela*, "to go far away."

## Chapter 7. The Undertaker Becomes a Big Man

1. This chapter is a somewhat revised version of an article that first appeared in *Indonesia* (Volkman 1979b).

2. Cf. Malinowksi (1954:48) on the contradictory "love of the dead and loathing of the corpse, passionate attachment to the personality still lingering about the body and a shattering fear of the gruesome thing that has been left over...."

3. That the spirit does have such needs is evident from the *to mebalun*'s actions. He offers the *bombo* food and drink, which he prepares; he makes its visual representation (the effigy) and feeds it; he brings its provisions to the grave. All these acts are carried out in silence while the *to minaa*, through long recitations, ensures the spirit's safe journey to the next world. Ritual speech thus also serves to bridge the living and the dead but without touching the corrupting physicality of eating or decay. Among the Bugis the *to meballung*, a low-status woman who wraps herself in cloths and sits constantly beside the corpse, is considered to be a bridge between the living and the dead (Andi Anton 1977, personal communication). This role also

resembles that of the Toraja *to balu* (widow/er) or *to ma'tongkonan* (substitute surviving spouse).

4. The carving of permanent effigies of jackfruit wood (*tau tau nangka*) is characteristic of the more southern stratified Toraja areas, where such expensive effigies are made only for the funerals of the highest nobility (see Volkman 1979a).

5. The only other silent *imbo* that I know of is performed by women, who are also publicly speechless in many senses. During the harvest ritual of *menammu* women *mangimbo dapo'*, "bless the kitchen," with a feather dabbed in chicken blood and touched to all the elements in the kitchen: post, the three firestones, serving spoons.

### Chapter 8. "Our Umbrella-dom Has Disappeared"

1. *Mabusung* may also result from an offense to a place, for example to an ancestral house considered sacred or potent (*kabusungan*), a house in which *ma'bua'* was once performed. Cf. Errington's (1983:567) description of *mabusung* in Luwu: "A lower person who has direct inappropriate contact with forces too potent for his or her own potency will become afflicted with malady or misfortune.... So, for instance, a person who looked directly at the Ruler, especially into his eyes, would suffer *mabusung;* so would a person who failed to get off a horse or close an umbrella when passing in front of a high noble's house." She notes that even poor or mad high nobles" are not to be trifled with, for, people say, 'even a dried-up chili-pepper is hot.' "

### Chapter 9. The Ritual Dilemma

1. The relationships between ritual, *aluk,* and the development of Toraja cultural identity are discussed in Volkman (1984), where a condensed version of much of the material in this chapter appears.

2. This publication (Salombe 1972) marked the beginning of a spate of indigenous books and pamphlets about Toraja culture coinciding with (and fostering) the new self-consciousness brought about by tourism, migration, education, and other changes. That year also saw the publication of a Toraja dictionary, the masterpiece of the Dutch linguist van der Veen (Tammu and van der Veen 1972). In the next year a bilingual (Indonesian/English) edition of "the secrets" of Toraja house-carvings was issued (Pakan 1973), followed by a massive study in Indonesian of "the Toraja and their culture" (Tangdilintin 1975a), a history of Pong Tiku's struggle (Tangdilintin 1975b),

and a compact English guide book, "an introduction to a unique culture" (Tangdilintin and Syafei 1977).

3. See Zerner (1982) on small-scale replication and other effects of tourism on the arts. Some of these effects are devastating, including the theft or decapitation of wooden effigies. A *Kompas* writer (Sandarupa 1981) reports that five *tau tau* were robbed from a single grave-site in February 1981. Wooden effigies have actually been on the art market for some time but never to this extent. In 1984, one appeared on the Parisian market for $75,000 (M. J. Adams 1984, personal communication). Several were on display in a recent traveling exhibition in major American museums (Stohr et al. 1982). See Ellis (1980) for examples of fine Toraja "objects" in a sophisticated, international art market.

4. To bypass the lowlands would also be to bypass tourist development in Bugis/Makassarese areas. See Volkman (1982a) on the possibility of heightened ethnic tensions arising from these plans.

5. See Adams (1984) for examples of this tourist literature. She argues that three elements of Toraja culture have been highlighted as "emblematic" by the tourist industry: the exotic mortuary complex, "boat-shaped" houses, and the notion of "heavenly kingship," derived from an implausible etymology of the name "Toraja."

6. The irony is that it was precisely the "paganism" of ritual that the early Europeans, the missionaries, tried to suppress (see Volkman 1982b).

7. One *to minaa* who was to be sent to study in Bali refused to go, fearing cremation if he should die there. At least one effigy carver, however, has studied sculpture in Bali and is now producing *tau tau* in a new, strikingly realistic style.

# Pong Sassan's Homily[1]

The Catholic church in Toraja, largely under the guidance of several Belgian priests, has made a conscientious effort to raise issues such as "feudalism," slavery, the family and *tongkonan*, and the role of ritual in Toraja life. Catechists meet in discussion groups at which these topics are considered, and they are now issuing printed booklets containing prayers and homilies dealing with their discussions. The selection below thus represents a Catholic-influenced Toraja view of the relationship between the family and rituals, well-being and prestige. The woman is presented as protecting the family while the man pridefully cuts.

On the house porch, Pong Sassan often sits catching the wind. On the last days of the month, he appears cheerful. His face beams, as if he had just received a large fortune. He turns here and there, and his wide smile decorates his face. His head is lifted a little, and his chest is swollen as he sits, leaning on the wall. Several times his wife is surprised to notice Pong Sassan's condition. Why is her husband like that, like a man who dreams in midday? What has happened, thinks Indo' Sassan.

After they eat that night, Indo' Sassan is a little nervous, because Pong Sassan begins to sing, which he rarely does. He only does this when he is extremely happy. And on the contrary, Indo' Sassan imagines the condition of their household that is washing away. The children no longer go to school, their clothing is in rags, and their thinness is no joke, because at most they

---

1. *Ibadat Umat Allah: Pa'rapuan Kristiani* (IKRAR, Rantepao), 2 July 1978, pp. 20–22 (my translation).

"chop cassava day and night" with a few friends, namely the vegetable *bulunangko*.

To see their house, oh, Indo' Sassan almost cried. The house was already half-roofed by the sky. When it rained, the children crowded together seeking shelter. Because she could no longer stand to imagine the household's suffering, Indo' Sassan reminded her husband directly of the situation.

But Pong Sassan, who felt annoyed with this reminder, became angry. Harshly he scolded his wife, "Hey, be quiet! Are you not proud of the ceremony we just attended? Are you not delighted with the spotted buffalo, big pigs, and giant procession (*rombongan*) of ours at that ceremony? Are you not pleased with the praise and whispers of people about our daring and wealth in that ceremony? Hmmm, it fits, your business is just in the kitchen, you don't understand the purpose of brave men losing in the ritual."

[commentary on the episode]:

Who do we want to side with, Indo' or Pong Sassan?

Pong Sassan feels that all is taken care of if he has tried with all his ability to follow in cutting or enlivening the death ceremony of his *nenek*. Pong Sassan feels he has succeeded in his household if he becomes number one at the family ceremony by cutting spotted buffalo, big pigs...and a giant *rombongan*. Most of all he is proud because his household is praised by people, meaning he obtains prestige as high as the sky.

It is clear that Pong Sassan dreams only of prestige. He is like a man who dreams beautifully in his sleep, but after waking he realizes that around him there are no changes, just emptiness. Moreover, Pong Sassan's dream about prestige does bring changes, that is the suffering of his household and his children. By gaining prestige, Pong Sassan thinks that he has fulfilled his responsibilities to his household....

Perhaps we could say that the prestige which appears smiling all day on his lips is paid for indirectly and very expensively with the suffering and misery of his household.

# The Death Ceremony in Tana Toraja

The article excerpted below (my translation), from the October 1978 issue of *Dinamika,* is a response to a nationally publicized funeral at which, by one estimate, animals valued at three hundred buffalo were slaughtered. Reporting this event, *Tempo* (Indonesia's equivalent to *Newsweek)* quotes a defense of this expenditure by Dr. Tandirerung, a prominent Toraja politician: "Don't view it just from an economic point of view ... but view it also from the angle of *adat,* inheritance, tourism, and so on. Westerners now return to spiritual and mystical worlds through material sacrifice" (Tempo 1978:27). In contrast, students abroad responded strongly to what they viewed as an extremely overblown affair. The passages below reveal some of the main themes—and confusions—in the students' attempt to "simplify" the ritual while still maintaining it as a crucial sign of Toraja identity; to reduce the disparity between rich and poor, high and low, while still maintaining "proper" *adat* levels; to draw tourists yet not lose the "essence" of what is Toraja; and to distinguish *adat* from religion. The terms of the argument are particularly Toraja, but at the same time the statement should be seen in the context of the wider student movement in Indonesia, and especially the demonstrations in early 1978 in Java against the Suharto regime and its nouveaux riches corruption and ostentation (cf. Anderson 1978).

### The Death Ceremony in Tana Toraja

The death ceremony, as one of the *adat* rituals in Tana Toraja, has recently become the subject of lively discussion, not only among the Toraja but also within social groups from outside Toraja. The recent death ritual of Ne' Atta' invited various questions, considerations, and evaluations, objectively as well as subjectively, for Toraja people themselves as well as for non-Toraja peoples.

The *Kompas* reporter, Mr. Sindhunata, together with his colleagues, has firmly immortalized this ceremony through his writings in *Kompas* (October 18–21, 1978). As a son of Tana Toraja, this writer expresses congratulations and thanks to him, although while giving his ideas he insufficiently probes several basic, hidden social values in Toraja *adat*, and within the society itself.

The death ceremony of Ne' Atta', with its expense of about 90 million rupiah [U.S. $225,000], and Lai Kanan's death ceremony, with one buffalo and ten pigs, are two *adat* ceremonies that are the same but very different in conditions and style. This writer takes these as the focus of his article, without giving a positive or negative evaluation toward either.

To speak of groups that live in Tana Toraja is complicated, because social groups are based on families or kinship, inhabiting certain areas, where one group and the next have a different *adat* and social structure. For example, we can see that there are several villages that claim the existence of a noble rank, commoners, and slaves. But in other areas (villages), such ranks are not known, or have a different status. However, in general ranks in society are acknowledged, and (especially before independence) felt to be very strong and clearly determining in social life.

*Adat* activities that are carried out in Toraja social life are very closely tied with social structure. The rules of *adat* are determined according to a person's social rank, although not in every matter. For instance, the death ceremony: the way it must be carried out varies according to the deceased's rank. The death ceremony for one of noble descent cannot be the same as that for a commoner, even if the material wealth of the commoner equals the noble's. The reverse is also true: a noble cannot be buried with the ritual appropriate for a slave.

If an infraction of *adat* occurs, it means that the harmony of social life is disturbed, and certain sanctions must be carried out to reverse or soothe the anger of the ancestors' spirits. On this basis we can explain why Ne' Atta' 's ceremony was not the same as Lai Kanan's, if it is true that their social levels differed. The disparity ... is based on a pure and consistently functioning *adat*, as the inheritance from the Toraja people's ancestors.

A person's funeral forms a statement of his social level for his circle, even if in daily life the level was already seen and felt. For example, when speaking with others, a slave will seek to use different words to address a noble, a person of his own rank, or someone below his rank. A commoner's house will also be different from a noble's house, etc.

But after independence the problem of rank in Toraja society underwent drastic changes, following the struggle for basic human rights. It cannot be said that this matter has been entirely eradicated: it can still be seen in certain *adat* rituals, and moreover there are still Toraja who are proud of this for one reason or another. In certain people a feeling is still implanted that this matter is natural law, especially for old people far from the city.

Other matters that we can see implicitly in the death ritual relate to religion, debts, and inheritance. From the moment a person dies, the family, relatives, and villagers begin to busy themselves preparing the ritual for the deceased. The bigger the ritual that will be held, the longer the time of preparation. Temporary houses begin to be built cooperatively, buffalo and pigs are readied for sacrifice. Those who feel that they have debts of buffalo, pigs, or a jar of palm wine begin plotting to find a buffalo or pig approximately the same size as their debt.... To cope with this one may be forced to borrow again from the others, debts that must be repaid when this other person faces a death ceremony. The paying of debts here is really no different from digging a bottomless pit....

Viewed from one aspect we can see that there is togetherness and mutual help and solidarity, so strong in Toraja society, as members of society feel happy and volunteer to lend buffalo or pigs for the needs of the funeral, although the time for repayment and the payment of interest are never counted....

The family members who slaughter the most buffalo or pigs are those who will inherit the most of the deceased's wealth.

As a consequence, the possibility of hoarding inherited wealth always exists for the rich and prosperous of the family, so that the rich will get increasingly richer and the poor will increasingly proliferate.

Conclusions ...

1. The death ceremony from an economic viewpoint is clearly not profitable for the larger part of Toraja society. The greater part of that society lives in spreading poverty, because of the lack of available fields of work. This is because the inhabitants of Tana Toraja lack a spirit of personal initiative to create new work fields. Perhaps this is caused by the persistence of remnants of influence of the Feudal system of the old days, in which most of the people submitted and surrendered to the situation created by those who dominated. And they always felt fear to take initiative or to face possible risks. The heart of their livelihood was from working the earth, whereas the existing *sawah* area cannot be relied upon to fulfill the whole population's needs for food....

The lack of work has caused many Toraja to migrate to other areas, and encouraged young children to continue their education in large cities. Of those who have migrated and have successfully accumulated some cash, even those who can be classed as intellectuals, it nonetheless is difficult to change their way of thinking or their orientation, especially about the problem of death ceremonies. In fact it is they who act as sponsors, relied upon by their families in the villages, to pay for funerals. It is deeply regrettable, but such is the reality.

This factor leads to competition in the family circle: who is the most extravagant, whose expenses are the largest in the funeral. So that we may draw the conclusion that "prestige" serves as the puppeteer (*dalang*) that must be maintained by every family and family member. Personal prestige victimizes all of society.... While at this time some people are fighting against poverty, still the opposite is true: there are several groups in Toraja society which are acting to fertilize poverty through the death ceremony.

Arrange for a simple life style and a simple death ceremony, so that the inhabitants of Tana Toraja may enjoy the fruits of this freedom which has already been dearly paid for with the blood and spirits of Pong Tiku and other heroes throughout our beloved Nusantara. This writer does not suggest that the death ceremony be eradicated, but rather simplified in accord with the capability of the masses, without diminishing the essence of the ritual itself, as a cultural value of which we are properly proud.

2. From the cultural aspect, it is clear that the death ritual must be maintained as the identity of the Toraja people. Among so many thousands of existing people, this is a culture unique, with noble values second to none on earth. But it must be remembered that we cannot allow ourselves to be lulled into sleep, fascinated in pride over the hysterical cries of foreign tourists—"Bloody," "Extraordinary," "Sadism" [English in original], etc., then sacrificing the values which exist in our own culture, or making the pride in our culture become a two-edged machete that *will slit our own throats.*

3. Considering the importance of tourism, the death ritual may invite a stream of tourists to Tana Toraja, which means that the earnings of the area may increase (or of the travel bureau?). But it does not mean that the simplification of the funeral will decrease tourism, and it also does not mean that the death ritual is the only tourist object in Tana Toraja. Nature in Tana Toraja sufficiently tempts the heart of the Tourist, and the same is also true of other customary rituals. And has the regional government ever counted the proceeds from tourists who want to see funerals, and then compared this with the cost that must be paid, the negative consequences that arise among the people, for example the mental disruption of society??

4. Seen from the mental aspect, clearly excessive rituals break the mentality of the people, because it is as if the death ritual closes the possibility for them to see other matters which could advance their way of thinking.

5. From the aspect of government policy, it is clearly opposed to a simple pattern of life and is not in accord with the evening out of livelihoods.

6. (To squat at a funeral for days and weeks very much wastes "working time" and drains mental and physical energy of civil servants. Editor)

*Proposals:*

1. To all the government apparatus in Tana Toraja, this writer proposes that policy steps be taken immediately to simplify the death ceremony in Tana Toraja, for instance:

a. Do not give permission to carry out funerals considered excessive (deviating from actual *adat*. Editor).

b. Do not use the ritual of death as an instrument to attract foreign tourists because this can cloud over noble religious values along with the essence of the customary ritual itself.

c. Actively carry out illumination/explanation in society concerning the good and bad and the results that may arise from the death ceremony.

d. Provide information in the schools.

e. Hold discussion forums.

f. Limit the cutting of livestock at death ceremonies.

g. etc.

2. To churches that are close enough to the people, that prohibitions be put forward against matters in connection with the funeral that are no longer in accord with the "christian" life. The authority of the church must be maintained even if it needs to be accompanied by church sanctions. For example, we read in *Kompas*, 18–21 October that a Christian man must be given an *adat* ceremony, whereas we know that the *adat* of the funeral is a product of the religion *Todolo* (animism). Many factors in the *adat* ritual are no longer fitting with the Bible, for instance the effigy of the deceased.

3. To the young generation who come from Tana Toraja and to the intellectuals from Tana Toraja as well as those from outside of Tana Toraja, let us open a discussion forum through the Media Bulletin of the Bandung Family of Toraja Students, so that through this discussion forum we can produce that which is beneficial to our society, our generation, and the generation to come.

Bandung, October 27, 1978

# Glossary

(Unless specified, all words are Toraja.)

*Adat* (Ind.). Custom.
*Aluk*. Ritual, symbolic action, religion; also defines "animists" in contrast to Christians or Muslims.
*Ambe'*. Father; village or group head.
*Ana' dara*. Effigy at *ma'bua'*; literally "sister" or "virgin."

*Balanda*. Dutch.
*Banua*. House.
*Bate*. Cloth and bamboo tower used in *maro* ritual.
*Bombo*. Ghost.

*Dama'*. Dammar, a colorless tree resin used in making varnishes.
*Dapo'*. Kitchen, hearth.
*Datu* (Ind. *raja*). Ruler.
*Deata*. Deity, spirit.
*Dodo* (Ind. *sarong*). Tube skirt.

*Ikat* (Ind.). Resist-dying technique.
*Indo'*. Mother.

*Kabusungan*. Powerful, sacred, dangerous.
*Kalaparan*. Smoke-rising ritual field.
*Kapayungan*. Power, glory ("umbrella-dom").
*Kapua*. Big.
*Kaunan*. Slave, dependent.

*Lolo tau*. Umbilical cord, descendants.

*Ma'bua'*. Highest smoke-rising ritual.
*Mabusung*. To transgress status boundaries.
*Mama'*. Mother (informal).
*Ma'nene'*. Ritual in honor of the ancestors.
*Maro*. Smoke-rising ritual; literally "crazy."
*Medatu*. Preplanting rite.
*Menammu*. Harvest ritual.
*Merantau*. To go abroad.

*Ne'*. Respectful title (short form of *nene'*).
*Nene'*. (Ind. *nenek*). Grandparent; ancestor.

*Padi* (Ind.). Rice, paddy.
*Pemali*. Prohibition.
*Penaa*. Breath, life-force, feeling.
*Puang*. Owner; master (of a slave); highest-ranking nobility in southern Toraja.
*Puya*. Land of the dead.

*Rapu*. family.
*Rarabuku*. Family; literally "blood bones."
*Rombongan*. Formal guest procession at a funeral.

*Sali*. Main room of house.
*Sangdadien*. Family; literally "one birth."
*Saroan*. Meat-sharing and labor group.
*Sawah* (Ind.). Irrigated rice field.
*Siri'*. Honor/shame.
*Sugi'*. Rich.
*Sumbung*. Southernmost room of house.

*Tana'*. Hereditary status; a tethering stake.
*Tau tau*. Effigy of the deceased.
*To*. Person.
*To balu*. Surviving spouse.
*To makaka*. High noble on Mount Sesean.
*To mebalun*. Undertaker, priest of the left; literally "the one who wraps."
*To mentaa*. Divider (of meat).
*To minaa*. Ritual specialist, priest of the right; literally "the one who knows."
*To'*. Place; clustered strands.

*Tondok.* Community, settlement.
*Tongkonan.* Ancestral house.
*Tumbang.* Highest female role in *ma'bua'* ritual.

*Warung* (Ind.). Coffee shop.

# Bibliography

Adams, Kathleen
  1984  Come to Tana Toraja, "Land of the Heavenly Kings": Travel
        Agents as Brokers in Ethnicity. Annals of Tourism Re-
        search 11(3):469–85.
Adriani, N., A. A. van de Loosdrecht, and H. van der Veen
  1916  Sa'danse Volksverhalen (Sa'dan Folk Tales). Tijdschrift voor
        Zendingswetenschap.
American Museum of Natural History
  1982  Indonesian Odyssey. New York: Discovery Tours.
Andaya, Leonard
  1979  A Village Perception of Arung Palakka and the Makassar
        War of 1666–69. In Perceptions of the Past in Southeast
        Asia. A. Reid and D. Marr, eds. pp. 360–78. Singapore:
        Heinemann Educational Books.
Anderson, Benedict R. O'G.
  1972  The Idea of Power in Javanese Culture. In Culture and Poli-
        tics in Indonesia. Claire Holt, ed. pp. 1–69. Ithaca, N.Y., and
        London: Cornell University Press.
  1978  Last Days of Indonesia's Suharto? Southeast Asia Chronicle
        63:2–17.
Barton, R. F.
  1963  Autobiographies of Three Pagans in the Philippines. New
        York: University Books.
Bigalke, Terance
  1981  A Social History of "Tana Toraja" 1870–1965. Ph.D. disser-
        tation. University of Wisconsin, Madison.
Bokko', Enos
  1978  Pesta Kematian di Tana Toraja (The Death Ceremony in
        Tana Toraja). Bulletin Dinamika, October. Bandung:
        Keluarga Mahasiswa Toraja.

Brooke, James, Esq.
　1848　Narrative of Events in Borneo and Celebes, vol. 1. London: John Murray.

Chabot, H. Th.
　1960　Kinship, Status, and Sex in South Celebes. New Haven, Conn.: Human Relations Area Files.

Coville, Elizabeth
　1982　"Mother of the Land": Gender and Generation in Tana Toraja. Manuscript, author's files.
　1983　Rice, Ritual, and the Good of Exchange in Tana Toraja. Manuscript, author's files.

Crystal, Eric
　1970　Toraja Town. Ph.D. dissertation. University of California, Berkeley.
　1974　Cooking Pot Politics: A Toraja Village Study. Indonesia 18:119-51.
　1977　Tourism in Tana Toraja (Sulawesi, Indonesia). In Hosts and Guests: The Anthropology of Tourism. Valene E. Smith, ed. pp. 109-25. Philadelphia: University of Pennsylvania Press.

——, and Shinji Yamashita
　1982　Power of Gods: The Ma'bugi' Ritual in the Sa'dan Toraja. Manuscript, author's files.

Decavele, Patrik
　1977　Mijn Broeder, de Vreemde (My Brother, the Stranger). Manuscript, author's files.

Echols, John M., and Hassan Shadily
　1963　An Indonesian-English Dictionary, 2nd edition. Ithaca, N.Y., and London: Cornell University Press.

Ecklund, Judith Louise
　1977　Marriage, Seaworms, and Song: Ritualized Responses to Cultural Change in Sasak Life. Ph.D. dissertation, Cornell University, Ithaca, N.Y.

Ellis, George R.
　1980　The Art of the Toradja. Arts of Asia 10(5):94-107.

Errington, Shelly
　1977　Siri', Darah, dan Kekuasaan Politik Didalam Kerajaan Luwu Zaman Dulu (Siri', Blood, and Political Power in the Former Kingdom of Luwu). Ujung Pandang: Bingkisan Budaya Sulawesi Selatan.
　1978　Genealogies and Society in Luwu. Manuscript, author's files.
　1979　The Cosmic House of the Buginese. Asia 1(5):8-14.

1983    Embodied Sumange' in Luwu. The Journal of Asian Studies 42(3):545–70.

Furnivall, J. S.
1939    Netherlands India: A Study of Plural Economy. Cambridge: Cambridge University Press.

Geertz, Clifford
1973    The Interpretation of Cultures. New York: Basic Books.

Geertz, H., and C. Geertz
1964    Teknonymy in Bali: Parenthood, Age-Grading, and Genealogical Amnesia. Journal of the Royal Anthropological Institute 94:94–108.

Gervaise, Nicolas
1685    Description historique du royaume de Macacar. Paris: Hilaire Foucault.

Godwin, Nadine
1981    In Indonesia's Toraja, There's Life after Death. San Francisco Examiner and Chronicle, travel section, November 29, 1.

Hamdan, Faisal
1976    Saroan: Sebuah Pranata Sosial di Tana Toraja (Saroan: A Social Institution in Tana Toraja). Ujung Pandang: Pusat Latihan Ilmu Ilmu Sosial.

Harahap, Parada
1952    Toradja. Bandung-s'Gravenhage: Van Hoeve.

Harvey, Barbara G.
1974    Tradition, Islam, and Rebellion in South Sulawesi 1950–65. Ph.D. dissertation, Cornell University, Ithaca, N.Y.
1977    Permesta: Half a Rebellion. Ithaca, N.Y.: Cornell Modern Indonesia Project Monograph Series.

Holt, Claire
1939    Dance Quest in Celebes. Paris: Les Archives Internationales de la Danse.

Ihromi, T. O.
1975    Sistim Kekerabatan pada suku Toraja Sa'dan (The Kinship System of the Sa'dan Toraja). Berita Antropologi 7(21):2–18.

Ikrar
1978    Ibadat Umat Allah: Pa'rapuan Kristiani (Religious Service for the Community of God: The Christian Family). Rantepao.

Kantor Statistik
1982    Penduduk Sulawesi Selatan Kelompok Umum. Ujung Pandang: Propinsi Sulsel.

Kato, Tsuyoshi
1982    Matriliny and Migration: Evolving Minangkabau Traditions in Indonesia. Ithaca, N.Y.: Cornell University Press.

Kennedy, Raymond
  1953   Field Notes on Indonesia: South Celebes 1949–50. New Haven, Conn.: Human Relations Area Files.
Kirsch, A. Thomas
  1973   Feasting and Social Oscillation: Religion and Society in Upland Southeast Asia. Ithaca, N.Y.: Cornell Southeast Asia Program Data Paper.
Kompas
  1978   Pesta Kematian di Tana Toraja (The Death Feast in Tana Toraja). October 18–20.
  1980   Tana Toraja Sebagai Daerah Kedua Sesudah Bali (Tana Toraja as the Second Area after Bali). May 21.
Koubi, Janine
  1975   La première fête funéraire chez les Toradja Sa'dan. Archipel 10:105–21.
  1982   Rambu solo', "la fumée descend": Le cult des morts chez les Toradja du Sud. Paris: CRNS.
Kruyt, A. C.
  1923–   De Toradja's van de Sa'dan, Masoepoe en Mamasa Rivieren.
  24      Tijdschrift voor Indische Taal, Land- en Volkenkunde 63:81–176, 259–402.
——, and J. Kruyt
  1922   Een reis onder de Toradja's van Sa'dan en Mamasa (Celebes). Tijdschrift Aardrijkskundig Genootschap 49:678–717.
Labby, David
  1976   The Demystification of Yap: Dialectics of Culture on a Micronesian Island. Chicago and London: University of Chicago Press.
Lieberman, Joseph
  1981   Sulawesi—Far From the Tourist Path. The Boston Globe, March 29.
Lineton, Jacqueline
  1975a  Pasompe' Ugi': Bugis Migrants and Wanderers. Archipel 10:173–201.
  1975b  An Indonesian Society and Its Universe: A Study of the Bugis of South Sulawesi. Ph.D. dissertation, School of Oriental and African Studies, University of London.
Malinowski, Bronislaw
  1954   Magic, Science, and Religion. Garden City, N.Y.: Doubleday Anchor Books.
Mauss, Marcel
  1967   The Gift. New York: Norton.

Metcalf, Peter
   1982   A Borneo Journey into Death. Philadelphia: University of
          Pennsylvania Press.
Meyer, Pamela, and Alfred Meyer
   1972   Life and Death in Tana Toradja. National Geographic
          141(6):793–815.
Millar, Susan B.
   1981   Bugis Society: Given by the Wedding Guest. Ph.D. disserta-
          tion, Cornell University, Ithaca, N.Y.
   1983   On Interpreting Gender in Bugis Society. American Ethnol-
          ogist 10(3):477–93.
Mills, R. F.
   1975   The Reconstruction of Proto South Sulawesi. Archipel
          10:205–24.
Noorduyn, J.
   1965   Origins of South Celebes Historical Writing. In An Introduc-
          tion to Indonesian Historiography. Soedjatmoko, ed. pp.
          137–55. Ithaca, N.Y.: Cornell University Press.
Nooy-Palm, C. H. M.
   1975   Introduction to the Sa'dan Toraja People and Their Country.
          Archipel 10:52–92.
   1978   Survey of Studies on the Anthropology of Tana Toraja,
          Sulawesi. Archipel 15:163–92.
   1979   The Sa'dan Toraja: A Study of Their Social Life and Religion,
          I. The Hague: Martinus Nijhoff.
Pakan, L.
   1973   Rahasia Ukiran Toraja (Secrets of Toraja Carving). Ujung
          Pandang.
Pelras, Christian
   1975   Celebes-Sud: Fiche Signalétique. Archipel 10:5–10.
Radin, Paul
   1972   The Trickster. New York: Schocken.
Radjab, M.
   1950   Dongengan Sulawesi Selatan (South Sulawesi Folk Tales).
          Djakarta: Balai Pustaka.
Rosaldo, M. Z., and J. Atkinson
   1975   Man the Hunter and Woman: Metaphors for the Sexes in
          Ilongot Magical Spells. In The Interpretation of Symbolism.
          R. Willis, ed. pp. 43–75. New York: John Wiley & Sons.
Salombe', C.
   1972   Orang Toraja dengan Ritusnya: in memoriam So' Rinding

Puang Sangalla' (The Toraja and Their Rituals). Ujung
        Pandang.
Sandarupa, Stanislaus
    1981  Pemerkosaan Nilai-nilai Budaya Tana Toraja (The Rape of
        Tana Toraja's Cultural Values). Kompas, March 9.
Sarasin, Paul, and Fritz Sarasin
    1905  Reisen in Celebes. 2 vols. Wiesbaden: C. W. Kreidel's
        Verlag.
Siegel, James
    1969  The Rope of God. Berkeley and Los Angeles: University of
        California Press.
Stohr, W., W. Marschall, J. P. Barbier, C. H. M. Nooy-Palm, J. B. Avé,
and J. de Hoog
    1982  Art of the Archaic Indonesians. Dallas, Tex.: Museum of Fine
        Arts.
Tammu, J., and H. van der Veen
    1972  Kamus Toradja-Indonesia (Toraja-Indonesian Dictionary).
        Rantepao: Jajasan Perguruan Kristen Toradja.
Tandilangi, Puang Paliwan
    1975  Les Tongkonan, maisons d'origine des Toraja. Archipel
        10:93–104.
Tangdilintin, L. T.
    1975a Toraja dan Kebudayaannya (Toraja and Their Culture). Ran-
        tepao: Yayasan Lepongan Bulan.
    1975b Sejarah Perjuangan Pahlawan Pong Tiku (History of the
        Struggle of the Hero Pong Tiku). Rantepao: Yayasan Lepon-
        gan Bulan.
____, and M. Syafei
    1977  Toraja: An Introduction to a Unique Culture. Rantepao and
        Ujung Pandang: Yayasan Lepongan Bulan.
Tempo
    1978  Mangrapai Nek Atta' (Ne' Atta''s Death Ceremony).
        35(8):26–27.
Turner, Victor
    1967  The Forest of Symbols. Ithaca, N.Y.: Cornell University
        Press.
van der Veen, H.
    1965  The Merok Feast of the Sa'dan Toradja. 's-Gravenhage: Mar-
        tinus Nijhoff.
    1966  The Sa'dan Toradja Chant for the Deceased. 's-Gravenhage:
        Martinus Nijhoff.

van Lijf, J. M.
1947– Kentrekken en problemen van de geschiedenis der Sa'dan-
48 Toradaja-landen. Indonesïe 1:518–35.
Vlekke, Bernard H. M.
1960 Nusantara: A History of Indonesia. Chicago: Quadrangle
Books.
Volkman, Toby Alice
1979a The Arts of Dying in Sulawesi. Asia 2(2):24–31.
1979b The Riches of the Undertaker. Indonesia 28:1–16.
1980 The Pig Has Eaten the Vegetables: Ritual and Change in
Tana Toraja. Ph.D. dissertaton, Cornell University, Ithaca,
N.Y.
1982a Tana Toraja: A Decade of Tourism. In The Tourist Trap:
Who's Getting Caught? Cultural Survival Quarterly
6(3):30–31.
1982b Mortuary Tourism in Tana Toraja. Manuscript, author's
files.
1984 Great Performances: Toraja Cultural Identity in the 1970s.
American Ethnologist 11(1):152–69.
Whitmore, T. C.
1981 Wallace's Line and Plate Tectonics. Oxford: Clarendon
Press.
Wilcox, Harry
1949 White Stranger: Six Moons in Celebes. London: Collins.
Yamashita, Shinji
1981 From Death to Life: A Ritual Process of Death in the Sa'dan
Toraja. Manuscript, author's files.
Zerner, Charles
1981 Signs of the Spirits, Signature of the Smith: Iron Forging in
Tana Toraja. Indonesia 31:89–112.
1982 Tourism and the Arts in Southern Sulawesi. In Ethnic Art:
Works in Progress? Cultural Survival Quarterly 6(4):21–23.
1983 Animate Architecture of the Toraja. Arts of Asia (Sep-
tember/October):96–106.
___, and Toby Volkman
in press The Tree of Desire: A Toraja Ritual Poem. In To Speak in
Pairs: Essays on the Ritual Languages of Eastern Indonesia.
James J. Fox, ed. Cambridge: Cambridge University Press.

# Index

Aceh, 29, 30, 125, 185
*Adat*, 6, 33, 36, 191
Address, terms of, 61, 66, 149, 158
Adoption: ceremony, 46; of Mama'
  Agus, 67, 105, 124, 156; affiliation
  through, 78; debts created by, 95;
  and inheritance, 105, 128; modes
  of, 178 –79
Age, 90, 98, 99
Agus, Mama': role of, in fieldwork,
  8, 12–19, 48, 103, 116; childhood
  of, 28, 67, 105, 124–25, 180; life
  of, during Japanese occupation,
  39–40; marriage of, 41, 123–24,
  126; family of, 56, 64–66, 86, 99,
  104, 106, 120–21, 158, 162–63,
  179; life of, in To' Dama', 60, 79,
  93, 101, 127, 129, 139–41,
  158–61; reflections of, 144,
  152–57
*Aluk:* funerals, 16, 84–91, 104, 150;
  contrasted with lowland kingdoms, 21, 28; defined, 33–35, 177;
  missionary response to, 35–37;
  ancestors honored in, 49, 144,
  165; smoke-rising rituals, 110–12,
  153; and religious differences,
  113–15, 161, 163; decline of,
  131–32, 136–37, 173; and tourism, 165, 167, 171; revitalization
  of, 167–69
*Ambe'. See* Big man
Ambonese, 28, 31, 35

Ancestors: and *aluk*, 33–34, 168;
  memory of, 46, 48–51, 74;
  honored in ritual, 49, 142–47,
  159, 162, 171; transformed,
  53–56; requests made of, 75; role
  in *saroan*, 77, 80, 141; invoked by
  women, 111
Andi Sose, 41, 130
Architecture: temporary, 78, 92,
  180. *See also* Granary; House
Army, national, 41, 155, 157
Arung Palakka, 23–24
Atta', Ne', 170, 192–93
Authenticity, 7, 44, 169

*Balanda,* 13, 19, 29, 125, 171, 176. *See
  also* Dutch
Bali, 7, 8, 43, 49, 166, 187
Balikpapan, 136
Balusu, 27
Bamboo: in landscape, 2, 3, 5; ritual
  uses of, 54, 55, 56, 69, 79, 83,
  86–93 passim, 111; everday uses
  of, 45, 53, 62, 103, 123; owner-
  ship and cultivation of, 90, 107,
  117
*Banua. See* House
Batak, 28
*Bate,* 54, 55, 176, 179
Batukamban, 101, 116–22 passim,
  128, 140
Betel: offerings, 28, 56, 90, 91, 92,
  144, 145; chewed, 47, 48, 68, 87;

exchanged 64, 66; pouch, 64, 86, 90, 146

Bigalke, Terance, 24–28, 35–37, 61, 63

Big man: changing roles and rhetoric of, 15, 43, 150–52, 170; defined, 22–23; Dutch relations with, 31; as rich men, 68; indebtedness of, 79; as *saroan* heads, 80–82; ritual responsibilities of, 94–99; role of, in meat distribution, 98–100, 106; and speech, 107, 152; and "small men," 109; of To' Dama', 118, 123, 128, 140–41, 150, 152, 159

Blessings: requested at *maro*, 54; wealth as sign of, 68, 146; requested at funeral, 90, 91; on rice seed, 110, 133; requested at *ma'nene'*, 144–47

Blood: as basis of hierarchy, 2, 60–62, 67, 68, 98–99; as shared substance, 46; of animals, 46, 57, 91, 96, 97, 111; not shed in trance, 55; and wealth, 59–63, 158–59, 161; redness of, 86

*Bombo*: transported to Puya, 33, 83–91; transformed into spirit, 53; effigy as receptacle for, 89–90; in this world, 142, 147

Bone, 23–28, 149, 150

Borneo, 3, 30, 183. *See also* Kalimantan

Breath (*penaa*), 50, 84, 88, 179, 182

Buffalo. *See* Water buffalo

Bugis: in South Sulawesi, 1, 3, 4, 10; relations with Toraja, 20–30, 107, 136, 137, 138, 170, 176, 177; conceptions of family, 45; status, 60; *siri'*, 74, 182; nobility, 80; language, 125; trade and travel, 132, 133, 177, 185; houses, 158

Cash: increasing importance of, 6, 32, 79, 122, 129, 159; obtained through migration, 135, 136, 158. *See also* Wealth

Cassava, 2, 5, 10, 62, 70, 86

Chickens: as ritual sacrifice, 2, 85, 90, 111, 151; at *maro*, 56; as wealth, 68, 69

Childbirth, 50, 71, 179

Children: value of, 50–51, 72; of *tongkonan*, 51–52; slaves referred to as, 65, 138; assume social roles, 74, 79; ritual pleasures of, 91, 111; ritual responsibilities of, 94, 104–6; in myth, 109–10

Chinese, 119, 120, 122, 137, 163, 167

Christianity: and cultural identity, 2, 130, 163, 167; conversion to, 6, 9, 30, 35–37, 42, 129–37 passim, 148, 149, 153, 169, 173, 178; and hierarchy, 6, 130–31, 149, 156; in To' Dama', 9, 113–15, 127–32, 134, 139, 153; and ritual, 17, 35–36, 113–15, 130–31, 136–37, 145, 150–51, 153, 161, 167, 169; and education, 37, 129, 132; and Islam, 30, 42; and migration, 132, 134, 136–37; and tourism, 167–69. *See also* Church; Funerals, Christian

Church: Catholic, 164, 189; Protestant, 11, 12, 15, 104, 113, 130, 145, 161, 164, 169, 178; Pentecostal, 113, 131. *See also* Christianity

Cloth, 38–39, 68, 85, 125; sacred, 47, 53–55

Cockfighting, 35, 62, 63, 158, 181

Coffee: trees cultivated, 5, 122; Japanese interest in, 10, 135; wars, 24–26; aroma, 34; served at rituals, 92, 93

Commoners, 6, 60, 66, 67, 98. *See also* Status

Communists, 42, 43, 178

Competition, 107, 108, 161, 164, 169

Cordyline terminalis: associated
with nobility, 53, 67, 127; associated with *deata*, 54, 55, 57, 117
Corn, 2, 56, 65, 83, 86
Corpse, 64, 83–91, 105, 151, 185

Dammar resin, 5, 39, 116, 117, 118,
133
Dana' stories, 20, 21, 108–9
Darul Islam, 41
Datu, 20, 21, 108, 110, 125
*Deata* (spirits): marriages with, 20,
83; nature of, 29, 33–34, 114, 117,
168; as transformed ghosts, 49,
53; called in *maro*, 54–55; offerings
to, 73, 75, 91, 110, 113; declining
potency of, 153
Death: preoccupation with, 5; and
life, 10, 110, 111, 113–14; "reversal" of, 53; and gender, 72,
110; as process, 84–91; role of *to
mebalun* in, 143–47, 150; and
*mabusung*, 154–55. *See also* Funerals
Debts: and slavery, 63–64; animals
as, 70, 73, 75, 163, 164, 183;
responsibility for, 79, 105; at funeral, 91–102
Descent group, 51, 53, 57. *See also*
Family; House, social significance
of; *Rarabuku*
Development, 151, 157, 159, 162,
164, 165
Divorce, 47, 60, 107
Dreams, 104, 183–84
Drums, 57, 85, 89, 103
Duri, 4, 41
Dutch: mission, 3, 32, 35–37, 129;
colonial period, 6, 10, 23, 24,
30–41, 122, 123; men, 11, 12, 13,
119, 120, 125; influence on To'
Dama', 11, 19, 126, 127, 129, 134;
invasion of South Celebes, 26–30;
Toraja perceptions of, 28–29;
return to Toraja, 171
Dutch Reformed Alliance. *See* Chris-
tianity; Church

Dyaks, 3

Education: in colonial period, 35, 37,
122, 185; and religious change,
131–32, 168; and migration,
134–36
Effigies: of deceased, 9, 15, 32, 71,
89–91, 143, 152, 185, 186, 187; in
*ma'bua'*, 56–58; Christian prohibition of, 131, 170
Elections, 178
Elite. *See* Nobility
Epidemics, 84, 107
Ethical Policy, of Dutch colonials, 29
Excrement, 22, 50, 100, 101, 109,
110, 184

Family, 46, 63, 85, 110, 114. *See also*
Ancestors; Descent group; Family
bamboo clump; House; Kinship;
*Rarabuku*
Family bamboo clump, 54, 67, 119,
171
Family planning, 168
Fertility, 50, 58, 69, 72
Firearms, 24, 26, 27
Forest: resources, 3, 20, 39, 61,
116–17, 133, 135; in myth, 20,
105, 109; otherness of, 124, 133
Funerals: focus on, 2, 5–8, 16;
Christian, 16, 91, 102, 148, 164,
170–71; headhunting for, 30; as
smoke-descending ritual, 33, 56,
114; critiques of, 6, 35, 161,
163–64, 170, 189–96; and changing status, 67, 76, 135–37,
148–53; gender distinctions at,
71–72; *siri'* expressed at, 74–76,
135, *saroan* functions at, 78–81;
stages of, 83–110; touristic interest in, 165–71

Galumpang, 133
Gambling, 28, 62, 63, 76, 107, 119
Geertz, Clifford, 7, 148, 152, 166
*Gelong*, 57

Gender, 71, 72, 79, 88–89, 110, 181
Ghost. *See Bombo*
Goa, 2, 4, 23
Gold: as tribute, 21; as metaphor, 54, 60, 107; as jewelry, 89, 106, 154–55
GOLKAR, 178
Gongs, 85, 89, 92, 103, 143
*Gotong royong,* 78
Government, 6, 96, 144, 157, 170
Granary: appearance of, 48, 52; and wealth, 68, 117, 123; ritual function of, 88; symbolism of, 180. *See also* Honor

Harvest, 58, 66, 110–11, 114
Headhunting, 2, 3, 24, 30, 71, 88
Healing, 32, 179
Heat, 55, 84, 147, 182
Hierarchy. *See* Status.
Hindu Dharma, 167
Honor, seat of, 48, 52, 66, 156, 164–65. *See also Siri'*
House: construction, 45, 78; replicas, 44, 166, 168; social significance of, 45–51, 77, 132, 140–41; ceremonies, 51–58; expresses status, 104, 123; in To' Dama', 116–28 passim; symbolism, 179–80. *See also* Ancestors; Descent group; Family; *Rarabuku*

Identity, cultural: construction of, 3, 6, 7, 161–62, 167, 195; and Christianity, 130; and migration, 138, 150
Ifugao, 84
*Ikat* cloth, 32, 133
Independence, Indonesian, 6, 40, 151, 155, 156
*Indo' padang,* 111, 184
Inflation, 7, 72, 161, 175
Inheritance: means of, 17, 46, 105–7; of status, 60, 142; of *saroan,* 79

Invulnerability, 118, 181
Irian Jaya, 43, 103, 134, 137, 138, 158, 159
Iron: swords, 54–55, 57, 68, 71, 89, 96–97; and status, 60; traded, 133
Islam, 2, 28, 30, 37, 130, 136, 167, 177
Islamization, 41, 178

Jakarta: Toraja in, 12, 121, 134, 158, 162; attempted coup in, 43; development plans of, 135, 165, 167, 168; visitors from, 170
Japanese: coffee factory, 10, 135; occupation, 13, 38–40, 126, 127, 149
Java: nationalism and revolution on, 38, 40, 41; possessions from, 59, 89, 123; travel to, 121, 138
Javanese: 28, 41, 43; conceptions of power, 68, 69, 176; marriages to, 136–37, 149; funeral, 148, 152

Kahar Mudzakkar, 41, 43, 178
*Kalaparan,* 117, 128
Kalimantan, 14, 43, 134, 135, 138, 148–50
*Kapa',* 60
*Kaunan. See* Slaves
Kickfight, 147, 163
Kila', Pak, 34, 167–69
Kinship, 48–50, 74, 77–78, 162. *See also* Ancestors; Family; House
*Kombongan,* 107, 155, 184
Kombonglangi', Ne', 123–24, 126, 159

Labor, 64–67, 71, 108, 128, 138–39, 182
Lale, Ne', 64–65, 118–20, 152
Laments, funeral, 87, 88, 142, 169, 183
Land: cultivation of, 4–5, 71, 138–39; ownership, 16, 35, 42, 61–67 passim, 128, 143; as

wealth, 70, 72–73, 182; inheritance of, 104–7. *See also Sawah*
Lande, Pak, 164–65
Langda, 169
Language: in fieldwork, 9, 11, 12, 14; in South Sulawesi, 3, 4
Leme, Ne', 13, 19, 97, 99–103, 118–29 passim, 139–41, 150, 159–62
Literacy, 22, 37, 68, 135, 160. *See also* Writing
*Lolo,* 50–51
Lombok, 125, 175
Lumbaa, Ne', 57, 104, 111, 180, 182
Luwu, 17–18, 20–27, 30, 40, 60, 82, 107, 110, 125, 153

*Ma'badong. See* Laments
*Ma'bua':* 43, 56–59, 72, 94, 151, 153, 154, 160
*Ma'londe. See* Laments
*Ma'nene',* 142, 144–47, 163, 165
*Mabusung,* 66, 154–56, 186
Magic, 69, 162
Makale, 4, 9, 30–31, 37, 41, 42, 61, 62, 78, 134, 158, 162
Makassar, 1, 4, 12, 23, 29, 39, 40, 126, 127, 133. *See also* Ujung Pandang
Makassarese, 1–3, 22, 23
Makassar Strait, 4, 24, 135
Malinowski, Bronislaw, 152
Mama' Agus. *See* Agus, Mama'
*Mangaru,* 100, 147
Mareks, Om, 119–26
Markets, 3, 4, 20, 32, 68, 116–17, 127
*Maro,* 53–56, 59, 94, 117, 153, 176, 179
Marriage: 47, 78, 79; in myth, 20–21, 83, 107; "returning to the house," 52, 122, 132; and status, 60, 67–68, 137, 154, 159–60, 179; in Mama' Agus's family, 118–24, 162–63

*Masero,* 91, 94, 183
Meat: symbolic importance of, 5, 7, 8, 23, 73, 75, 84, 131; Christianity and, 36, 113; distribution of, 42–43, 65, 69, 72, 75, 76, 79–82, 96–104, 106, 109, 139–41
*Medatu,* 21, 110
*Menammu,* 111–15, 140
Migration, 6, 43, 132–38, 149, 154, 167, 185
Minahasan, 35, 41
Minangkabau, 132, 185
Moluccas, 23
Monoliths, 90
Mount Sesean: introduced, 5, 9, 12, 17; history of, 25–26, 28–29, 32, 39, 42, 128–30, 169; marriage on, 52; ritual on, 53; status on, 60–61, 63, 68; land on, 61–62, 71; *saroan* on, 77, 79, 82; in myth, 108. *See also* Tondoklitak
Mourners, 86, 90, 183
Multinational corporations, 43, 135, 139
Myth: 14, 15, 29, 54, 72, 105; of Karaeng Dua', 20–21; of Puang Matua, 34, 61; of Potto Kalembang, 61; of Pong Pa'pak, 68, 69; of Polopadang, 83; of Lando Rundun, 107–8; of Indo' Orro Orro, 109–10; of Pong Bulu Pala, 184. *See also* Dana' stories

Names, 48–50, 79, 98, 152
Navel post, 57, 180
New Order, 43, 167, 178
NICA, 40
Nipi, Ne', 13, 119–21, 124, 125
Nobility: changing experience of, 6, 37, 76, 152, 154–56; role of, 9, 18–19, 31, 53, 59–68, 80, 98; slaving activities of, 25–26; in Pantilang, 120, 123

Omens, 114

*Padi:* traded, 3; measured, 16, 72; processed, 64, 68, 133; exchanged, 79, 111–13, 143, 154; origin of, 108. *See also* Rice

Palimbong, Ne', 170

Palopo: trade in, 3–4, 20, 24, 133; Mama' Agus's family in, 121–26, 159

Pancasila, 156

Pangala', 26, 62, 93, 118, 148, 165

Pantilang: location of, 17; controlled by Kahar, 41; status in, 60, 64, 66, 98, 120, 122, 123, 127; political organization of, 82; myths, 107–9

Papua New Guinea, 32, 71, 80, 162

Paretasik, 120–21

Pare Pare, 4, 24, 29, 126

Pentecostal, 113, 131

Pigs: role of, 2, 8, 62–72 passim, 99, 118, 181; in myth, 20–21, 109; sacrificed, 23, 50; sacrificed at *ma'bua'*, 57–58; as debts, 75, 79, 91–96, 101–2, 151, 162; sacrificed at funerals, 85–90; sacrificed at *menammu*, 111–13; sacrificed at *saroan* formation, 140; sacrificed at *ma'nene'*, 144; sacrificed at hotel ceremony, 169

*Piong*, 110, 111

Polina, 121, 124–26

Politics of meat, 14, 81, 82, 97–98, 100–102, 107. *See also* Meat, distribution of

Polotondok, 116–22 passim, 128–29

Pong Maramba, 26, 27, 42

Pong Pindan, 96, 141–42, 147–53

Pong Tiku, 26–28, 42, 118, 120, 166

Population, 11, 42, 61–62, 135

Possession. *See* Trance.

Poverty, 3, 17, 62, 63, 68, 79

Power: loss of, 6, 7, 55, 152, 153; organizaton of, 21, 23, 30, 31, 52, 66, 82, 96; sources of, 37, 41, 58, 63, 69, 76, 124, 140, 144, 157, 159; conceptions of, 68, 76, 161

Prestige, 6, 56, 67, 76, 82, 106, 136, 189–90

Prostitutes, 39, 125, 133

Protestant. *See* Christianity; Church, Protestant

*Puang*, 27, 61–67 passim, 123, 128, 155. *See also* Nobility

Puang Laso' Rinding, 165

Puang Matua, 34, 61, 168, 169

Puya, 33, 34, 84, 88–91 passim, 104

*Rante*, 90, 145

Rantepao: as urban center, 4, 8–11, 31, 37; tourism in, 44, 166, 168; *saroan* in, 78; To' Dama''s ties to, 120–23 passim

*Rarabuku*, 46, 50, 54, 106, 108, 128. *See also* Ancestors; Descent group; Family; Family bamboo clump

Religion, 33, 113, 191. *See also* Aluk; Christianity; Church; Islam

Rice: fields, 2, 4–5, 10, 12, 22, 42, 53, 61–62, 128, 139; and fertility, 21, 50, 56–58; cooking, sharing, and eating, 47, 64–68, 74, 110, 112; at funerals 86–93; and community, 109–12. *See also* Padi

Ritual: transformations, 6–10, 43, 131, 136, 148–54, 157, 161–71; in fieldwork, 16–17; agricultural, 21, 110–15, 184; and status, wealth, and *siri'*, 23, 32, 48, 59, 67–76; smoke-rising, 33, 36, 53–58, 70, 72, 94, 117, 144, 150; smoke-descending 33, 70, 83–110, 144; Dutch approach to, 35–36; affirms social and ancestral ties, 46, 49, 53; animals used in, 68, 85, 90, 170; food served at, 92, 93, 101–3; music played at, 151, 169. *See also* Aluk; Funerals; Ma'nene'; Speech, ritual

Ritual specialists. *See* To minaa; To mebalun

*Rombongan*, 65, 91–96, 102, 108

Rongkong, 21, 133

Sa'dan, 2

Sacrifice: and Christianity, 36, 131, 164, 168; symbolism of, 71–73, 84–86; and *siri'*, 75, 138, 149; at funeral, 81, 85–91 passim, 96–97, 108, 150–51, 189–96; and inheritance, 104–6, 136; and *saroan*, 111, 140; at *ma'nene'*, 144–45; cleansing, 147; at wedding, 162; and tourism, 169

Sandalwood, 5, 53, 67, 117, 123

*Sarita* cloth, 54

*Saroan*: described, 59, 77–82; prohibitions, 90, 140; and meat, 94–95, 101–3, 128; community as, 111–15, 144; changes in, 139–41, 150–51, 159

*Sawah*. *See* Land; Rice, fields

Schools. *See* Education

Seko, 2, 118, 133

Seventh Day Adventists, 161

Shame. *See* Siri'

Sharecropping, 62, 66, 78, 128, 129

Siblings, 49–52 passim, 62, 64, 74, 104–5, 109, 128

Sidenreng, 24–27

*Siri'*: problem of, 8, 59, 163–65; significance of, 73–76, 92, 140, 155; expressed in ritual, 95–102, 104, 108, 135, 138, 157

Slaves: sale of, 3, 4, 10, 25–26, 133; ritual status and roles of, 6, 43, 84, 86–87, 98, 104, 106; daily life of, 18, 22, 53, 117, 123, 127–29, 139; in myth, 20, 108–9; in colonial era, 30, 37, 40, 41; changing status of, 60, 76, 136–38, 141, 153–60, 163–64; varieties of, 62–68, 180

Songkok Borrong, 23, 25

Speech: 80, 152, 186; ritual, 29, 33, 37, 54, 151, 168, 174, 185

Spirits. *See* Deata

Status: elaboration of, 2; changing, 6–7, 152–58; and fieldwork, 16–19; in colonial era, 30, 32; in

Puya, 33; and social organization, 52, 59–80 passim; and ritual, 91–96, 146; and Christian ideology, 130–31; and migration, 135–37

Suharto, President, 43, 135, 191

Sukarno, 40

Suloara, 5, 33

*Sumange'*, 179, 181

Sumatra, 29, 30

Suroaco, 40, 121

Taboo, 33, 46, 54, 56, 65, 111, 128, 140, 143, 147

Tampang. *See* Polina

*Tana'*, 59. *See also* Status

Tandi Allo. *See* Leme, Ne'

Tandi Allo, Ne', 65, 132

Tandi Bua', 149

Tandi Datu, Ne', 14, 113, 114

Tarakan, 122, 136

Tawao, 158

Taxes, 16, 32, 96, 122, 133, 157

Tikala, 62, 106, 123–24

Timor, 23; troops from, 28; East, 149

*To barani*, 66–67, 71

*To ma'tongkonan*, 86, 183, 186

*To makaka*. *See* Nobility; Status

*To mebalun*: introduced, 14, 33; role of, in funeral, 86–98, 131, 136, 185; changing status of, 142–53, 157. *See also* Pong Pindan

*To minaa*, 14; ritual speech of, 37, 54, 140, 152, 174, 185; role of, in smoke-rising ritual, 54, 55, 57, 110–11; role of, in funeral, 80–99 passim; in Mama' Agus's family, 118, 119, 128; and change, 114, 131, 136, 167–69, 173. *See also* Lumbaa, Ne'; To Napa, Ne'; Suloara

To Napa, Ne', 32, 118–19, 121, 128, 151, 173

To Pare, Ne', 118–19

*To parengnge*, 31

To *sallang*, 28
Tondok, 22–25, 82, 118
Tondok Diongan, 102, 140–41
Tondok Doan, 102, 140–41
Tondoklitak: location of, 5, 11; status in, 31, 52, 61, 99; conflict in, 101, 113, 140; change in, 129–30, 134–38, 165
*Tongkonan.* See House
Tourism, 2, 6, 9, 44, 152, 161, 165–71, 186–87, 195
Trade, 1–2, 11, 23, 118, 120, 122, 133. See also Markets; Slaves, trade in
Trance, 54–56, 153, 179
Transportation, 4, 8, 114, 122–23, 126, 166
Tribute, 21, 110, 133
Trickery, 29, 176. See also Dana' stories
*Tuang tuang,* 88, 90
Tumba', Ne', 106, 119–21, 129
Tumbang, 56–58, 160

Ujung Pandang: transportation from, 4, 65–66; Toraja in, 12, 14, 114, 134, 138, 149, 158, 162–63. See also Makassar
Umbrella-dom, 6, 7, 152–53, 158
Undertaker. See To *mebalun*

Unity, ideal of, 46, 79, 110, 112, 115

Van de Loosdrecht, A. A., 35–37, 129–30

Wajo, 24
War: late nineteenth century, 24–26, 62–63, 72, 118, 176; guerrilla, 41; and "heat," 84. See also World War II
*Warung,* 11, 18, 127, 158
Water buffalo: raised, 2, 65; importance of, 8, 23, 181; as wealth, 16, 67, 68, 69–73; ownership of, 61, 65; and inheritance, 62, 104–7; displayed, 66, 75; *bonga,* 70–71; and *saroan,* 79–81; sacrificed, 85–102 passim, 143–44, 151, 157, 163–64, 169; in myth, 108; traded, 120; fight, 181
Wealth: and status, 6–7, 67, 99, 161; assessment of, 16; children as, 51; consolidation of, 52, 163; and land, 62–63; and rich men, 68–70, 76, 151; inheritance of, 104–5; new, 136, 150–59; of *to mebalun,* 144–52 passim
World War II, 12, 40, 119
Writing, 4, 96, 112. See also Literacy

# A Note on the Author

TOBY ALICE VOLKMAN is an anthropologist with Documentary Educational Resources, of Watertown, Massachusetts. She earned a B.A. from the University of Chicago in 1969 and a Ph.D. from Cornell University in 1980. She has done fieldwork among the Toraja since 1976 and has published articles based on that work in the *American Ethnologist, Asia, Indonesia, Dialectical Anthropology, Pacific Linguistics,* and the *Journal of American Folklore.* She is also the author of a monograph about the Namibian San (Bushmen) in transition, and a catalog of ethnographic films. This is her first book.